To Margaret -

Best Wishes,

Alvin Green

We Who Believe in Freedom

Activism and the Struggle for Social Justice

KING JESUS PRESS LLC

WE WHO BELIEVE IN FREEDOM

ACTIVISM AND THE STRUGGLE FOR SOCIAL JUSTICE

A MEMOIR BY

ALICE P. GREEN

FOREWORD BY PAUL GRONDAHL

ISBN: 978-0-9998489-3-7
(Soft cover)

ISBN: 978-0-9998489-5-1
(E-book)

ISBN: 978-0-9998489-4-4
(Hard cover)

Library of Congress Control Number: 2021923425

Author photo courtesy of: Colleen Ingerto

Cover illustrator: Mahodd Harvin

PRAISE FOR WE WHO BELIEVE IN FREEDOM

Alice Green's memoir, "We Who Believe in Freedom: Activism and the Struggle for Social Justice," reveals that her life journey resembles Harriet Tubman's herstory; Tubman, the renowned antebellum activist who fought to abolish the enslavement of 4 million imprisoned on southern plantations, and Green, the respected Albany, New York-based activist who has battled boldly to abolish the plantation-like prison incarceration of men and women, mostly descendants of the enslaved Africans which Tubman sought to liberate.

She has penned a narrative as captivating and significant as Frederick Douglass' and Malcolm X's life chronicles: namely, her unflinching confronting of callous, power- gluttonous, bigoted male police chiefs, district attorneys, and mayors about police brutalizing, murdering, racial profiling, and incarcerating Albany's African American citizenry because of their facial appearance.

Green's soul journey truths include organizing, educating and empowering disenfranchised residents of Albany's underdeveloped communities regarding the power of the vote, assisting them to shred the shackles of fear that froze their ability to think independently and critically. Readers witness her civil rights and human rights work to eliminate covert apartheid in New York State's capital and overt apartheid in South Africa.

What is equally impressive about "We Who Believe in Freedom: Activism and the Struggle for Social Justice" is Green's escape from political, social and economic incarceration in Greenville, South Carolina, an overground undertaking by six million Africans locked in cotton and tobacco fields to actualize their constitutional rights up North during the Great Migration. We feel for an adolescent traumatized by racism and identify with her finding healing in the arms of her great grandmother,

grandmother and mother. The strength of her father and other men in the family is soul-inspiring. We smile with pride as Green, raised by illiterate parents, receives an earned doctorate degree.

Overall, "We Who Believe in Freedom: Activism and the Struggle for Social Justice" offers readers an extraordinary and adventurous opportunity to journey Green's happiness and heartaches, her triumphs and defeats, health and illness, loyalty and betrayal, courage and fear, the bitter and sweet - all of which have assisted and sustained the maturation of one of America's notable social justice advocates.

Yusef Salaam, Freelance Writer
New York Beacon

Dr. Alice Green's memoir provides a vivid and gripping portrait of the injustices faced by many as a result of racism, the prison industrial complex, and police brutality. She ends her stirring and poignant memoir with the words, "We who believe in freedom cannot rest until it comes." These words embody how Green, beginning with a racist incident that occurred when she began her first job, committed to living a life of activism. This unforgettable incident left an indelible mark on her life; she determined that she would never allow herself to be subjected to overt racism without fighting back. The seeds of activism were thus sowed and became a central part of Alice Green's DNA.

Green has used her voice and her writing to become a strong advocate for prison reform, fairness and equity in voting, housing, employment, and education, and a revamping of the criminal justice system. Readers will be inspired and saddened by her persistence in the face of many obstacles, her description of politics and civic unrest in Albany, and her portrayals of the many black people who have been victims of social, economic, and political injustice.

Brenda M. Greene, Founder and Executive Director of the Center for Black Literature and Professor of English at Medgar Evers College of the City University of New York

Dr. Alice Green's narrative tells about the evolution of an activist---and better yet, it is a well-researched, fascinating personal story of historical events, told within the broad context of racism in America, juxtaposed with insights about Albany's long history of dealing with racial issues in community policing and the criminal justice system. This is a good story loaded with interesting facts and anecdotes. It is a personal account of Alice's long life's journey that has concluded with her belief in "walking the walk" as an activist.

Barbara Delaney-Author of Paths to the Past, Hudson River Valley etc. and Follansbee Pond Secrets

DEDICATION

This book is dedicated to all those central to my being who are no longer here, but their spirit lives on deeply within me and guides me in my activist work: great grandmother Cicely Cawthon, grandmother Alice Moore, parents William and Annie Payton, beloved brothers Raymond and Ralph Paden, and sister Geraldine Wood. Then there are the friends and advocates who taught me so much about injustice and how to work for freedom: Boji Jordan, Vera Michelson, Eddie Ellis, Scott Christianson, and Jonathan Gradess. As well, my heart aches for all those who have and continue to be harmed by a legal system blinded by injustice and racism and dedicated to punishment and suffering instead of love and caring.

CONTENTS

Part III – The Center for Law and Justice

FOREWORD

By Paul Grondahl
Director, New York State Writers Institute and
Award-winning Journalist

I first met Dr. Alice Green when I wrote a profile on her for the Times Union in the mid-1980s. I decided to go running with her as a way to see her in action doing something she was passionate about. Staying fit and strong was very important to her. She woke up each morning before dawn to run several miles through the quiet streets of Albany. She set a fast pace, and I struggled to keep up. Her grit and determination were on display as she churned up hills without slowing down. I also remember the heartache I felt when she confided to me that on more than one occasion, passing motorists had shouted racist slurs at her as she ran through the city's Pine Hills neighborhood in the early morning hours. That is the terrible reality of racism that Alice Green has been confronting as the leading black activist in Albany since her involvement in the civil rights movement in the late-1960s.

For the past half-century, Alice Green has toiled on the front lines of the struggle to abolish systemic racism and to gain equality for black people. As the founder and executive director of the Center for Law and Justice, she has taken on that role in the style that defined her as a runner: tireless, determined and committed for the long haul. She is the conscience of Albany's black community. She gives voice to the voiceless. She speaks truth to power. She stands up for Albany's marginalized black residents, serves as an advocate for the oppressed, and fights on behalf of prisoners of color who are disproportionately incarcerated in New York State's prisons. She has never wavered in her belief that police in Albany must be reformed because they have undermined trust and created animosity in the black community. She argues that police have caused disenfranchisement through racial profiling, arrest blacks significantly more often than whites, and engage in police brutality against blacks with distressing frequency, including fatally shooting unarmed black men.

I walked alongside Alice Green as she marched in demonstrations against racial injustice and to celebrate the life of slain civil rights leader Reverend Dr. Martin Luther King Jr. I have heard her make impassioned speeches at rallies and stand in silent vigil at makeshift memorials to victims of gun violence and police shootings. I observed her trying to console grieving family members and friends of black men who died or were gravely wounded after being shot by Albany police, including Jessie Davis, Nah-Cream Moore, Dontay Ivy, and Ellazar Williams. I wrote numerous stories about those controversial cases, in which a grand jury each time called the shootings justified and failed to indict the police officers. I saw her heartache and outrage as she struggled to bend the long arc of the moral universe toward justice. I have walked with her through black neighborhoods in the city and watched how residents respected and revered the woman they address as Dr. Green and refer to as "a genuine freedom fighter."

Alice Green is the real deal. I have witnessed firsthand how she not only talks the talk, but walks the walk. She is fearless, relentless and convinced in her very marrow that she is on the right side of history and that there will be redemption for black people and that they will overcome someday.

Now, in this sweeping new memoir, *We Who Believe in Freedom: A Memoir of Activism and the Struggle for Justice,* we are offered a full portrait of Alice Green in all her complexity. Those who have known her well for many years, including myself, will learn new insights and be astonished by some of the revelations. Green reveals intimate instances when she has been harassed or mistreated because she is black, beginning when she was a teenager. The bigotry she has endured forms the foundation for the lifelong battle she has waged to demand racial equality and to challenge white supremacy and white privilege wherever she finds it. This unflinching memoir also describes her long career fighting for prison reform through the Center for Law and Justice that she established in Albany in 1985. She has worked tirelessly on behalf of prisoners of color who are disproportionately imprisoned and helps them gain employment and housing to assist their transition into meaningful, productive lives after incarceration.

The mistreatment based on the color of her skin began in her early teen years living in the Adirondack hamlet of Witherbee, Essex County, where hers was one of the only black families. Her father worked in an iron ore mine after their family migrated from the Jim Crow South in search of economic opportunity and to escape discrimination and overt racism. In the North Country, it was a more subtle form of exclusion based on race.

In her memoir, Alice Green weaves historical accounts with personal narrative, and she includes chapters on the horrible treatment of enslaved people in Albany, the impact of The Great Migration on the capital city, and the long tradition of police terrorizing the black community. She describes her work at the Trinity Institution empowering black people amid grinding poverty and disinvestment in the city's South End. She recounts her involvement with Albany's black militant group, The Brothers, and her decades of work laboring to reform the state's criminal justice system and to end racist policies governing its correctional facilities. She builds her arguments with scholarship, data and knowledge gained while earning a doctorate in criminal justice and three master's degrees – education, social work and criminology – all at the University at Albany.

Since she was a young girl, Alice Green has stood up to racism, looked racists directly in the eye, and made it clear that nobody was going to treat her like a second-class citizen. Her inner activist has remained unbound. Of course, her righteous indignation has earned her plenty of critics and opponents. I have spoken to elected officials who consider her a thorn in their sides and who actively try to discredit her and her work. I also know that she gave up her writing as an unpaid blogger for the Times Union because each and every day she was assaulted with the most vile, ugly and threatening racist attacks. She did not leave because she was afraid of these cowardly racists who hid behind the anonymity of the online world. Rather, the unending racist vitriol eventually wore her down. The repugnant comments depressed and exhausted her, and she had enough.

Alice Green practices what she preaches. In the closing chapter, she offers 10 lessons and takeaways from her journey of confronting social, racial and criminal justice in the black community. I choose to highlight three that seem central to who she is. **Do not be afraid to call out the injustices you see; Find good allies; Develop a thick skin.**

These are just a few of the attributes that make Alice Green an Albany original and an American treasure. This memoir hopefully will inspire the next generation of genuine freedom fighters.

Alice's childhood friend, Myrtle; Alice; and Alice's sisters, Joan and Geraldine in Witherbee circa 1958

INTRODUCTION

It was the dawn of the 1960s Civil Rights Movement. My family had moved to Witherbee, a small iron ore mining hamlet nestled in the Adirondack Mountains, where few blacks resided. The few who were there were beckoned from the South to work in the dangerous mines along with mostly first- and second-generation European immigrants. These blacks also came to escape Jim Crow oppression and find a land free from racism. We soon learned our new home was no panacea, but displays of racism were more subtle. At the age of 15, I had a brutal and abrupt awakening to the evils of racism and white supremacy that would shape my view of the world and the work I would devote my life to doing.

Strong friendships were hard to come by in Witherbee, but I was fortunate to live next door to white twin girls who were my age and became like sisters to me. We were inseparable. Now that we were of working age, one of the twins, Myrtle, and I decided to seek employment in the tourism business to earn money for needed school clothing and supplies. We knew how to clean, wash dishes, and make beds, just the skills needed for a chambermaid position. We landed a position at Clautice's Motel and Restaurant in Paradox Lake, near Schroon Lake, but some 40-miles from our homes. The job offered free food and housing. So, we accepted the maid positions and looked excitedly toward working and living together as roommates.

We arrived at our work location where the white southern owner, Mrs. Clautice, greeted us. During the summer tourism season, she and her family resided in the main house on the property in a large, well-furnished second-floor apartment, which was part of the introductory tour she gave to her new employees. Myrtle and I thought we had struck pay dirt.

Following the tour, we met her regular summer help who she brought with her from the South - a married black couple who cooked for the restaurant. They were assisted by a young, well-built black teenager. We also met the bartender and waitress staff who were all white; they lived together in a nice little staff cottage.

The time came for Mrs. Clautice to show us to our room. Myrtle and I could hardly contain our excitement about living together during our first stay away from home. Mrs. Clautice showed Myrtle to her room, located in the family's luscious living quarters. We explained how we expected to live in a shared room. Mrs. Clautice quickly told us that was impossible. Then, she led me to my room. We walked to the back of the building to a large barn with steps leading up to its unfinished loft, a space with a high-pitched ceiling and no furnishings. Mrs. Clautice explained that a section of the loft would be my room. The other black staff worked a night shift. They were housed in the barn as well. I stared in disbelief and fear.

Because I was black, I had to live in a barn while my best friend, who was white, would live with the owner's family in a large, furnished room in the big white house. I became numb with anxiety and anger. Myrtle seemed dumb founded as well and begged to room with me. Mrs. Clautice reiterated how our request was out of the question. I was being told I had to live like the animals who once occupied the space now reserved for me and the other black staff. What should I do? I kept asking myself, knowing my mother desperately wanted me to work for the summer to help her get the things my siblings and I would need for the coming school year. I did not want to disappoint her and add to the stress my family was undergoing due to our poverty situation. Added to these concerns was the fact that I had no way to get home short of walking 40 miles.

I waited until the black night staff came on duty to ask them how they felt being housed in a barn and segregated from the rest of the staff. Seemingly bewildered by my question, they simply dismissed me by replying, "This is the way it is."

Fearing a night alone in the big barn and confused about what to do about the situation, I slowly made my way up the stairs as night was falling. A single cot awaited my anxiety-ridden body. Reluctantly, I crawled into it.

Unable to sleep, I noticed something perched on a high beam above my bed. What was it? Soon others joined it. Although fearful of them, I had never seen live ones in my life – bats. Bats were circling the room. I sat in that room and cried until dawn. I had my answer about what to do.

I marched down to the big house and asked to see Mrs. Clautice. I relayed how angry I was over her display of racism. After I finished my loud, angry ranting, she told me, with a flushed face, I was fired. My response to her was, "Too late! I already quit!" Myrtle had joined us in the room. She chimed in that she was quitting too. We gathered our belongings and headed for the highway to go home.

I took along my dignity, self-respect, and commitment to fight racism and white supremacy. My promise to myself at 15 years of age was to never again allow white people to demean, disrespect, or devalue me or other blacks, particularly those in poverty and under the control of our legal and criminal justice systems. After all, my Dad left the South primarily due to his fear of convict leasing and chain gangs, so much a part of the criminal justice system.

"We Who Believe in Freedom: Activism and the Struggle for Social Justice" exposes readers to weighty topics such as police abuse and accountability, criminal justice and prison reform, and political abuse of power. In this book – part memoir and part history - I demonstrate these topics through my life experiences as a lifelong advocate, highlighting the impact they have had on Albany's black communities since the early days of enslavement up to the present day where we still have so many racial and criminal justice issues before us.

Along the journey, I introduce you to people I have known and respect who love freedom as much as I do and have actively devoted their lives to the work of achieving social justice, racial equity, and freedom for all people. I saw them as kindred spirits who shared my commitment.

This book is also an exercise in remembering, praising and thanking many of those who blazed the trail to achieve justice for blacks and other people of color, particularly those who came to Albany during the early 20th century. Then there are those who came immediately following the Second World War, when a steady stream of black families and individuals started arriving from the South as part of the Great Migration. Black and brown people now make up more than a third of Albany's population. Their arrival generated much friction and tension between them and whites at times. In a city dominated by a Democratic political machine and government officials eager to control these newcomers, it became clear they would have to continue their struggle for freedom in their new home. And, the police would, in large measure, define the nature and character of their new struggle. But, the new wave of blacks paved the way for the current struggle to dismantle white supremacy and the systemic racism that continue to define our community institutions and keep us in bondage. I found much to celebrate and honor in this continuing struggle for freedom and justice.

A large segment of this book is devoted to the work of the Center for Law and Justice, an organization I founded in 1985 to actively work for transformative change in criminal justice and the elimination of structural racism.

Although my memory of events and circumstances may not always be completely accurate, I believe them to be truthful.

My thoughts are mine, even though they may differ from the recollections of others.

In looking back, I give mention of several black Albanians who experienced life in early Albany going back to the 18th century and through the mid-20th century. Perhaps, the most telling historical document about black life in Albany comes from a 1928 Urban League report titled, "The Negro Population of Albany, New York." But, my attention is heavily focused on black Albanians who lived and struggled here during and following World War II, when most of them migrated from the South looking to escape the harsh and often deadly treatment they experienced there. Every 10 years, their numbers doubled. My knowledge of their experience in Albany was gleaned from stories, writings and conversations with many who I met upon my arrival in the city.

My personal recollections begin in the mid-1960s when I permanently settled and started working in the city, equipped with a bachelor's degree and trying to shed my upstate rural identity and lack of knowledge about black history. I was fortunate enough to get started while the Civil Rights Movement was in full swing, and Albany was beginning to change geographically and demographically. It was a time when a growing number of Albanians began thinking about how to make social, political and economic changes that might free residents from the control of the Democratic political machine that had controlled the lives of ordinary people for far too many years. Albany County Democratic Chairman Dan O'Connell and Albany Mayor Erastus Corning kept firm control of the city for more than half a century.

Here, I also share my thoughts, knowledge, perceptions and experiences that shaped my life as an activist and inspired me to form the Center for Law and Justice. This organization gave structure and support for my lifelong participation in the struggle for social justice and freedom. I also share my recollections of the many dedicated community leaders and social activists I learned from and was fortunate enough to work with side-by-side. There are so many who fought courageously for justice, including those who died for the cause.

For a long time, I rejected the label "activist". It sounded mundane at one point. But, after years of struggle, I now embrace that label with great pride and joy. I actively work to promote change. Unlike some of my intellectual and professional associates who are expected to adhere to a definite structure and set of principles and maintain a defined decorum, activists can go beyond those expectations. They can often throw all caution to the wind and move instinctively ahead with what they believe to be right to relieve pain and change the social structure without worrying about acceptability of their actions by others.

I conclude with a brief discussion of where I believe we are as a nation and community when it comes to destroying white supremacy, structural racism, poverty, and other oppressive forces that have been operating to harm and oppress black people since 1619. How were we affected by the brutal murder of George Floyd right before our eyes and the coming together of millions who finally understood the dilemma of black folks in America, recognizing that the battle for true freedom is not yet won?

After looking back over my life and that of so many fellow activists, I wanted to title this memoir, "We Who Believe in Freedom" after a song – Ella's Song - written by Bernice Johnson Reagon for my idol, Ella Baker. Bernice paid great tribute to Baker, who gave so much to the Civil Rights Movement without fanfare, just strong persistent activism without resting. This is how I see the commitment and work of so many tireless souls committed to continuing the struggle for freedom that began in 1619 and continues today. The song goes on to highlight the killing of black sons, which is solemnly appropriate for this time in our country. After the murder of George Floyd and countless others, we know we cannot rest or give up the struggle until we are all free, no matter how long it takes. This song also speaks to the work of activists who I feature in this book and the work left to be done by our young people. Read these words below, and let them penetrate your soul. May they ignite the activist in you.

Ella's Song
Refrain:
We who believe in freedom cannot rest
We who believe in freedom cannot rest until it comes

Verses
Until the killing of Black men, Black mothers' sons
Is as important as the killing of White men, White mothers' sons

And that which touches we most is that I had a chance to work with people
Passing on to others that which was passed on to me

To me young people come first, they have the courage where we fail
And if I can shed some light as they carry us through the gale

The older I get the better I know that the secret of my going on
Is when the reins are in the hands of the young who dare to run against the storm

Not needing to clutch for power, not needing the light just to shine on me
I need to be just one in the number as we stand against tyranny

Struggling myself don't mean a whole lot I come to realize
That teaching others to stand up and fight is the only way my struggle survives

I'm a woman who speaks in a voice and I must be heard
At times I can be quite difficult, I'll bow to no man's word

PART I

History of African Americans in Albany

New York State Capitol Building
Photo courtesy of King Jesus Press LLC

Groans from the Grave:
Caesar, Pompey and the Negro Girl

The City of Albany. Birthed by charter in 1686. New York's capital city. Home to the majestic New York State Capitol adorned with stunning, 19th century architecture and a million-dollar staircase. A historical showcase of culture, commerce and transportation. A city that owned enslaved Africans.

It is no surprise to me that the city I work in, where I have dedicated my life to criminal justice advocacy and reform, used brawny Africans torn away from the thrones and fields of a mighty continent to serve a life sentence of enslavement. Two known enslaved Africans owned by the City of Albany were Caesar, sold December 5, 1794, and Pompey, sold June 22, 1795. Although my research does not tell me details of their lives and all they endured in bondage, I wonder if they suffered from constant beatings to 'whip them into shape' or were exposed to grisly events like seeing others maimed or hanged. I wonder if they worked inside the comforts of City Hall or if the sun darkened their already black hue from working outdoors from sun up to sundown.

We have all heard stories about the abominable atrocities black people suffered and endured at the hands of white slave masters who considered them to be no more than chattel or personal property. History tells us of an unjust slavery system that, on one hand, valued black bodies, and on the other hand, devalued black bodies.

During slavery, black men, women and children were a commodity, or a product. And just like any other commodity, such as precious metals, produce, or raw materials, they had monetary value. While slaves were of value to their owners because of all the money they were able to make off free labor, blacks were treated like they weren't even human or worthy of the same liberty and pursuit of happiness enjoyed by others. They were bought, branded, beaten, and berated. They were treated like soulless bodies, dispensable after the useful life cycle. They were as valuable as sugar, and as devalued as an old workhorse.

After all the physical, emotional and psychological pain that my imagination tells me Caesar and Pompey suffered under a system of oppression in Albany, I want to believe their souls are resting well now. But I can't. I want to believe that every scar from the branding iron or whip that cracked against their bodies was not in vain. But I can't. I want to believe the sound of the drumbeat led their spirits safely to their ancestors from the citizenry of Africa. But I can't.

I believe they are full of sorrow, knowing that the same soil they treaded, the same city where they suffered, is the same city where blacks like them continue to suffer under another system of oppression. While enslaved people in New York State became free in 1827, the economic system in the state - and later in the country - evolved from free labor under the legal act of slavery to free labor through mass incarceration. They traded one set of chains for another.

Criminalized Movement

For Ellazar Williams, a young black man in Albany, those chains came in the form of racial stereotypes that led to a police detective mercilessly shooting him in the back and leaving him paralyzed from the chest down in August 2018. Ellazar was 19 years old when he and two friends were at a convenience store on Central Avenue in Albany. The store owner had a dispute with one of the friends, and as they walked away, a store employee called the police and claimed one of the young men in hoodie had a gun. Unfortunately, this is where the tragedy began for Ellazar.

Detectives in an unmarked car were nearby and responded to the call. Fearing the police, as is common in predominately black communities, Ellazar ran away instead of heeding the officer's command to stop. Across a school concrete courtyard, and with the agility and motion of a football player, Ellazar ran as if his life depended on it. And it did. Moments later, the detective fired two shots - I believe without provocation - with one striking Ellazar in the back. The crippling bullet is still lodged in his spine. Why? Because society is conditioned to believe black boys and men are all menacing thugs that we should be afraid of. Because it was easier for the detective to pull the trigger on the questionable claim of fearing for his life, than to utilize other tactics to apprehend Ellazar. Because the color of Ellazar's skin determined his guilt before he even stepped into a courtroom.

Anger consumed me when I heard about Ellazar's story. An oppressive force, once again, had control over the life and wellbeing of a black person. The detectives were operating on stereotypes that are deeply embedded in the police department, and this goes all the way back to slavery. Blacks were seen - and are still seen - as lazy, worthless and shiftless. Stereotyping is the only way I can explain why the police acted this way. They did not value Ellazar's life, and they used a weapon to take him down.

I felt helpless and powerless as this situation unfolded. Here we have a young man who is paralyzed, and I cannot do anything about it. Ellazar, who grew up in foster care, now has a life forever altered from August 2018. His financial and medical needs are mounting, and he requires caregiver assistance to get him through life every day. My heart mourns his dire circumstances. My head swirls from the fathomless actions of this officer of the law who shot a black man recklessly and without cause. But my fight muscles are strengthened by my resolve to create transformative change in police/community relations in Albany.

After an investigation, the Albany Police Department issued a report and cleared the officer of any wrongdoing, but brought criminal charges against Ellazar, the victim. The report detailed the events as the police saw it, yet it was full of apparent contradictions. The most obvious contradiction said Ellazar was coming toward the officer brandishing a weapon. If that was the case, how was he able to shoot Ellazar in the back? To understand how police in the City of Albany can get away with shooting a black man in the back as he runs away, you first must understand the history of black people here.

The criminal justice system has been impacting the lives of blacks since enslaved Africans first arrived in Albany. A report published by the National Urban League in December 1928 gives a historical account and timeline of some of these early individuals. In 1650, the Dutch West India Company (WIC) sold an enslaved African in Albany. The WIC was a trade or charter company of Dutch merchants and investors, and it was largely responsible for the Dutch colonization of North and South America. And even though Albany was not an official city yet, records indicate blacks were in this area even as early as 1628.

When Albany formed its government in 1686, its by-laws stipulated, "That no Negroe or other slave doe drive any carte within this citty under the penaltie of Twenty Shillings to be paid by the owner of such slave for each offence. Brewers, drays or carriages for beer only excepted, etc." Even at the very foundation of our city's structure, black people's movements were criminalized, much like Ellazar's. Old English and misspelling aside, this law dictated their "place" in the city and reinforced their station in life. It established a hierarchical society that ranked blacks at the bottom. It planted the seed of viewing blacks as inhumane, and sprouted a tree of racism, bigotry and intolerance that stands tall today.

Not only did Albany's early by-laws control and criminalize the movement of blacks, they assessed a penalty for those who got caught. In this case, the penalty was twenty shillings, the currency used at that time. Enslaved people were already confined by the nature of their existence, so jailing the offenders was not an option. That punishment for frivolous offenses would come later. Instead, slave owners had to pay.

Without Retribution

In addition to our city's history telling us blacks were not welcome in certain areas, it also demonstrates that whites could cause harm or death to blacks without consequences. In 1687, a slave owner named John Caspers was indicted for causing the death of one of his slaves. "His Negro girl" is what the records call her. I do not know why this unnamed girl lost her life. Maybe she rejected him after her pubescent curves aroused John's senses, causing him to force himself on her. We know it was common for slave masters to rape their slaves. Maybe her debilitating menstrual cycle caused her work production to slow down, triggering angry John to lash out with rage. But what I do know is, he got away with it. Yes, he was *indicted*, and ordinarily, the sounds of an indictment would be a sweet melody in our ears. It would be the beginning of justice to come. After all, an indictment is a criminal accusation that a person has committed a crime. But research indicates there is no evidence of a *trial*. A trial would mean John would have had to appear before an all-white jury of his peers. His peers were other esteemed landowners. Parishioners at his church. The affable woman he waved to when he passed by the general store every day. The rambunctious men he hung out with at the tavern. John's peers would have never convicted him even if he had a trial. His life meant more than the life of his dispensable property. No trial means no conviction. No conviction means there was no justice for "his Negro girl".

I have seen this somber scenario play out repeatedly in the black community over the past 40 plus years that I have been on the forefront of social and criminal justice reform. Reflecting on injustices that have become commonplace in the black community, raw emotions swell in me as I recall Donald "Dontay"

Ivy, who died at the hands of white police officers in 2015 after they tasered the 39-year-old black man who had been diagnosed with mental health issues. His crime was walking home from the store on a frigid night in his Arbor Hill neighborhood.

Nah-Cream Moore was riding in a car parked on South Pearl Street when police approached and ordered him out of the car. After 19-year-old Moore exited the vehicle, police fatally shot him three times in the chest. Police said Moore was reaching for a gun, but an eyewitness accused the officer of shooting Moore while he was unarmed and on the ground. Moore's crime was the assumption of guilt because he was a parolee.

On April 11, 1991, 30-year-old Raymond Stallings, an ex-marine and correctional officer, left the Grand Union store in Elsmere – an Albany suburb – when a detective in an unmarked car followed him because he "appeared nervous and ill-at-ease." I can only imagine what Stallings' thinking might have been at a time when Rodney King had just been beaten in Los Angeles by the police, a high-profile case. When the detective ran the plates on the car Raymond borrowed from his sister and found that they did not match the car, he called for backup, and Albany city and county police joined him. With red flashing lights and three police departments in pursuit of him, Stallings jumped out the car and ran across a field - panicked by all the commotion – and dropped dead from a heart attack. This black man from Albany's crime was buying groceries for his wife's birthday celebration in a suburban, white community. His grieving wife said he was frightened to death.

Just like John Caspers got away with murder, so did the officers who caused the deaths of Dontay Ivy, Nah-Cream Moore, and Raymond Stallings.

Albany's historical treatment of blacks has its genesis rooted in the idea of supremacism. Throughout time, we have seen how groups have had an inherent desire to dominate and control other groups. Their sense of superiority, or "I'm better than you," is a survival stance. Something in their psyche tells them they need to dominate or be dominated. Perhaps Albany's growing black population in the 18th century had something to do with this thinking. In 1771, the number of enslaved people in Albany County increased from 187 to 3,887. While this may seem like a small number, it still shows significant growth. And when you have shown cruelty to a whole race of people for so long and they begin to multiply, you scramble to maintain control by any means necessary.

This way of thinking did not dissolve with time. Centuries later, it still shows up in our halls of government, courtrooms and classrooms. It breeds in our police departments and district attorneys' offices. It takes on the form of unjust laws, inconsistent penalties, double standards for whites versus blacks, closed doors, substandard housing, and decreased opportunities. It results in economically depressed inner cities, low graduation rates, fewer job opportunities, and psychological damage.

I am committed to destroying negative stereotypes of black people and insisting we be treated as equal, human beings in American society. I owe that to people like Caesar, Pompey and the Negro girl.

Alice's parents on their wedding day, Circa 1940,
Greenville, South Carolina

The Great Migration

Early Influences

People often ask me to explain why I engage in social activism and racial justice work. The question sparks reflections on my early childhood and the four family members who played a major role in my life. They have shaped my decision to do what I am committed to - social justice. I did not realize the great influence these four people had on my life until I completed my formal education in 1982 with a doctorate in criminal justice. Then, my life took on new meaning. My education gave me a deeper and more balanced understanding of black history in America, particularly what my parents and grandparents endured during the enslavement, Reconstruction, and Jim Crow periods. Their experiences and treatment at the hands of white supremacists affected my life and perspectives on the cause of the black divide in America, how it must be addressed, and the role black individuals should play in correcting the problem. I also came to realize that I personally embody, in some fashion, the major historical forces that dramatically influenced the lives of black Americans – enslavement, Reconstruction and its demise, Jim Crow segregation, the 60s Civil Rights Movement, and mass incarceration.

Looking back at my four family members and the influence of these forces, my maternal great grandmother was first. Her name was Cicely Cawthon. She was born enslaved around 1859 in the state of Georgia, we reckon. No one knows for sure. But, she recalled a lot about her early life as an enslaved person living on a plantation owned by a white family. This I know, because she was interviewed by a writer from the 1930s Federal Writers' Project, developed to put unemployed writers to work during the Great Depression. It was part of the Works

Progress Administration (WPA) from 1936-38. This means that my great grandmother Cauthon was in her late 70s when she was interviewed.

Most of what I know about Cicely Cauthon I learned from that recorded interview.

"I think I was about five or six, but I can remember nearly everything that went on about the last of the war. I was one of Marster's born slaves, but my father come from Charleston, South Carolina. He was sold to my master," explained my great grandmother when she was interviewed. *"He paid $1,000 for both him and his mother together. My daddy come out of the drove. His name was Charlie Hames, and he was what you call the butler now. He tended around the house. He never did go to the field. He drove the carriage too. My mother's name was Harriet. She was a house girl. She had nine boys and two girls. My mother was raised there on the plantation. Marster's father raised my mother. She was one of his born slaves. My mother's mother was the cook; Icie was her name."*

After giving us a glimpse of her genealogy - my genealogy - Great Grandmother Cauthon continued with stories of the scare tactics overseers would use on the plantation.

"Overseers didn't do no more than what Marster told him to. He'd come to the field and if he saw a slave sitting under a tree he'd ask him if he was sick, and it was all right if he was sick, but if he was well and laying out under a tree, he got a whipping. The overseer would go back and tell Marster, and that night he'd give them just as many licks as Marster said, but he was careful with the darkies. I never seed the overseer have a billie in his hand. His whip was wrapped around on the side of his saddle. He'd unwrap it and put you on the clock and give whatever Marster said. Overseers didn't have no rules, but if you resisted him, he'd double your whipping. For killing time or being lazy, you get twenty-five licks; for stealing, fifty licks; and for running away, that was the worst, if they got you back, you got a hundred licks. I had a cousin to run away, and they got her back from

Charleston. The overseer give her a hundred licks. One lick cut the blood, and my Mistis got so mad she throwed that long hair back, I can see that long hair now, and quarreled at Marster. He said he had to make an example for the other slaves. Mistis said it injured the woman to whip her that way, so then Marster made them be more careful. Even that warn't as bad as going to the chain-gang now."

I have only the vaguest memories of her, but I do recall more vividly her wake, which was held at the family home in the small town of Taccoa, Georgia. As her lifeless body occupied the casket in the living room, I didn't want to look. Five-year-old me was petrified. Even though my parents wanted me to, I didn't want the last image of her to be one as morbid as that. To find out she was dead and not moving was very scary to me, as it probably would be for any child. That fear still invades my memory.

Great Grandma Cauthon's large, white house with a swing on the porch sat back from the dirt road on a small hill of red clay dirt that many blacks were fond of eating. Some say it's a tradition carried over from West Africa. A huge pecan tree sat in the backyard and provided shade and the most delicious nuts. Both offered added pleasure to her great grandchildren's infrequent visits to her house.

My Mom's visits to Great Grandma Cauthon's home were much more frequent. After all, my Mom thought of her as "mother" because Granny Cauthon, as we knew her, raised her oldest grandchild, who learned how to survive and manage a household in the Jim Crow South, something all black females were required to know.

When I became an adult, having learned about enslavement, I became deeply troubled and angered by the fact that my great grandmother had been owned by someone and was considered property like a pig or a chicken, or more infuriating, a table or chair, but not an equal human being.

My paternal grandmother, Alice Moore, was a southern sharecropper, born in 1871 during Reconstruction in South Carolina. She bore and reared several sons (we never knew exactly how many), two of them ventured North as young men. No one in our family ever mentioned a grandfather on either side.

Grandma Alice was a tough cookie. We were told that she partied and was a heavy drinker, but a hard worker. Then, she found religion, which turned her life around, and she became a community leader, industrious and a businesswoman of sorts. Her hard work and determination to climb out of poverty paid off when she earned money sewing, taking in white folks' laundry, making wine from locus leaves, and scavenging. Not only did she make money, but she gained the respect of blacks and whites alike.

As her namesake, she treated me royally, which irritated my five brothers and sisters. She gave me everything she thought I wanted and was often called upon to help our family with financial support to ward off the ever-threatening criminal justice system that seemed bent on controlling the behavior of her youngest son, my Dad. He made little money at his cotton mill job, drank alcohol as his mother had done before him, and resented and feared a criminal justice system bent on using a chain gang and conducting a convict-leasing system designed to legally return black men and women to enslavement by arresting, sentencing, and, in turn, leasing them out to private companies that exploited them by using their labor to satisfy their unjust jail sentence.

Perhaps my clearest and most enduring memory of Grandma Alice is of her taking me along with her before dawn on her weekly scavenging trip to the garbage can in the back of a local white-owned grocery store, where she always found something that could be rescued for food or used for some other purpose. Sometimes, it was a grapefruit gone a little bad or an apple with a brown spot that she would simply cut away. After filling her handmade gunny sack shopping bag, she and I would head home as the sun would begin to rise. I held on to her long flowing skirt while she carried the bag of questionable goodies in one hand and her walking stick in the other.

Everyone seemed to know that Grandma Alice had money when no one else on our dusty, country road did. We shared a small, two-family house with Grandma living next door. This arrangement allowed me to watch my father and a string of neighbors stop by her house hoping for a loan or a handout. She was tight, yet firm and generous. Our small, segregated neighborhood street in Greenville, South Carolina appreciated and respected her for her generosity, ingenuity, and leadership.

Grandma Alice left me with much more than her name. She taught me the value of family, hard work, persistence, conserving resources, sharing, challenging injustice, and community leadership. Her life had shaped mine in so many ways.

My Dad had a much more subtle, but substantial influence on my life. He was not close to his children, but he was committed to providing for our care even though major roadblocks were placed in his way. To escape slave wages, Jim Crow segregation and the threat of imprisonment under the South's convict leasing system, he fled to the North to raise his family. But there, he found only limited relief, due largely to racism and poverty that proved detrimental to his health, welfare, and level of employment.

But, it was my Dad's hard work and insistence on being treated with dignity and fairness that sharply defined him. For example, he stubbornly refused to accept derogatory name-calling that other black men in the area allowed in order to *keep the peace*. For him, they were *fighting words* that could never be allowed. I came to respect and embrace his approach to life, which helped shape my intolerance for attacks on my dignity and that of others.

Perhaps my Mom had the greatest impact on my life. We were close to each other. By the age of six or seven, I observed and recognized her tough struggle to survive and care for her children. I sensed when she was unhappy, hurting physically and emotionally, fearful, and determined.

Mom gave her children not only the gifts of life and love, but also how to cope with poverty, rejection, and racism. Rearing her seven children *was* her life. She sacrificed so much for us, even in poor health and while abused occasionally by my father and our much older half- sister much of her life. Yet, she carried on nurturing and protecting her six younger children. From her, I learned the values of education, hard work, compassion, family, persistence and caring. She did all the things caring and attentive parents do. She never missed a parent open house or consultation with our teachers, attended my brothers' sporting events and competitions, insisted we attend Sunday school and church services, made sure we were in the house at her specified time, assigned work details to us all, taught us about our changing adolescent bodies, constantly advocated for our safety and well-being, and did so much more to keep our family healthy. Most importantly, she taught me to be kind and caring, yet assertive in my beliefs. She was a gentle woman.

I do the work of social justice due to the influence of these four giants in my life and the resolve to eliminate all those oppressive forces that shape and restrict the life chances of black people.

From Enslaved to Imprisoned

It was oppressive forces that drove black families to the North en masse during the Great Migration from around 1916 – 1970. The end of slavery left a gaping hole in America's economy. Our nation's early political leaders knew ending slavery meant there would be a shift in America's economic foundation-- a foundation that created generational wealth for so many corporations, institutions and white families. Their solution was to end slavery and just criminalize being black. That way, the nation could continue to profit from free labor, while rebuilding the southern economy post-Civil War.

In her criminal justice documentary titled *13ᵗʰ* – a nod to the 13ᵗʰ Amendment to the Constitution of the United States - award-winning filmmaker Ava Duvernay brilliantly explains how blacks continued to endure systematic hardships through the criminal justice system, even after slavery in the United States was so-called abolished in 1865.

The 13ᵗʰ Amendment reads:

Neither slavery nor involuntary servitude, **except as a punishment for a crime whereof the party shall have been duly convicted,** *shall exist within the United States, or any place subject to their jurisdiction. Congress shall have power to enforce this article by appropriate legislation.*

This "except as a punishment for a crime" loophole in the 13ᵗʰ Amendment had a two-fold, detrimental impact on black men, women and youth that we still feel more than a century and a half later. First, this continuation of bondage prolonged black servitude. As Duvernay's documentary highlights, four million people who were formerly property were now free. Our government activated that criminal clause immediately after the Civil War to rebuild the economy in the South using these very same people who just gained freedom under the Constitution. To achieve this, police would arrest black men for minor crimes like loitering and vagrancy. They got away with this by instituting Black Codes – restrictive laws designed to control the movement and conduct of blacks. Can you imagine being a black man who just gained freedom, but have no home to lay your head, so you are arrested for being homeless? Or, a black man who is no longer obligated to sow in the fields, but is jobless, so you're arrested for loitering as you stand around contemplating where your next meal will come from? These frivolous arrests that unfairly targeted blacks were just enough reason to bind freed blacks in chains once again, forcing them to work for free through the criminal justice system.

Society created this narrative of blacks being criminals who needed to be controlled; menacing savages who went around pillaging homes, raping white women and breaking laws. These myths permeated every part of southern culture – entertainment, arts, politics, religion, education, law enforcement – and were just enough to create disdain for blacks. The rhetoric swayed public opinion, and it led to many arrests. Through the centuries that followed, we continued to see a structure controlling the movement of blacks and enforced by the criminal justice system.

The other reason for criminalizing blacks was to shut them out of the political system by impacting their ability to vote. I thought a lot about this when I started my graduate studies at SUNY Albany where I was a part of the Blacks in Criminal Justice project. It was an aha moment when I realized that the disproportionate incarceration of black men and efforts to curb their right to vote went hand in hand. I have been speaking about this issue for a long time and only recently have others adopted this reality and perspective. I was delighted to see Duvernay address the issue in *13th*.

I experienced a feeling of hopelessness when I started thinking about that clause in the 13th Amendment because racism is so deeply imbedded and hidden in our history, and most of the people I knew were happy to point to the amendment as a real source of freedom. I saw it as having won something on one hand but lost something else on the other. I also realized that the South could never accept losing the war and their billions of dollars of property. They had to find a more *subtle* way of bringing back enslavement, while adhering to the Constitution. This increased my mistrust of white America.

Neither the 13th Amendment (granting freedom), 14th Amendment (granting citizenship) or 15th Amendment (granting voting rights) have provided true freedom and equity to black people. There is no equal protection of the law under the 14th Amendment, and the states could determine the criteria for voting under the 15th Amendment. With the latter, we got poll taxes, grandfather clauses, literacy tests, and felony convictions as limits on the right to vote.

Poll Taxes and Grandfather Clauses

Beginning in the late 1800s, many southern states required people to pay a poll tax before they could **vote**. This fee to vote was clearly enacted to keep black men from voting, even after the 15th Amendment was supposed to give them this civic right. Most of them were poor and unable to pay a tax. To maintain the privilege of being white, many poor whites were excluded from paying a poll tax because of a **grandfather clause**, which said adult males were exempt from the tax if their father or grandfather had voted before. Obviously, no black fathers or grandfathers had been able to vote.

Literacy Tests

As another deterrent to voting, the government implemented literacy tests in the 1890s. These tests supposedly analyzed voters' ability to read and write, and they were given to anyone who could not prove a fifth-grade education. Below the surface, it was another legalized method of keeping blacks – who were historically shut out of education - from voting. These tests were nearly impossible to pass, and while whites also were subjected to them, blacks were given harder tests, or administrators would mark their answers wrong intentionally.

Questions on literacy tests could be anything *from: interpret a section of the state constitution and write an essay on the responsibilities of citizenship,* to: *If a person charged with treason denies his guilt, how many persons must testify against him before he can be convicted?* Then, there were literacy tests that were not designed to test literacy, but to intentionally confuse blacks taking the test. Louisiana had questions such as: *Draw a figure that is square in shape. Divide it in half by drawing a straight line from its northeast corner to its southwest corner, and then divide it once more by drawing a broken line from the middle of its western side to the middle of its eastern side.* The anxious, would-be voter had a mere 10 minutes to complete about 30 convoluted questions, and one wrong answer resulted in a failed test. In Great Grandma Cauthon's state of Georgia, they had questions such as: *What does the Constitution of the United States provide regarding the suspension of the privilege of the Writ of Habeas Corpus? What does the Georgia Constitution provide?*

Felony Convictions

Being shut out of the voting process because of felony convictions was yet another voting deterrent, and one we still see today. Section 2 of the 15th Amendment allowed states to enact such legislation.

White America created all these barriers for the sole purpose of voter suppression - to keep blacks disenfranchised - and if those methods did not work, good old-fashioned physical threats and acts of violence by white-hooded Klansmen or angry mobs were the next tactic of choice.

Escaping Southern Oppression

The hostility toward blacks was unbearable in the South. The disparity in treatment was inhumane. The looming thought of getting arrested, or worse – killed, was frightening. After all, Grandmother Alice's home state of South Carolina, along with Mississippi, were the first to enact Black Codes in the South in 1865. My family did not have to look too far to find examples of the type of brutality and calamity blacks feared. On February 17, 1947, in my hometown of Greenville, South Carolina, a mob of white men lynched a 24-year-old black man named Willie Earle. Earle had been jailed in the Pickens County jail on charges of assaulting a white taxicab driver. Law enforcement, which has historically failed blacks, allowed a mob of white men to take him from his jail cell to a deserted country road, where they viciously beat him, slashing chunks of meat from his body before blasting him with a shotgun. Thirty-one men were charged with murdering Earle, but an all-white jury acquitted them three months later, even after most of them confessed to his murder.

My father was hard working, and he demanded respect. Grandmother Alice grew increasingly fearful of what might happen to him if he remained in Greenville. My mother was also fearful. She was scared to death every time he went to his job at Dunean Cotton Mill where he worked for very low wages. I heard stories growing up of my Dad having to walk to the cotton mill before daybreak - not to escape the sweltering heat that interrupted pre-dawn's gentle coolness – but because my mother was petrified of him being falsely accused of making eye contact or whistling at a white woman. A light penalty for such an act of defiance and aggression was jail time. The grave penalty that unfortunately fell on some was death by lynching.

Because of the fear of police, my father decided to follow the sweeping migration North to escape the oppressive forces in the South and to search for better opportunities. In 1949, he relocated his family to Witherbee, New York, or what we like to call it, the North Country. Although my mother was saddened to leave her family and support system behind, it was safer than living in the South. She was reared by her formerly enslaved grandmother, so she knew very well the horrors that could fall upon black families. Neither she, nor my father, wanted our family to get caught up in the convict lease system in the South where blacks were snatched off the streets and leased out to work for free. Once you were in the system, you could not get out of it.

My father's older brother, Herman, had already moved North to work in the iron ore mining industry after serving in World War I. His employer, Witherbee Sherman – later named Republic Steel Corporation - used to travel South to recruit. Working in the mines was a very hard and dirty job, and southern blacks were used to hard work. By this time, immigration from Europe had slowed down, and the company needed to find another pool of candidates to work in this laborious and dangerous industry. So, my father joined his brother in the mines.

There were very few people of color in Witherbee. It was much different from the communities in Greenville we were used to. Witherbee is in the Adirondacks, where pristine and expansive mountains nestle rural communities. We did not see the other black families in the area much. They were probably just as curious about us as we were about them.

Witherbee was an all-white, Catholic town. There were many first-generation European immigrants, and they connected very well together. Blacks stood out, not only because of our color, but, because we were non-Catholic. After a time, the community came to tolerate our presence, but we were still not treated like equals. There was very little interaction between blacks and whites back then. There were some racists, and they did not hide it. They had a posture of white supremacy, and they wore it like a badge of honor. It was the familiar tone my parents had grown accustomed to back home. Others whites were more covert. In school, they would try to touch my hair and skin out of curiosity. Did they think my smooth black skin was painted on and the color would rub off on their fingers as they swiped my face?

My mother just wanted me to fit in. She would straighten my hair to replicate the silky tresses of the white girls in school. The routine to tame my coils was all too familiar to little black girls everywhere. A hot, metallic comb heating up on the stove. A greasy hair dressing for that desired sheen. Smoke emitting from the comb right before it makes contact. And the sizzling sound of burning hair as the comb snags then glides through my hair. My mother expected us to "act white." I suppose she thought it would help us assimilate in our new North Country environment.

While we and other families were relocating to the Adirondacks, blacks were also moving two hours south of Witherbee to Albany. It was not just my family seeking a better quality of life. Details from the 1928 National Urban League survey documents – among other trends – there were 1,239 blacks in the City of Albany in 1920. While they only made up about one percent of the population at the time, their numbers had grown steadily over the previous decades. In 1900, there were 1,178 blacks in Albany. Ten years earlier, in 1890, there were 1,122. In 1880, there were 1,048. And in 1870, there were 764.

The movement of black families to Albany and other areas across the country during the Great Migration was no different than the migration of other ethnic groups. History shows us that all people who are oppressed try to leave. Just like the Irish left their homeland because of the Potato Famine in the 1800s, the Italians who were war refugees or trying to escape an unfair taxation system, and the Jews who left Europe after a rise in antisemitism, they also were looking for a destination with better conditions and opportunities.

Most of the black population that moved to Albany during the Great Migration was from southern states. This is no surprise since every **United States Census** prior to **1910** shows more than 90 percent of the black population in the U.S. lived in the South. These families arrived from places like Georgia, Alabama and Tennessee. But, the states where most of the population came from were Virginia, North Carolina and South Carolina. And, although a smaller portion came from Mississippi, the migration of blacks from "The Magnolia State" has been well documented in books and film.

Shubuta, a small town in Clarke County, Mississippi, is where many blacks in Albany can trace their family roots. Shubuta is on the eastern border of the state, and in 2010 had a total population of only 441. This number dwindled from Shubuta's heyday in the late nineteenth century when it experienced prosperity from the booming economy as a result of the railroad. People would travel for miles to visit its shops and commercial district. Shubuta's port was important to the cotton industry, as cotton was shipped downriver from Shubuta to Mobile, Alabama, and then to other major ports.

For such a small town that most people probably have never heard of, Shubuta has six houses and an old railroad bridge that are listed on the National Register of Historic Places. The railroad bridge, nicknamed the "Hanging Bridge", is recognized for its ghastly past. It is where several young people were brutalized and lynched. In 1918, four black farm workers: two brothers ages 16 and 20, and two sisters, also ages 16 and 20, were hanged. They were accused of murdering a white dentist on the farm who, allegedly, impregnated both sisters when he raped them. At the time of their deaths, the sisters were six and nine months pregnant. Witnesses claim they saw one of the sister's unborn baby move in her belly the next day when she was buried. That poor baby was buried alive. If only these grisly events took place two weeks later, baby Jane Doe would have been born, albeit raised without a mother or a father.

In 1942, two other black males, ages 14 and 15, also took their last breath when they were lynched at the Hanging Bridge in Shubuta. An eyewitness spotted them talking to a 13-year-old white girl they knew from around town. And since this was frowned upon, the young men were arrested after being accused of attempted rape. The town marshal handed the boys over to a white mob who mutilated their bodies by cutting off their genitals before hanging them from the bridge.

In both the 1918 and 1942 murders, law enforcement officials colluded with angry mobs so they could dish out justice on their own. Much like we see today in Albany, these young people's lives were not valued, and the criminal justice system failed them when they were supposed to get due process. It's no wonder why blacks were eager to leave Shubuta.

In Jennifer A. Lemak's book, "Southern Life, Northern City: The History of Albany's Rapp Road Community," she details how and when blacks started leaving Shubuta for Albany. Louis W. Parson, a logger and part-time preacher from Buckatunna,

Mississippi, was instrumental in this migration. He and his wife moved to Albany after he received a large sum of money from his employer because of an on-the-job injury. He did not want to stay in Mississippi with that kind of money, so they drove North and eventually settled in Albany.

Upon arrival, they joined a small church in need of a full-time pastor. Parson was the man for the job, thus establishing the First Church of God in Christ on Franklin Street, before it eventually moved to Hamilton Street. The church experienced even more transition when the building was demolished for the South Mall project in Albany. With a slightly different name, Wilborn Temple First Church of God in Christ moved to Jay Street and still stands tall in Albany as a beacon for those seeking salvation and spiritual nourishment.

In need of members to grow this small church, Reverend Parson traveled by car back and forth to Shubuta and other nearby areas to recruit church members. He wanted his fellow Mississippians to have access to better jobs, housing and education. This could not have been an easy feat for Reverend Parson. In today's automobile, the trip would be a long, 18 and a half hours with cold air blowing in through the vents to counter the sweltering heat outside, especially in the summer. But in the 1930s, the drive would have been even longer since his Buick would not have gone as fast, hotter since he would not have had the luxury of air conditioning, and uncomfortable with more people piled on top of each other than the car is designed to carry.

As he traveled through the South, I imagine he had vittles in tow to provide him sustenance for the journey, knowing that he may not be able to find a white-owned restaurant on the way that was friendly toward blacks. He may have even had a *Green Book* - a guide published until the 60s that helped black motorists find food, lodging, gas stations and other businesses that would serve them while on the road. After all, this was the Jim Crow era where blacks encountered legal discrimination, hostility, and open violence. I picture Reverend Parson being strategic about his travel, mapping out routes that avoided "sundown towns" – all-white municipalities throughout the U.S. that enforced restrictions against blacks. If "colored people" were caught in *their* town when the sun set, the result could have been intimidation, jail, violence or worse. Despite grueling travel conditions and potential dangers, the betterment of his people was more important than the fear of what could happen. Besides, being a preacher, he put his faith in God to carry him through.

John (Jack) Johnson and his family were among those Reverend Parson brought to Albany from Mississippi. Johnson was a youth leader back home, and even helped Reverend Parson with the voyages when law enforcement started harassing Parson. Lemak accounts in her book how Johnson would make the trip in Reverend Parson's place. He strategically signaled when he arrived in town with a beep of his horn. Once eager southerners heard that, they knew he would be back later in the middle of the night to quietly whisk them away from the plantations where some were sharecroppers. They had to sneak away because some owed unfair debts to landowners that were difficult to pay. The sound of the car horn was freedom. To the north-bound individuals and families, it meant the end of peonage and back-breaking farm work. They would exchange their field clothes for britches fit for city life.

Together, Reverend Parson and Johnson helped increase the black population in Albany. With courage like Harriet Tubman and perseverance like their ancestors that came before them, Reverend Parson made countless number of trips until his death in January 1940, and Johnson was responsible for rescuing 100 blacks from the South between 1937 and 1957.

The Making of a Community

With the influx of families that arrived in Albany from Mississippi and other areas, securing housing was a priority. Many of the new transplants settled in the South End where

Reverend Parson's church was; an ethnically diverse area occupied by immigrants. This was a side of town where the German immigrants co-existed with the Irish immigrants. Where the green, white and red flag representing Italian descent indicated you were patronizing a restaurant serving authentic Italian cuisine reminiscent of Sicily. Small businesses that lined the streets often exchanged goods instead of money. Everyone was like family in this tight-knit community.

In between American Revolutionary War General Philip J. Schuyler's mansion — now a State Historic Site — and the factories and businesses that lined the port, you would find an array of houses. Blacks occupied houses that were very old, brick structures and had seen decline and decay. There were not a whole lot of available housing for blacks, as white landlords were reluctant to rent to them. The National Urban League survey indicates that these houses were in such bad shape that landlords either did no repairs or did some essential repairs to prolong the life of the buildings, but they were not up to Albany's building code standards. The city tolerated these conditions because the increased population of blacks were the ones moving into them. These types of houses were unlike anything the southern blacks had seen before. Some were a series of rowhouses attached to one another and spanning an entire block, where the only access to the backyard was through a back door.

The newcomers were not happy with the housing situation. In addition to still experiencing the racial discrimination they thought they left behind, some longed for the ability to grow their own food and raise cattle on farmland — something they could not do within the limited acreage in their new urban environment. Others were not happy with living in a seedy area where they were subjected to gambling, prostitution and bars — all prevalent in the South End.

Reverend Parson set out to remedy the housing situation his church members faced. He - along with his wife, Frances — and a gentleman named William Tolliver, purchased a total of 28 acres of land in the Pine Bush in 1930 and 1933. Reverend Parson subdivided the rural land and sold tracts to members of his congregation to get them out of the city and into an environment better suited for them. There, they cleared the land and built houses that would be the beginning of the Rapp Road community. And what a close community it was! Neighbors helped other neighbors build their homes, as banks were not dispensing mortgage loans to black folks. They had to erect their homes little by little as they were able to pay for materials.

This herculean, yet selfless effort, truly embodied what would later be called the seven principles of Kwanzaa: 1 - *Unity or umoja* - They relocated together, knowing there was strength and protection in numbers. 2 - *Self-determination or kujichagulia* – These families didn't let their humble beginnings, or the injustices of the world stop them from building their own community. 3 - *Collective work and responsibility or ujima* – Knowing that it truly takes a village, neighbors and family members pulled together to pool their resources and time to help each other achieve a better quality of life. 4 - *Cooperative economics or ujamaa* – With the space they were accustomed to in the South, families on Rapp Road were able to grow their own crops in the fields and raise animals, making them self-sufficient. They were able to share their bounty with others in need. 5 - Purpose or nia – The Rapp Road families knew there was dignity in home ownership, and they migrated North for the opportunities they were denied back home. 6 - Creativity or kuumba – When some lacked building materials because of the scarcity during World War II, they used whatever materials they could find to complete their homes, even if it meant building temporary shotgun houses until they had enough money for a more permanent, bigger house. 7 - Faith or imani – The church was a central part of the lives of the Rapp Road families. They worshipped together, and Reverend Parson ensured he met the needs of his congregation.

Rapp Road is sort of tucked away in the Western Part of Albany, lying between Washington Avenue Extension and Western Avenue. Residents did not experience much traffic because anyone who was driving through lived there or had family that lived there – that is, until the commercial development from Washington Avenue Extension took place in 1971. That is when people realized there was a black community living and thriving in the Pine Bush.

The children on Rapp Road attended School 27 for elementary school, and W.S. Hackett for junior high, before they moved on to Albany High School. This was quite a distance, so transportation for the students was necessary. Unfortunately, the city failed these youngsters by refusing to provide bus service. The official excuse from the city was the streets around Rapp Road were too narrow for a bus to navigate. In the spirit of unity and in true Christian fashion, the church community stood in the gap by working with Rapp Road residents to purchase a bus. One of the community residents drove the school bus, ensuring one less obstacle to a quality education for the black children on Rapp Road.

The confines of this new community were relatively safe. Children were free to run around and play outside. They darted from one house to another in their rural oasis until it got dark. The adults enjoyed their liberties as well, doing life together. Within their safe boundaries, the Rapp Road residents did not really encounter law enforcement. In this all-black community, the police did not concern themselves with what the residents were doing, as long as they were in *their* community. But once these residents ventured outside their bubble, the police were at hand to control the movement of blacks and make sure they were not anywhere the police thought they didn't "belong". I guess you can say Rapp Road was self-policing. In the absence of law enforcement, the church was the moral force that influenced their behavior and decisions. Religion was a central part of their lives, just as it was back home in Shubuta.

In addition to churches, social clubs also served as an integral part of the lives of blacks in Albany. Some of their origins date back to the 19th century. According to the National Urban League survey from 1928 titled, "The Negro Population of Albany, New York":

- The Female Lundys was the oldest women's club in Albany, organized in 1822 to care for the sick and bury the dead.
- The Lawton Club was another women's club for civic and social engagement. They were especially active in relief work during the World Wars.
- The Home Social Club, organized in 1887, was a men's group who socialized monthly.
- The Negro Welfare Association was dedicated to social, economic, and educational improvements of blacks.
- All Buddies, created in 1923, was an organization of black youth under adult management to develop character through mental and physical channels.
- Book Lovers and The Literary Round Table were literary clubs.

Blacks were involved in fraternal organizations as well, including:

- Improved Benevolent Protect. Order of Elks
- Knights of Pythias
- Court of Calanthe
- Ancient, Free and Accepted Masons
- Prince Hall Masons
- Eastern Star (female)
- Independent Order of Odd Fellows
- Household of Ruth

The checks and balances of the black churches and social clubs served as a deterrent that helped some blacks avoid negative law enforcement interactions. They were **there working with the community when the police were not present. They**

30

provided positive social interaction for this growing population when they were shut out of other opportunities.

In my many years advocating for social and criminal justice reforms, I have always recognized the role the community at large could play in helping to prevent blacks from succumbing to negative statistics. We grow when organizations get involved. We thrive when we are living purposefully. We excel when we are given the same opportunities as our white counterparts, and we produce when we have accountability partners.

Grandmother Alice Moore

Families who migrated to Albany from Mississippi with the help of Reverend Parson and Rev. John (Jack) Johnson

Reverend Parson

Patrons at the Blue Note on Green Street in Albany's South End,
Circa 1958

3

Police Terror in the Black Community

The South End

The Red-light district. Most urban areas have them. If they don't currently exist, they used to before government officials rid cities of their most tantalizing pleasure areas. In Manhattan, it used to be 42nd Street. In Buffalo, it used to be Chippewa Street. In Albany, it was the South End. That is how Albanians familiar with the area would describe it mid-century in the 1900s. Most of the black population in Albany lived on the South End, although others lived in Arbor Hill as well. The people in Arbor Hill were considered *elite*. It was not because they had more money or education. The central stratum was determined by how people conducted themselves; how they lived. The optics of Arbor Hill residents were that they were more refined than their South End counterparts. They had low paying jobs and did menial work too, but they were involved in the church, especially Israel AME on Hamilton Street.

"Everything was jumping off down there. The city didn't close. You had prostitution. Gambling. After- hours joints. Downtown, from Dongan Avenue to Green Street and Herkimer Street. The activities started Wednesday night. It was unbelievable! It was like Time Square," Former Police Officer Bill Payne reminisced when I interviewed him in 2010.

On a beautiful, spring day in May, we talked for a good while near Central Avenue and Henry Johnson Boulevard at the Townsend Park Homes where he shared with me his memories of Albany's South End. As a retired narcotics detective, he knew the area all too well. For a little "hick town" – as Payne called it –

Albany had a nightlife back then that rivaled even today's larger metropolitan areas. Constitution Hall – or the Hall as everyone called it - was on Beaver Street. That is where all the big-time entertainers performed: Fats Domino, Little Richard, Etta James, Mickey & Sylvia, and more. Sometimes they would stick around and stay for weeks.

One of my favorite singers was James Brown. I saw two of his electrifying performances, once at the Palace and another time at the Hall. I was a teenager, about 16 or 17 years old, the first time I saw the *Godfather of Soul*. Then, there was the time I saw Jackie Wilson when I was a college student. Jackie was a tenor with a four-octave range. What a voice! When he came to perform in Albany, I made it my mission to see him. I was with a female friend, and together, we devised a plan to sneak backstage to meet him. Our only obstacle was a young police officer named John Dale whose job was to protect Jackie. Our stealth movements paid off, and we successfully snuck into the dressing room to see our celebrity crush. John was nice about it. He could have kicked us out, but he allowed us to relish in the moment. I was absolutely delighted. I made a new friend in John Dale that day who later became the first black police chief in Albany.

This was quite an exciting experience for me – a black girl from the North Country - to see black performers whom I have always read about or saw on television but never thought I would see in person. It was a whole new world that opened for me, and I loved seeing these people that I had only dreamed about. Not only did I not see black performers where I am from, but growing up in Witherbee, I did not see a lot of other black people in general. So, making the trek into Albany and seeing other blacks expanded my horizons.

The South End was the place to be if you were looking for fun. There was a jazz café downtown called the Blue Note at 111 Green Street. A black entrepreneur named Jack Dozier and his wife Luella owned this spot from 1953 to 1965. I would say this

36

was the most popular place in Albany at the time. All the younger people hung out there. Although I have never been there, people say it was a great place to drink and listen to live music and relax. Jack was a former musician, and he also had another place on Westerlo and South Pearl streets.

Other entertainment establishments where blacks hung out included the Down Beat in the South End, Kittle's in Arbor Hill, and Dorcey's and the Two Sisters downtown on Broadway between Maiden Lane and Clinton Avenue. These spots were east of the Kenmore Hotel located downtown on North Pearl Street. Few knew that this hotel where big bands graced the stage had been black owned at an earlier period. Mike's Log Cabin at 23 North Swan Street was also in Arbor Hill, but blacks were not welcome there. There were no segregation signs denoting it as a whites only spot like one would see in the South, but it was apparent just the same. The Log Cabin is where all the white college students went. Their entertainment was vastly different, and they often longed for the sounds and beats they could only find where they followed the melanin. So, they would leave the Log Cabin sometimes and go party at Kittle's nearby.

So many forgotten-about businesses thrived on the South End once upon a time. Vastly different from the neglect you see today, this economic hub included Freeman's Department Store on South Pearl Street, William's Department Store, Paragon Paint Store, The Economy Restaurant, New York Bakery, Zucker's Bakery, Capital City Bakery, Schuyler Pharmacy, Candino's Pharmacy, Wisteria Barber Shop, Floyd's Barber Shop and Stancil's Barber Shop owned by Willie Stancil, Sr. Many indulged in billiard games at Scotty's Pool Room on Madison Avenue.

Not all enterprises were legal though. Brothels were prolific on Albany's South End. They were just as part of the community as any other business. They were next door to residences where children lived and played, and they were across the street from churches where people worshipped. One such church was the Church of God in Christ (COGIC) #3. Elder John (Jack) Johnson was the pastor, the same Johnson that helped bring black families in droves to Albany from the South.

"Our church was a three-story building located at 7 Dongan Avenue. My father [Elder John Jack Johnson] bought it from Irving Kirsch – the well-known slumlord - remodeled it, and opened a storefront church in 1952," said Reverend Sam Johnson, associate minister at Greater St. Johns COGIC and the son of Elder John Johnson. "It was located directly across the street from five houses of pleasure. I know firsthand because my father was a painter, plumber and carpenter. He was hired to paint the inside of these houses, and I helped him. My father received flak from some folks, but he would say, 'You can't criticize and talk about people. As far as I'm concerned, you have to help people where you can.' My father prayed for them and even invited them to church," explained Rev. Johnson as he reminisced about his father whom everyone affectionately called Brother Jack. According to Rev. Johnson, these houses of pleasure were also located on Herkimer, Franklin, Bleeker and Division streets.

My friend Alice Wicks, who was an Albanian and a black World War II Army veteran, once provided me with additional insight on South End illicit activities.

"Ms. Pauline was the only white madam they ever had here. She made money because she had white girls in her house. I lived right across the street on Division Street. I saw everything sitting right here on my stoop. I was only about 6-years-old, but I knew something was going on. Big cars would drive up, and the chauffeurs would let the men out. And then, they would come back and pick them up. Albany was really bustling, but everybody was making money. And the police got their cut," explained Wicks so matter-of-factly. It was well known that white police officers were frequent guests at the brothels. I guess that is how they were able to operate their forbidden businesses.

The City of Albany saw a steady increase in the black population in the 1930s, 40s, 50s and beyond. In 1930, there were 2,324 blacks who called Albany their home. In the decade that followed, there was a slight increase at 2,929. They represented only two percent of the population. Still climbing, there were 5,759 blacks in Albany by 1950, and 10,736 in 1960. The population growth wasn't surprising, considering southern turmoil and the Great Migration North. In some ways, blacks fared better in their new northern surroundings. This new population gave rise to black professionals and those who achieved trailblazer status by becoming the first in their respective fields. Sure, there were still black women who worked as housekeepers for white people and black men who worked long hours doing strenuous work in factories, but there were also those who would shatter glass ceilings and surmount tremendous difficulties to help write Albany's history of diversity.

Leroy Logan and Larry Johnson were the first black police officers in the City of Albany. John Dale climbed through the ranks to reach the highest level of law enforcement when he became the city's first black police chief, not to mention the first college-educated chief. In 1870, James C. Matthews, Esq. became the first black person to graduate from Albany Law School and the first black graduate of a law school in the state, but Peter Pryor, Esq. was the first black lawyer to graduate from Albany Law in the 20th century. His expertise would later aid in the struggle for social justice. The first black schoolteacher was Harriet Van Vranken. She taught at School 5.

William Fletcher Brown was the first black dentist, and Joe Robinson was the first black doctor here. The first black chaplain to offer prayer for the New York State Senate was the Reverend Jeremiah Smith. Garland Brothers Funeral Home is the oldest minority-owned business from Monroe County to Westchester County and the oldest black-owned funeral home in the Northeast. Benjamin G. Garland's wife, Jeanette, was the first black woman to graduate at the school of Mortuary Science from Hudson Valley in 1972.

Their successes did not come without struggle. Just as blacks were treated poorly in the South, blacks in Albany also experienced racism and injustice. This rang true in all areas, especially criminal justice and housing. After he retired, my friend Chief Dale told me how difficult it was coming up through the ranks of the Albany Police Department because of the color of his skin.

Society reinforced the notion of keeping blacks in their place. They were relegated to black neighborhoods – mostly South End or Arbor Hill – and it was unacceptable to live anywhere else, regardless of their socio-economic status. John Jennings, a prominent black attorney in Albany, was a perfect example. He bought a house in the New Scotland Avenue area in the 1960s. His dream of homeownership turned into a nightmare when, evidently, an arsonist let him know he was not welcome there. The symbolism was like that of crosses set ablaze in the South. The message was very clear. He did not belong in *their* neighborhood.

Dr. Brown also knew this harsh reality when he tried to find office space for his dental practice. White landlords did not want to rent to him. A black practicing physician and friend of Dr. Brown, Dr. James Spencer, attempted to assist him find space for his dental practice in the office he rented on Central Avenue. When Dr. Brown arrived, the landlord refused to rent to him because of the perception of two black professionals in the same building. Dr. Brown was forced to open his office in his new home on South Pearl Street.

Peter Pryor experienced housing discrimination as well. When he went to buy a house in the exclusive Loudonville area, the builder claimed he did not have the house anymore, after Pryor gave a down payment. As any good attorney would, Pryor took the seller to court, and he was fined and found guilty of blatant discrimination. That was a landmark case. Over the years, the movement of middle-class blacks to uptown Albany and into the suburbs is something Peter Pryor can take a great deal of credit for.

I too, got the message that I did not belong. In the 1970s, I was working at Trinity. Someone who worked in my office gave me a ride uptown to the Pine Hills neighborhood. After he parked, we sat in the car to finish whatever conversation we were engrossed in. Suddenly, the police showed up out of nowhere as we sat there talking. It was that moment most black people dread – a white officer walking slowly toward the car with one hand on his holstered gun and the other hand on his hip, the universal body language of someone taking assertive action. The tapping on the window and the motion to lower it is enough to throw your secretion glands into overdrive and to bring your anxiety level up. The surly officer told us we could not park there. Now, we were not illegally parked. We were not breaking any laws. Yet, he did not want us to be on a tree-lined street with well-manicured lawns filled with residents that looked nothing like me. This incident reinforced to me that there were places in Albany where black people were not allowed. It also demonstrated the constant police surveillance of blacks. I wonder if someone was peeping out of the window with suspicious eyes and called the cops on us. If this happened in today's culture, someone would have been on the sidelines recording on his cellphone camera, and it would have gone viral on social media. We have all seen videos circulating online of whites calling the cops on blacks for frivolous things like barbequing in the park - #BBQBecky - or lawfully swimming in their apartment complex swimming pool - #PoolPaul. My incident would have definitely been worthy of its own hashtag - #ParkedcarPaula.

This sentiment of *staying in your place*, even if you had achieved career goals that would afford you the opportunity to live in the more affluent neighborhoods, created communities where black entrepreneurs and professionals lived in black neighborhoods and had strong connections with the residents there. The unintended, yet positive consequence of this invisible

41

segregation was that little boys and girls had role models in their community; positive people they could one day emulate. Residents had black-owned establishments in their neighborhood; thus, circulating black dollars within the community. I spoke to Ben G. Garland in May 2009, and he echoed the importance of community.

"We, as a people, can't forget where we come from. I treat everyone the same. I can relate to some of these families [that come to my funeral home]. When they come in, they're crying. When they leave, they are laughing. I'm a part of the community. I go to affairs with them. I go to church with them. I go to restaurants with them. They come and borrow my chairs when they have functions. This is a personalized business," Garland explained as he talked about customers who patronize his funeral home business.

Tony Dean

Large gatherings of black people in *the hood* enjoying themselves was the type of environment that attracted police attention. So, the nightlife in the South End - with its girls, gambling and grooving – put a target on the backs of all those who indulged. The most famous Albany police enforcer, known throughout the black communities, was undoubtedly, Tony Dean. Dean, who grew up in Arbor Hill, became a legend by physically threatening and abusing blacks. Tony Dean was a detective in charge of the infamous Night Squad. He eventually rose to become the deputy chief of police. He was the guy with a night stick who used it to keep black folks in line. Dean's abuse and terror in the black community was commonplace, and to this day, everyone I speak to about him echoes the same message, whether they knew him personally or just heard of his notoriety.

"Tony Dean had a relative who was a detective in Troy. He didn't want to be on the force here in Albany because they hated Tony. Everybody hated that man," one confidante told me. "He was just a nasty man," another said. "Tony Dean was a rotten so and so, and he abused our people," said another friend of mine familiar with Dean. One thing is for sure, Tony Dean did not treat white people in other parts of town the way he treated blacks. I never met the man but have only heard chilling tales of his bloody reign here in Albany.

Hollywood loves to create mobster characters, and society is consumed with these bad boys of the underworld. That is why movies and shows like "The Godfather", "Scarface", "American Gangster" and "The Sopranos" have done so well. Right here in the State of New York, we had real life mobsters. Dutch Schultz was one such gangster. A Jewish boy from the Bronx, Schultz ran in the same circles as the infamous Five Families – the five major New York City organized crime families of the Italian mafia. He associated with people such as Lucky Luciano from the Genovese crime family, and Legs Diamond, an Irish gangster who spent so much time in Albany and other Upstate New York areas, he was considered a local celebrity.

Dutch Schultz only lived for a short 33 years before he suffered the same violent fate in 1935 that he often inflicted on others. But in such a small amount of time, he amassed a reputation for being a ruthless, murderous gangster whose illegal enterprises included bootlegging and gambling, as well as partnering on an illegal saloon.

As Pulitzer prize winning author William Kennedy alleges in his book, "O Albany!", Dan O'Connell – Albany's long-serving chair of the County Democratic Committee – said Jimmy Hines, the Tammany Hall leader, called him for a favor sometime in the 1930s. Hines wanted permission from O'Connell to allow Dutch Schultz to come to Albany and stay for a while. O'Connell declined because he did not want any trouble to fall upon our great city. Schultz was already on his way to Albany, and therefore, did not get the message to stay away. Now, the process of calling up the Democratic Party political machine for such a thing is a story for another time. O'Connell wanted to ensure Schultz came nowhere near Albany, so he sent the one cop he knew was tough enough to handle the situation. Detective

Tony Dean. He sent a savage like Dean to face off with a brutal gangster like Schultz. Dean met Schultz's train at Union Station to prevent him from getting off. Reportedly, Schultz did not get off the train.

This is the same Tony Dean who, with men on the Night Squad such as Detective Ted Flint and others, were ready for party goers looking for debauchery in the South End. Flint was one of Dean's loyal followers who adopted his modus operandi which was to instill fear in people, not to protect and serve.

The Night Squad, commanded by Dean, was notorious for waiting to round up blacks in the South End. During an acceptance speech in 2015 where he was honored at the Ancient Order of Hibernians, Attorney Peter Pryor spoke about Tony Dean.

"There was one person who made a name for himself as far as conduct in the South End. Tony Dean. Thank God there's no flag flying for Tony Dean! He was noted for his brutality as far as blacks are concerned. That was Tony's contribution to the City of Albany. It was one of those things that turned blacks bitter in Albany," Pryor explained.

William Brown Murder

Peter Pryor became involved in the first notable police brutality case – or what he called police assassination case - in the City of Albany. William Brown was a 23-year-old black man who was shot and killed by police on July 17, 1959. Newspapers reported police were trying to arrest Brown after another black man accused Brown of threatening him with a knife. During that same acceptance speech where he expounded on his life's work in civil rights, Pryor described the shooting that snuffed out Brown's life.

"Willie Brown was 23 when he was shot down after having been searched by police at Madison Avenue and Green

Street. After being told he could go, he was called back. They said, 'We're going to have to take you to the Second Precinct.' The first thing that came to Billy Brown's mind as a young 23- year-old was, 'You're not going to take me down there to beat me!' And he started running. Then there was a hail of gun fire on Green Street. Police started shooting. He [William Brown] was shot three times in the back. One woman told me, and I will never forget her words, 'Lawyer, I ran after them. I begged the police not to shoot anymore because he's been hit. I took Billy's head in my hand. He tried saying something, Lawyer Pryor, in a tiny voice. And he just laid there. Then the ambulance came and took him.'"

Doctor Wright, who was chief of pathology at Albany Medical Center at that time, described the wounds in Billy Brown's body. According to a conversation Pryor had with him, he said, "I don't know why this one wound went right through the groin. The exterior indicates it was a wound from the front." Pryor explained that Emma Mill - a bystander - said she asked the police, "Why are you shooting him?" And, supposedly the police said, "Get away! You're interfering with an officer!" Then he fired a shot into Brown's abdomen.

William Brown, like others, knew the reputation of the police. The thought of going into custody and facing possible brutality at the hands of those who were supposed to protect and serve was terrifying. An anxiety-filled situation, such as the one Brown faced, can trigger stress hormones that produce physiological changes. A combination of reactions to stress is also known as the *fight-or-flight* response because it is a survival mechanism, enabling people to react quickly to life-threatening situations. The sequence of hormonal changes and physiological responses help people to fight the threat off or flee to safety. Brown thought he had better odds if he fled. Running cost him his life.

Sam Clark Beating

Peter Pryor, a World War II veteran born in Savannah, Georgia, has an impressive resume as a celebrated civil rights attorney and community activist. He has worked in several capacities under New York Governor Nelson Rockefeller, worked as a consultant to the state comptroller, became assistant attorney general, chaired the consumer protection board, founded the Albany Urban League, and served as president and general counsel of the Albany chapter of the NAACP. He is also trustee emeritus at Albany Law School and Siena College. Pryor did so much work in the South End early on after he graduated law school. He recognized the oppressive condition of his clientele who really did not have any means of compensating him for his savvy legal work.

Judge Russell Hunt encouraged Peter Pryor to take a job as an assistant district attorney. The idea of having the type of money that would come with such a job, plus still being able to practice law if he did not handle any criminal matters, piqued his interest. When he realized he was not making any money on criminal cases, he decided to accept the position. That is, until he met Samuel Clark.

"A nice guy, army vet, postal worker - living over in Stratford, Connecticut - came to visit his mother in Albany. He returned from Six Mile Waterworks where his family had a Memorial Day picnic. He double parked in front of his mother's home to unload the picnic gear. The police sped up behind him and said, 'You can't double park here.' He said, 'I just want to unload.' So, there was an exchange. Sam Clark, 39, was arrested for disorderly conduct. It was sort of like driving while being black. Disorderly conduct covered just about everything. There was no crime. He was beaten while in police custody and carried to St. Peter's Hospital. If you were to read the Knickerbocker News from June 1, 1962, for three months consecutive, that's all you would read about – Sam Clark," explained Peter Pryor about his client.

The Knickerbocker News reported Clark's account of what happened to him in police custody on May 30, 1962. "Mr. Clark said the blow was open handed. He said the blow stunned him. 'I asked him why he hit me,' he said. He quoted the officer as saying, 'Why can't you answer a damn question.' 'He slapped me a second time. He took his foot and came down on my right foot. It was the same officer. He kicked me in the instep of my left foot. One officer held me. The officer who slapped me, punched me in the stomach five or six times. He stomped on my foot. I was barefooted,' Mr. Clark continued. 'I was still in front of the desk in Division 2. The same officer twisted my arm around my back. He said as he twisted my arm, 'I'll break your g_____ d_____ arm off' and he twisted. He then pushed me forward and rammed my head against the wall. 'You black n_____ you, I'll kill you,' he said.'"

The incidents with William Brown and Samuel Clark are a small sampling of the conditions blacks suffered through law enforcement interactions. Anyone with a soul was infuriated by the disproportionate way police treated blacks in the 1900s, especially black men. Back then, we did not have social media to amplify these acts of violence like we do now. We did not have a Black Lives Matter movement to stir the community and call for change. Instead, we had organizations with a purpose and churches with a following. That *was* our Black Lives Matter movement.

The Albany chapter of the NAACP (National Association for the Advancement of Colored People) was founded in 1935. One of the primary goals for this civil rights organization was ending police brutality toward blacks. So, it was fitting for the NAACP to step up and act after Brown was struck down by police bullets. The organization protested the 1959 police killing and met with Albany Mayor Erastus Corning to discuss the case. The Rev. Louis C. Brewer, president of the Albany Chapter of the NAACP, and other organization leaders wanted the case discussed publicly and wanted an investigation into one eyewitness's account of the officer shooting Brown in the abdomen after he was already on the ground and immobilized. They also wanted Leamon Grady, Brown's friend who made the original knife complaint, questioned about the incident. Rev. Brewer, who was also pastor of Union Missionary Baptist Church and the Rev. Charles M. Walker of Faith Baptist Church attempted to locate Grady, and they spent hours talking to South End residents. They could not find him.

A group of Albany religious leaders – consisting of the Capital Area Council of Churches, Jewish Community Council of Albany and First Unitarian Church of Albany - and representatives of the State Commission Against Discrimination met with the NAACP to get briefed on the organization's meetings with Mayor Corning. They stood united with the NAACP and wanted "the mayor's expression of official interest in this matter." Mayor Corning stood firm on his belief that the eyewitness account was just a rumor and there was "not the slightest shred of truth". The acting police chief at the time echoed the mayor's position. He was, none other than Tony Dean. But the community did not expect anything differently from Dean.

"We met with Mayor Corning," Peter Pryor explained. "And we wanted a public hearing, but Corning said, 'These are matters that are not handled by a public hearing. They're handled by the grand jury.' I said, well forget the public hearing, let's have a preliminary hearing. I knew what the grand jury was going to do. My fear was they were going to turn back a no bill – justifiable – because the mayor had already said the shooting was justifiable by the police officer. He decided to think about it over the weekend. On Monday morning, someone hand-delivered to me a letter from the mayor saying he had gotten District Attorney John Garry II to turn this matter over to the grand jury for an investigation. And it was a no bill."

No bill is a legal term that refers to a grand jury's notation that insufficient evidence exists for an indictment on a criminal charge. The foreman of the grand jury writes across the face of a bill of indictment, *no bill* to indicate that the criminal charges alleged therein against a suspect have not been sufficiently supported by the evidence presented before it to warrant his or her criminal prosecution. In laymen's terms, the cops got away with murder in the William Brown case.

Unfortunately, the outcome in the Samuel Clark case was no different. The community did, however, unite on behalf of the injustice Clark endured. A reported 350 individuals gathered before Albany City Hall to protest at a rally following Clark's beating by the police. It was a combination of prayer and meeting led by the Rev. Dorman Avery of Temple Baptist Church. Some of the other notable clergymen on the frontline were: the Rev. Thomas Hunter of Temple Baptist Church, the Rev. Louis Brewer, the Rev. James Smythe of Mount Zion Baptist Church, the Rev. Val Mendes of the Mount Olivet Church, and the Rev. Robert C. Lamar, pastor of the First Presbyterian Church.

Those at the rally were not only protesting the incident, but they were seeking social action. The coalition wanted a better police department with better standards, better pay for them so they would not have to work a second job to make ends meet, better housing and better schools in Albany. During the protest, they adopted a motion to establish a Citizens' Committee on Police Brutality, headed by James Lockhart, president of the Troy branch of the NAACP.

Sam Clark's nephew, Bill Clark, was interviewed for a documentary released in 2018, *More Than Words: The Photography of Newsman Bob Paley*. The documentary focused on the many photos former Knickerbocker News Photojournalist Paley took throughout his career capturing images of Albany's marginalized residents in the mid-20th century. Sam Clark was one of the subjects Paley captured with his camera while he was still in the hospital recovering from his wounds. In the black and white photo, the hospital room walls are sterile. Clark lay helplessly in the bed with a white bandage over his eye concealing the trauma. A woman sits in the chair next to him, as if she is keeping watch. Her head is turned away from him, giving us a side profile of her. It is probably his mother, as any loving mother would have difficulty gazing at her son in that condition.

In the film, Bill Clark spoke about visiting his uncle in the hospital after the police beating. Sam Clark recovered from his physical wounds, but the experience left emotional scars. The officers were never punished for what they did. And Clark's family "never went on a picnic again," Bill Clark said.

James Q. Wilson

The tragedies of William Brown, Sam Clark, and countless others are examples of how Albany's police department dealt with people of color. Those in the community knew this behavior was deeper than just a few bad apples, but rather, was systemic and embedded into Albany's law enforcement culture.

The City of Albany's policing approach was scrutinized by James Q. Wilson, a social scientist who spent most of his career as a professor at UCLA and Harvard University. In his 1968 book, "Varieties of Police Behavior," he examines the character of policing in several cities including Albany. Through his writing, he explores what he calls the legalistic style, the service style, and the watchman style.

The legalistic style relies heavily on handling commonplace situations as if they were matters of law enforcement rather than order maintenance. For example, officers in a legalistic department will issue traffic tickets at a high rate, detain and arrest juvenile offenders in great numbers, act vigorously against illicit enterprises, and make a large number of misdemeanor arrests even when the public order has not been breached.

The service style responds to all calls for law enforcement or order maintenance but are less likely to make an arrest or impose formal sanctions. For example, officers in a service style department will avoid making arrests for minor infractions of the law when possible. They will issue warnings to motorists and refer fewer juveniles to family court. You will usually find this style in middle-class communities where residents agree on the need for public order, but do not want a legalistic approach.

The watchman style primarily emphasizes order maintenance rather than law enforcement when dealing with non-serious crimes. Officers in a watchman style department will use the law more as a means of maintaining order than of regulating conduct and will judge the requirements of order differently depending on the character of the group in which the infraction occurs.

Wilson described Albany's policing style as watchman - or controlled-oriented - meaning the department was less concerned about protecting rights and the welfare of residents and more concerned with controlling their behavior and keeping the peace. This was interpreted by many as confining blacks to certain neighborhoods and providing tight surveillance and the use of excessive force to achieve that goal. Residents reported personal experiences of brutality, arrests, and even killings by police that supported the department's style of policing. From the very beginning of my introduction to Albany and throughout the 60s, 70s, and 80s, complaints of police abuse of power were bantered about with many ending in formal complaints and even lawsuits.

Peter Pryor, Esq., prominent black attorney in Albany

Former Albany Deputy Police Chief Tony Dean

Reverend John (Jack) Johnson with his sons (from left to right) - Eddie, John (Jack), Sammy, McKinley and Ted

Albany's First Black Police Chief John Dale

Part 2

African Americans and the Social Justice Movement in Albany

Alice, newly appointed executive director of Trinity
Institution.

Trinity Institution: Albany's Response to the
War on Poverty

Equipped with my ancestral and strong parental values, the lessons of poverty, and a limited understanding of structural racism, I set out on my own to become educated, to work, and most importantly, to find out who I am. It was the time of the Civil Rights Movement with Dr. Martin Luther King, Jr., black voter registration, Vietnam War resistance, the death of Malcolm X, black urban uprisings, increasing police brutality, political assassinations, the Civil Rights Act, War on Poverty, Black Power Movement, Attica Uprising and much more. Aside from my formal college education, these events provided me with a more involved education in reality - lessons in community involvement and organizing - that put me in the middle of the struggle for civil and human rights.

There was no better place to be than at Trinity Institution in Albany's South End. Trinity was a settlement house founded by Episcopalians in the 1920s to support primarily poor white immigrant children and families. By the time I arrived in the mid-60s, it was experiencing a major transition and serving primarily black youth throughout the area that included public housing residents. Its leaders, social workers Richard Collins and later Michael Nardolillo, were committed to social change and the reduction of poverty. So, with funds from the federal government-sponsored Great Society Program – that included the War on Poverty - they introduced Head Start, community organizing for change, developing neighborhood associations, welfare rights, tenants' rights, voting rights, interfaith and affordable housing, cooperative food programs, youth development, mentoring programs, and much more.

What an education Trinity provided through human experiences, political struggles, community leadership development, community organizing, and radical change efforts! So much flowed from that space and time. Although I was hired as a group worker for youth, I was so fortunate to be an integral part of the change that was taking place. I developed valuable knowledge, understanding and involvement in real social change.

I was soon called upon to take on more responsibility and get involved in other aspects of the Institution's programs including community action activities. One of my lasting contributions to the change effort was improving the way residents received information and communicated their feelings and concerns to the public and political officials with the power to make changes in their lives. I started a mimeographed newsletter called The Voice of the South End.

Writing, publishing and distributing The Voice of the South End was a major undertaking for me. I had to gather information by talking to people, find event schedules, and confirm community programs. Once that was done, I had to write articles by long hand and type the material on a typewriter using mimeograph paper which was like carbon paper, but worse. Any mistakes required great skill and patience to erase, dry and retype the information. Severe frustration was always a companion during this part of the process. Sometimes it required exhausting work into the middle of the night. Once the copy was complete, reading and editing was even more painful.

The next step was to attach the completed mimeograph copy carefully and perfectly onto the machine where a drum held the required ink. The slightest mistake could ruin the copy and require that I repeat the process. Once I successfully completed this process, I began to print. But often, something disastrous would happen to delay print completion. The machine would run out of ink, it would stop for seemingly no reason at all, or the master mimeograph sheet would develop a tear which meant going back to the drawing board.

Once I completed the printing, I stapled the double-sided pages together. Then, the most important and taxing work began – I distributed the paper to as many residents of the area as possible. I chose to start with the Albany Housing Authority buildings because they had the highest concentration of residents. There were four, 10-story towers with 10 apartments on each floor, or 400 apartments in the Green/Rensselaer Street apartments alone. Although delivery was taxing, it allowed me the opportunity to connect with and talk to many residents, which, in turn allowed me to promote Trinity and community programs, spread useful information, and receive feedback about Trinity and other important civil and political issues.

After President Lyndon B. Johnson released his War on Poverty initiative, college students and uptown residents started coming to Trinity to volunteer their services. A couple of them became interested in assisting me with the Voice of the South End. With their input, advice, and support, we decided to revamp the paper, make it look more professional, and cover more topics of interest, particularly local politics and issues related to the War on Poverty. First, we renamed the paper, The South End Scene. Then, we attracted local businesses who were willing to pay for advertisements. This allowed us, in due time, to hire a publisher - The Jewish World.

The South End Scene became a staple in the community, and I published it until the late 70s before a new publisher took it over and renamed it The Scene to attract and *satisfy* a broader city audience. The paper finally folded in 1997. A new effort is underway by the Albany Public Library to relaunch the paper. As I write, they have published two editions, each in hard and electronic copy. My involvement with The Scene taught me how valuable and powerful the press could be. It was an effective informer, educator, and organizing tool I learned to use in my social justice work.

Trinity was at the forefront of social justice. Its community organizing work included hiring two professional social workers trained in community organizing and case management. They were schooled in the approach and philosophy of Saul Alinsky, a radical activist whose approach to running a movement for social change called for leaders to involve community members in their own change efforts. Trinity was a perfect field placement location for students enrolled in the new SUNY School of Social Welfare. Trinity had already taken on Siena student Jack Mayer. He proved to be a highly effective community organizer who was hired after completing his internship at Trinity. The other social worker was Michael Nardolillo, who eventually became executive director of Trinity after Collins.

A yearning to become a professional social worker to gain legitimacy and learn useful community organizing techniques grew inside of me. The desire was so strong that I could not ignore it. So, I enrolled in the SUNY program at the time Attica erupted.

Attica is a maximum-security prison near Buffalo. About 2,000 people are incarcerated there. Situated in a quaint, suburban area with a small-town charm, Attica Correctional Facility has housed some familiar names since its construction in the 1930s. Remember David Berkowitz? Perhaps, you know him by his other name – Son of Sam, a serial killer who terrorized New York in the 1970s. Mark David Chapman, who pleaded guilty to murdering John Lennon, once stayed there. Terrorist El Sayyid Nosair, responsible for the 1993 World Trade Center bombing, spent a short time in Attica for a different assassination. David Sweat, whose infamous escape from Clinton Correctional Facility in 2015 led to movies depicting the ordeal, was rehoused in

Attica in 2017. That manhunt had the North Country on high alert for about three weeks. Amongst the prisoners who were serial killers, terrorists and mobsters, there were also people like Valentino Dixon, a black man from Buffalo convicted of murder who served 27 of his 38 1/2 year-sentence for a crime he did not commit. Thanks to some intrigued Georgetown University students who produced a documentary about his case, Dixon was exonerated in 2018.

Attica, which housed many people convicted of violent crimes – often people transferred from other facilities because of behavioral issues – was a breeding ground in the mid-60s and the early 70s for some of the most egregious and inhuman practices against prisoners. Those imprisoned there were frustrated with chronic overcrowding, censorship of letters, and living conditions that limited them to one shower per week and one roll of toilet paper each month. People were fed up. The conditions formed a pressure cooker environment where tempers were inevitably going to manifest into something bad.

That *something* happened in September 1971, when those imprisoned started an uprising on their way to breakfast and seized control of the prison. They took more than four dozen staff hostage for four days. Those imprisoned - armed with homemade weapons - beat guards, burned down the prison chapel, and even threw a guard from a second-story window. The imprisoned made 27 demands during negotiations. When it looked like New York Corrections Commissioner Russell Oswald was going to honor most of the demands, Governor Nelson A. Rockefeller, who refused to visit the prison as requested by those incarcerated, ordered Attica to be retaken by force. A helicopter dropped tear gas into the prison, and state troopers and correction officers used the cloud cover to storm the prison, shooting indiscriminately, killing 29 imprisoned and 10 hostages during the raid. Many consider the Attica uprising to be the most notorious prison uprising in U.S. history, and it was instrumental in the Prisoners' Rights Movement.

The Attica uprising piqued my interest in prisons, and I was anxious to know more about the cause of the uprising and basically what prisons were like and what people incarcerated there were experiencing. With this new interest in prisons and moved by the vast experiences I gained from working with and connecting to community people, professionals, and human service providers, I decided to improve my skills and knowledge about community organizing, social change, structural racism, and criminal justice to become an effective change agent.

While continuing to work at Trinity, I again enrolled as a student at the SUNY School of Criminal Justice which established the Center on Minorities and Criminal Justice. In 1978, the school recruited about 10 black students into the program so that we could pursue a field of study that included very few blacks across the country. Scott Christianson, a doctoral student, researcher, and former newspaper reporter, was a mentor to the new students. He eventually edited a volume titled, *Index to Minorities & Criminal Justice*. I was fortunate enough to become an associate editor of the volume published in 1981.

Through this program and the work of Scott Christianson, I was introduced to the phenomenon of the disproportionate incarceration of minorities in our criminal justice system. The topic fascinated me. But it took me awhile to connect it to the underlining causes of the Attica uprising in September 1971. It would be years before I understood more clearly the nature of that connection and the connection between prisons and black and brown communities.

Governor Mario Cuomo spoke at the 1982 SUNY Albany graduation when I received my PhD in criminal justice. He would soon ask me to join his administration, which I did after working for the New York Civil Liberties Union managing its Albany office. While there, I also took on the task of serving as chairperson of the local NAACP's Legal Redress Committee. While heading these two programs, I was in the thick of most of the criminal justice, civil and legal rights, and race-related issues of the time. Soon, I added to my agenda, issues related to the state's prison operations and its impact on the imprisoned, their families, and communities. This meant lobbying on related issues of concern to both groups.

It did not take long for me to develop a reputation as a strong community advocate. I was everywhere speaking out on police abuse, violations of the Bill of Rights, racism and discrimination in employment, education and housing, the death penalty, and many other political, economic and social issues. With Sol Greenberg as the Albany County district attorney who lacked legal and racial knowledge, and Erastus Corning as mayor, there were always issues for me to fight and address. Greenberg had expressed many racist ideas, and he once told me that blacks have no morals and stated the reason they were arrested more is because they were more visible. What an insult! Mayor Corning had a reputation for being a control freak who salivated over power like a dog chomping on a bone. He had full control of the city – housing, employment, voting and policing - especially policing people of color.

Mayor Corning died in 1983 after a 40-plus year reign, and Thomas Whalen became mayor, which brought some relief to countless oppressed residents. Many people saw Mayor Whalen as a breath of fresh air. He did not crave power as his predecessor did. Instead, he was more about running the city as a business. Mayor Whalen stopped the practice of no-bid contracts that led to city deficits. He was also more sensitive to issues in the black community. He created a community/police relations board and, of course, appointed the first black police chief. However, Mayor Whalen was not the most politically progressive person. He did much of what he thought was good for the city.

When I received Governor Cuomo's job offer in 1986, I was deeply torn. My case management work, civil and legal rights advocacy, and community organizing was enjoyable, satisfying, exciting and challenging. I was deeply engaged in it all, working nearly 17 hours a day on it. The work of challenging the police and the governmental power structure fit me like a glove. Staring me in the face, I saw the opportunity to change a power structure that had enslaved my great grandmother, exploited my grandmother as a sharecropper, forced my parents to leave their families and flee from Jim Crow only to be met in the North by a different form of racism and oppression – more subtle, but every bit as harmful.

Because the police were omnipresent in the life of the community and that of the people I worked for in the community, my focus for change shifted quickly toward policing like the needle of a compass. Not only did I hear complaints of police brutality streaming from the mouths of people on the street, but national researchers and writers backed up these claims and drew a direct correlation between the growing urban upheavals and police brutality and racial injustice.

In July 1967, President Lyndon B. Johnson appointed an 11-member Kerner Commission to expose the causes of urban uprisings, specifically the violent 1967 uprisings that killed 43 people in Detroit, 26 in Newark, and many others around the country. The Kerner Commission published the 708-page Kerner Commission Report condemning white racism as the primary cause of the recent surge of uprisings.

What looked like a scene from a movie, was a sobering reality in our country. Thousands of protesters marched with amplified voices, fists in the air and waved signs with calls for justice. Storefronts with smashed windows lined commercial districts. Vans set ablaze as the fire's warmth satisfied protesters' insatiable appetite to exhibit rage. Police officers struck peaceful protestors with batons and rubber bullets. American military police forcefully removed American citizens with pepper balls and tear gas. Law enforcement officers cloaked in riot gear stood watch as they intimidated crowds. Officials in authority overtly incited violence with phrases like, "When the looting starts, the shooting starts."

No, I am not recounting events from the 60s that led up to the Kerner Commission Report. I am describing more current events we saw in 2020 because of George Floyd's murder, a 46-year-old unarmed black man in Minneapolis who cried out for his mother as a police officer kneeled on his neck, restricting his breathing. As much as the Kerner Commission Report revealed the flaws in policing black communities across the country and right here in Albany and the correlation between race and poverty, very little has been done since the government released the report and its recommendations more than 50 years ago. This is why I believe the work I do is so important. And, this is why Trinity Institution was and is a beacon in the community.

Trinity was the center of the social justice movement in Albany. Its director, Richard Collins, was a white, progressive man, and he understood the power of community organizing. He embodied the slogan, "Power to the People" and knew that people from the community had to start getting involved in the movement to see real power, real change. With War on Poverty grant money from the federal government, Trinity was able to pull in people who lived in our impoverished neighborhoods and train them in community organizing. The experienced organizers worked behind the scenes to identify and train the right people. Through these efforts, we identified Olivia Rorie as the perfect community spokesperson and leader to grab the baton and run for social justice. Rorie was an articulate mother with nine children who was not shy about rattling off all the problems she observed in the South End. She knew the damage that poverty was doing, and she accepted the challenge to be a part of the solution.

Like any mother who wanted a safe place for her children to play, Olivia Rorie and other volunteers fought for more playgrounds in the South End. She was also instrumental in getting Giffen Elementary School's playground opened for community use after school hours.

Rorie tackled many pressing issues throughout her career and life's work, but inadequate housing was the cornerstone of her efforts. Facing crowded housing herself, she talked to other residents in her neighborhood and discovered they also had housing concerns. Residents refused to pay rent because slum landlords were not making needed repairs to bring their properties up to code. Rorie served as a mediator between tenants and landlords, convincing the landlords to make repairs and convincing tenants to resume paying rent.

Olivia Rorie served as a member of the Interfaith Better Homes Development Corporation. This community group formed to build and sell low-income housing to community residents. It accomplished just that as it constructed eight housing units in the South End and five in Arbor Hill.

Rorie also became president of Better Homes Neighborhood Association where she used coordinated efforts to attack housing, recreation, employment, and other community problems. In this role, she was no stranger to the power structure and people like Mayor Corning. Armed with a list of housing complaints from 45 South End families, Rorie met with Mayor Corning in July 1965 to lodge those grievances. Since it was the city's jurisdiction to address housing code violations, there was no better place for them to land but in the mayor's ear.

Broken windows. Non-working sinks and bathtubs. Missing toilet seats. Collapsed ceilings in bedrooms and hallways. No bath or hot water. Standing water and sewage in the cellar. Holes in the walls. Missing door locks. Rotten wood around windows. Leaky ceilings. No fire escape. Rickety stairs and bannisters. Roaches. This was just a fraction of the problems tenants endured. Who would want to live like this?

Unfortunately, the burden of being black means institutions we rely on for our very existence reinforce a belief system about blacks in this country that started in 1619 and was passed down through the centuries. It is the belief that the black race is an inferior race, and therefore, do not deserve the same high standards in the quality-of-life whites enjoy. That is why the slum landlords who owned property in the South End and rented to blacks thought it was acceptable living conditions for them.

Being black in the 60s meant you often secured low-wage jobs so, essentially, you were poor. Being poor meant you lived in a crowded, urban community with deplorable living conditions and substandard schools. Even if you could afford to move out to other neighborhoods, you had discrimination, unwelcoming neighbors, and police intimidation. Therefore, we cannot talk about one societal ill without addressing these problems in totality.

Coming out of Trinity in 1966, an organization called the South End Neighborhood Community Action Program – or SENCAP – served to address these various issues at a micro level. It was federally funded under the Economic Opportunity Act – the law that created the War on Poverty. One of the roles of SENCAP and Trinity was to develop local neighborhood associations to address problems in their own neighborhoods. SENCAP, chaired by Earl Thorpe who was a surgical technician at the Veteran's Administration at the time, hired George Bunch as a coordinator of the neighborhood groups. He was a psychology and sociology professor, and also taught a social action course at Russell Sage's Junior College of Albany. Bunch, viewed as a radical by some, caused a stirring in the city in October 1966 when he was accused of slapping a 12-year-old white girl after she called him a derogatory name. According to Bunch, he asked her to leave Trinity's main building three times. That is when she unbridled her tongue and unleashed her offensive language. SENCAP, along with Trinity, became embroiled in a lawsuit as a result because the girl's parents alleged the organizations should have known Bunch was a violent man when he was hired.

While no one condoned the alleged act of striking a 12-year-old girl - no matter how sassy she was – the community was enraged by the court's decision to jail Bunch without bail, a pretty harsh determination for a third-degree assault charge. More than 200 people protested outside of Albany's State Capitol to bring attention to this injustice. Being thrown in jail without bail is an action we see far too often in the black community. This highlights the importance of bail reform. Without it, the scales of justice will continue to be unbalanced.

Like many other civil rights protests, the rally was filled with songs, prayers and speeches. One of the speakers, psychology professor John Delonas, was quoted in the Times Union as saying, "As a psychologist I say we must try to prevent this mental examination farce. Sending a man to a psychiatrist is a way of preventing him from coming before a jury of his peers, a way of getting him out of the way. We must not let this happen to George." He was referring to the court-ordered mental examination that Bunch was to undergo because of the incident.

SENCAP tackled many issues at the height of its existence, including the firing of Lola Johnson, a black teacher at Phillip Schuyler High School. Johnson asserted she was fired unfairly and without cause by Principal Ben Becker and the Albany School Board. The community united to support Johnson, and the Federation of Community Organizations held a rally at Trinity Institution on her behalf to raise funds and awareness. Olivia Rorie, whom you now know was an outspoken community organizer, spoke candidly at the rally as a SENCAP member and hurled accusations that Johnson's firing was a discriminatory action.

Fifteen groups came together on this issue. You had the usual players who were visible on every issue. You also had students from Siena College, Albany Citizens Against Poverty, Students for a Democratic Society, and The Brothers - a newly formed civil rights group. Together, they understood the power of raising a unified voice.

At a time when black teachers were as rare as a unicorn, we could not lose Lola Johnson. The black girls in her class who saw themselves when they looked at her brown face with hopeful eyes could not lose her. The black boys who felt safe in her class could not lose her. I, along with 36 others, in a visual display of disgust over the school board's decision, picketed in front of school board President Dr. Arthur Wallingford's nearly 5,000 square-foot home. Holding signs with messages of support, we demanded he do the same, and reinstate Johnson. The police kept a watchful eye on our protest at 32 Marion Avenue, a tree-lined street in the sought-after Buckingham Pond neighborhood. They did not dare try any brute force on our peaceful demonstration in front of the news cameras and reporters that were present. Onlookers with arms folded gazed at us as if we were alien invaders.

Johnson believed she was dismissed because of her civil rights activities, so she filed an appeal with the State Commission for Human Rights. Her dismissal letter listed too many failures in her class as the reason why she was not granted tenure. Suspicious of this reasoning, Johnson said the Board of Education made the decision at its June 1 meeting when final exams and grades were not even given yet. Ultimately, Johnson lost the appeal. This would not be the last time the system failed the community.

In 1963, Dr. Martin Luther King, Jr. wrote in a letter from a Birmingham jail, "Injustice anywhere is a threat to justice everywhere. We are caught in an inescapable network of mutuality, tied in a single garment of destiny. Whatever affects one directly, affects all indirectly." The ecumenical community of Albany understood Dr. King's words. They were very much active in the War on Poverty, helping in every step toward a more just society, especially in the lives of South End and Arbor Hill residents. It was, after all, the Episcopalians who started Trinity to aid the poor. This was a time when white church leaders worked alongside black church leaders. It did not matter if they were Catholic, Baptist, Presbyterian, Methodist, or Jewish. They protested together. They fought against social inequalities thrust upon the people by the established democratic political machine that ruled Albany like the mafia. They abhorred racial disparities and understood that it did not just affect blacks, it affected humanity.

Father Bonaventure O'Brien, a theology professor at Siena College and a Franciscan of the Holy Name province, was an important figure in the War on Poverty movement. He knew social and civil rights work was God's work. He was instrumental in helping to form a neighborhood association in the Philip Street area, worked with Better Homes Neighborhood Association, and labored as a member of the Inter-Faith Task Force. On campus, he was also a student counselor, and some students described him as the most popular priest at Siena. Off campus, he was an outspoken voice for the voiceless.

The church frowned upon Father Bonaventure's social justice activities and, ultimately, moved to silence him. He was no longer allowed to engage in public speaking or talk to the media, and he had to quell all his community work. As a Franciscan priest, he was not directly controlled by the diocese, but Siena College had an allegiance to both the Franciscan order and to the diocese. The order came down from the diocese and the provincial of the Franciscans executed the request.

To those in the community who worked side-by-side with Father Bonaventure and had been involved in the civil rights struggle, the church's motive was obvious. Father Bonaventure was an outspoken critic of the city administration. He often "poked the bear" with published letters and speeches attacking the Albany Democratic machine for neglecting the black community and not addressing the disgraceful conditions that existed. He also urged residents to join the Albany Citizens Against Poverty, which was at odds with the city administration in the quest for federal anti-poverty funds. But the unspeakable act that curtailed Father Bonaventure's involvement was empowering residents to become poll watchers on Election Day – a duty that entailed monitoring polling sites to ensure adherence to voting laws. He even showed up to a polling site to lend moral support to the novice poll watchers, only to be harassed by other poll workers who questioned why a priest would be involved in politics. The orders to end his work came shortly after, and many believe Mayor Corning was the man behind the curtain – an accusation he denied.

It was not long after the church's decision to suppress Father Bonaventure's voice that we saw politics rear its ugly head again. The City of Albany decided to abruptly cut its financial support to Trinity Institution, a decision made solely by Mayor Corning without explanation. Trinity, *the* organization at the center of social action, was receiving $16,898 from Albany, plus another $6,000 in rent the city paid Trinity for classroom space in its building. It was the only community organization with such an arrangement with the city. A great portion of those funds paid workers' salaries. I was one of them.

The money directly supported services to youth and families. Did Mayor Corning not believe children in the South End needed the enrichment Trinity provided? Was he able to sleep at night after he snatched the books and pencils clutched in their little, tiny hands? Was the mayor indicating he did not believe in helping the poor and working-class families get the resources they needed for a better quality of life? By yanking the financial contribution away from Trinity, these were the messages he was sending.

It was time to battle. We could not just let the mayor get away with using Trinity like a pawn in his political chess game. At this point, we were organized. Trinity already formed four neighborhood groups, churches were united through the Inter-Faith Task Force, and other organizations like the NAACP lent its voice to the cause. College students were energized and ready to join us on the frontlines, especially after what happened to their beloved Father Bonaventure. We engaged in a campaign that included writing opinion editorials and submitting them to The Knickerbocker News and The Times Union. Because of the pressure the community applied and our demand for answers, the mayor agreed to meet with representatives from the four neighborhood groups. It was a rushed and half-hearted meeting - if you could call it a meeting. The mayor emerged out of his office to address the group, saying he was in the middle of another meeting with another to follow. But in the brief exchange, he promised to provide answers by Christmas to our very direct questions, which were:

1. "Why was the money taken away from Trinity?"
2. "You said you felt poverty funds could do the job better. Are you aware you cannot replace existing programs with anti-poverty funds?"
3. "What projects were you talking about when you made that statement?"
4. "When will members of the (Albany) poverty committee be appointed?"
5. "Will people from the four associations represented here be appointed?"
6. "When do you expect the first federal money will be available?"

Our questions were in response to Mayor Corning's public statements he eventually made about why he stripped Trinity of its funding. His rationale was that the organization should use federal funds earmarked for anti-poverty initiatives instead. We were not buying that argument, especially since we could not use that money for existing programs. He also stated the contracts were canceled because Trinity failed to provide reports on how the money was used. That was not accurate.

While community representatives met with Mayor Corning inside, we protested outside of City Hall. I was among the 125 or so people raising a picket sign and my voice. "Albany New York or Albany Georgia" is what my sign read. "Why punish the poor," read another. In a picture captured by Knickerbocker News, you could see blacks and whites together, dressed in heavy coats, as we demonstrated. Not even Albany's bitter December cold could keep us from speaking truth to power. When community members concluded their time with the mayor, they left with little hope of restoration.

What was meant to immobilize an organization, failed. The mayor's attempt to slap us on the wrist for not playing nice did not halt our efforts. Today, Trinity is thriving and still serving the community in an expanded way. Once a settlement house to help newly arrived immigrants acclimate to a new world, Trinity morphed into a one-stop resource agency for the entire family. It now offers prevention services that include grief counseling, crisis intervention, couples counseling, youth anger management, parenting skills, mental health counseling, household assistance and help transitioning back home from foster care. Funding from the United Way and Albany County makes this possible.

Trinity also has a wellness program, food pantry, anti-violence initiative, re-entry services, workforce development, literacy initiatives, early childhood & family support services, after-school care & summer camp. Lives are being transformed through the many partnerships Trinity formed, and they are truly empowering people for brighter futures.

I was privileged to play a part in the transformation and evolution of Trinity. From my humble beginnings as a youth worker, to my rise as executive director in 1975, I have seen firsthand how the work at Trinity had a direct and positive impact on the lives of countless youth and families. The impression we made by starting a program for early childhood education and having the first Head Start Program in Albany is everlasting. The youth who hung out at Trinity after school and engaged in basketball, boxing, mentorship and other activities, embraced it like their second home. Families formed bonds over sewing classes, cooking classes, and more. The newspaper I started brought the community together, not only informing residents about community matters, but about what was happening across the state with policing, incarceration, and race relations. Veterans returning to the community after the Vietnam War ended could pick up a copy of The South End Scene and catch up on issues that mattered the most. Trinity prepared me for what was to come as my profile increased in criminal and social justice work here in Albany.

Alice holds a sign at a rally in support of Lola Johnson.

Alice and others picketing outside of Albany City Hall
protesting cuts to Trinity Institution's budget.

The Brothers - Leon Van Dyke, Purcell McDowell, Alice, and
Earl Thorpe. Photo courtesy of Paul Grondahl.

The Brothers

In the 1960s, black men and women across the country and right here in Albany were more mobilized than ever to stand up against racial inequalities. They were no longer just standing on the sidelines singing old Negro spirituals and praying their problems away. People started fighting back. They understood their rights, and they started asserting themselves in a way they had not done in the past. The community started rising.

While sitting around a table at Trinity Institution in 1966, three men gave birth to an organization designed to be more vocal and speak out on what blacks were experiencing. Black men, as heads of households and leaders of their community, wanted to come together like brothers to accomplish this mission. Non-related, yet still familial in every sense, these men took the idea of brotherhood seriously. They were allied by nature - not kinship - yet they looked out for one another; they had each other's backs. Those three men were Earl Thorpe, George Bunch and Leon Van Dyke, and they decided to name the new group *The Brothers*.

The Brothers were at the center of the northern Civil Rights Movement in Albany. When they first emerged, the media described them as a secret, militant group. "The Brothers, an organization of militant young Negro men in Albany's South End, swore in three new members last night. But before the oath was administered on a Bible, a fourth candidate for membership, a Negro who decided at the last minute not to join and a white newspaper reporter were asked to leave. It is a secret organization and meetings are closed to non-members, both Negro and white," said Richard Gaikowski, reporter for The Knickerbocker News. While the details of their strategies behind closed doors may have been off limits to non-members, their work was far from secret. They were very much involved in the protests when SENCAP's George Bunch was jailed without bail and when Lola Johnson was dismissed as a teacher from Phillip Schuyler High School.

To fortify this rising group, The Brothers aimed to recruit young, black men. At the inception, there were between 15-20 members including: Gordon Van Ness, Clarence Williams, James McBride, John Williams, Sam McDowell, Robert Gene Dobbs, William Gibson, Peter Jones, Les Davis, Purcell McDowell, Kenny French, John Rollins, and Herman Washington. They paid $5 a month in dues, and the chairman of the organization changed every week to ensure no one could "be bought".

I sat down with Earl Thorpe recently to get more insight into this pioneering group in Albany. He described how they grew big quickly and gained the attention of the Albany Police Department. "We initially held our meetings at Trinity. There was friction with the cops. John Dale was a detective then. He knew us, so he would be outside in the car to identify us. We would say, 'Hey John!' They wanted to know who all these guys were, because we would come out of our meeting with about 40 or 50 guys, and the police considered us a threat."

Some people compared The Brothers to the Black Panther Party for Self-Defense that had also formed in 1966 in Oakland, California by Bobby Seale and Huey Newton. The Black Panthers were known for openly carrying weapons to patrol and monitor the behavior of Oakland Police Department officers and challenging police brutality. Like The Brothers, law enforcement also considered the Black Panthers a threat. In fact, Federal Bureau of Investigation Director J. Edgar Hoover in 1969 described the party as "the greatest threat to the internal security of the country." But, The Brothers were not tied to any national organization. They were even intentional about not using the term *black power* because they did not want to incite tension between the races. In an interview with The

Knickerbocker News in 1966, Leon Van Dyke said, "We are religiously non-violent, but we're not afraid of violence. It's unnatural to turn the other cheek." Or as Earl Thorpe described it, "We weren't militant. We just didn't believe in turning the other cheek. We were about protecting our people. If we got smacked, we would smack you back. We would protect ourselves."

Jobs

The 1960s was a fertile decade for construction in Albany. Two major capital projects were underway. In 1962, Governor Rockefeller broke ground for the SUNY Albany uptown campus.

In 1965, the other capital project plan was a complex of multiple state government buildings with a $2 billion price tag. The plans called for four 23-story agency towers and an egg-shaped performing arts venue called – surprisingly – The Egg. The Egg and the Empire State Plaza Convention Center, as it stands today, hosts a throng of people every year for various affairs, so I have been there on many occasions for community or government events. My activism and calls for change in the criminal justice system have even gotten me escorted out of an event there – kicking and screaming - by state troopers. This was under the Pataki Administration, a pro-death penalty governor who wanted to build more prisons. My "no more prisons" banner was frowned upon and, I guess, seen as a distraction.

The complex also has a 44-floor Tower Building with an observation deck. This skyscraper that soars 589 feet into the sky towering over several reflective ponds is the tallest skyscraper in New York outside of New York City. Today, we know it as Corning Tower, named after Mayor Corning. The Cultural Education Center sits prominently on the south side and houses the New York State Museum, the New York State Archives, and the New York State Library. These buildings have a series of interconnecting concourses underground allowing people to conveniently access the New York State Capitol, the Legislative

Office Building, and the Alfred E. Smith Building. With Albany's winters being what they are, these tunnels have become a necessity to shield state workers from the harsh weather outside. The complex, completed in 1976, is the Governor Nelson A. Rockefeller Empire State Plaza.

The state constructed the Empire State Plaza in the footprints of where a residential community once stood. Through eminent domain, the state seized control of the 98.5-acre site, demolishing 1,200 structures where many black and poor people lived. Some of those families were moved to public housing.

With all the capital projects, it was, indeed, a good time to work in the construction field in Albany – that is, unless you were black. Like other aspects of the black experience, employment injustice permeated black communities. Those searching for a good job with the unions on these construction sites were shut out. Union managers would hand pick people to work on these capital projects, and very few blacks, if any, were chosen. This did not sit well with The Brothers. While the state and city were breaking ground, they decided they were going to break the law.

"When they were building SUNY Albany on Washington Avenue, we tried to block the entry to the construction site – about 15 of us. At the time, I had a job. I was just a concerned citizen," Earl Thorpe explained when I interviewed him. He continued, "Our protests started out with one or two people picketing the union halls. Then it grew. By two months, we were picketing and closing down all of the construction sites in the capital district. The Catholic church came to help picket as well. Father Trembley, Father Young, and more. We had this coalition that came from nowhere. People I didn't even know joined us. They came because we were right and just in what we were pursuing.

"We also saw that [coalition building] with the anti-apartheid movement in South Africa, we saw that with Gandhi, and others. This wasn't just happening in Albany. It was happening across the nation and the world. I argue that this was the beginning of the rainbow coalition that got President Barack Obama elected. People came to help us from Siena College and the suburbs. They came because of our moral authority. The church's involvement was instrumental. They put everything on the line, but they were still out there with us."

The Brothers spread their fight for jobs beyond the construction sites. They also picketed places like Shaker Brewery. They had no black people employed there, and The Brothers were instrumental in getting blacks hired there too. "I went to Shaker Brewery. Moses Thomas, one of the other Brothers went too. We saw how the hiring practices were. You had to work 90 days to make the union. I got my cousin a job there. He worked there for 86 days, then they let him go. So, I fought that," Thorpe explained. Practices like this also kept blacks from joining unions, those bargaining units meant to offer protections for workers.

This moment of protest in Albany also signaled a change in how blacks viewed law enforcement. Where blacks once tried to avoid police and evade going to jail for any reason, they were no longer afraid of getting arrested. It was like a badge of honor. Thorpe described to me how he and other members of The Brothers would repeatedly go to jail.

"It was always a peaceful arrest. The cops didn't use any brutality on us because they knew us and knew we would retaliate. You get us today; we'll get you tomorrow. That's the attitude we had. We knew we would get arrested, but we protested anyway. When we got arrested, we got out the same night or the next day."

The Brothers knew the cops would arrest them, and it was a means of control. The confrontation with them would start with commands to get off the corner. Remember, we saw these same antics after slavery was abolished in this country when police arrested blacks in large numbers after accusing them of loitering. Then, it would escalate to claims of The Brothers resisting arrest and assaulting an officer after – as Thorpe puts it

– the cops were the ones doing the pushing. What would start as something minor, would result in arrest. The Brothers would go to jail, but they continued to go back to the same frontlines that got them in trouble in the first place. Luckily for them, they had good attorneys.

The Brothers reminded me of another "brother" who pushed the boundaries of personal freedom in the name of seeking those unalienable rights our founding fathers affirmed in the Declaration of Independence. He was not a part of The Brothers in Albany, but he was number 20886 – at least that is what the placard read that hung around his neck in his black and white mug shot on May 24, 1961 when he was arrested for using a "white" restroom in Jackson, Mississippi. This young 21-year-old brother was John Lewis, who later became a civil rights icon and served in the United States House of Representatives for Georgia's 5th congressional district.

Like Thorpe, Van Dyke and others, Lewis was not afraid to come face-to-face with law enforcement officials. I could see that in his expression as he smiled for the camera in his 1961 mug shot. Dressed in a suit and tie, he had a smirk on his face that, to me, said he would not accept defeat, and he would not stop pressuring local and national government to end practices that demonstrated racial inequalities. As one of the original Freedom Riders, at the time Lewis was arrested, he was riding an interstate bus from D.C. through the segregated south with others - including white supporters - to challenge local municipalities that did not uphold laws that made racial segregation in public transportation illegal. This would not be Lewis' last protest or arrest. His civil rights work included chairing the Student Non-Violent Coordinating Committee, helping coordinate the March on Washington with Dr. King and others in 1963, participating in lunch counter sit-ins and voter registration drives, and, of course, leading 600 protesters across the Edmund Pettus Bridge in Selma, Alabama in 1965 where he suffered a fractured skull at the hands of police – all in the name of securing voting rights.

I have been so inspired by Congressman Lewis because of what he had been through. I truly admired him because I heard so much about him and his life-long accomplishments. That is why I was elated when I finally got a chance to meet him here in Albany when he spoke at Mount Olive Southern Missionary Baptist Church on July 9, 2010. Our encounter was brief, but it was a cherishable memory. I only wish I had spent more time talking, sharing stories, and connecting with this gentle giant.

Rep. John Lewis succumbed to cancer in July 2020, but not before he made his mark in Congress for 17 terms. He encouraged the world with these words from a 2018 tweet, "Never, ever be afraid to make some noise and get in good trouble, necessary trouble." This is the sentiment in which The Brothers lived by. They got into *good trouble* and went to jail for the sake of others. They fought the unions and construction sites because it was necessary to ensure employment for those who had been shut out for so long. They stood up to power structures when it was not popular because it was necessary to break through the reigning control Mayor Corning and the democratic machine had over the police department, jobs, and the entire city.

Housing & Trash Removal

By now, you know of the deplorable housing conditions that existed in the South End. I have already written extensively about it. Earl Thorpe was chair of the Housing Committee for The Brothers, so housing was one of his passion areas and one of the other social issues The Brothers decided to tackle head on. In addition to landlords neglecting properties, residents had to deal with a major trash issue. There was no garbage pickup in the South End. The City of Albany did not provide this service, and it was the residents' responsibility to pay for private trash collection. This was, obviously, a problem for some in the community who could not afford groceries, let alone trash pickup. Who knew proper waste management was such a luxury?

Have you ever tossed chicken packaging in your garbage can, letting it sit there for one night? How about scraps from a fabulous seafood dinner where all that remained were the garlic butter covered shells from the mollusks and crustaceans you devoured? If so, then you know the garbage stench in your kitchen will leave an offensive, lingering odor until you remove it. Now, imagine creating garbage – especially smelly garbage - but not having anywhere to dispose of it. I do not know what you would do, but some residents in the South End started tossing garbage in their backyards. They had no choice. I imagine this accumulation was not only unsightly, but a health concern as well. Just think of the rodents that were likely scavenging through the yards and carrying diseases. They likely scurried across the same areas where children played hide and seek, hopscotch, and jump rope. Or, maybe the plot of soil where families planted vegetable gardens was where rodents ate too.

The South End became a dumping ground for others who lived outside the community as well. People who *could* afford to pay a trash removal company used to bring their garbage to the inner city to dump it. Arbor Hill also saw this form of neighborhood degradation, not just the South End. Without regard for the residents, outsiders would pollute the community with garbage as if these areas were void of people.

The Brothers knew they had to take action to address this neighborhood blight. They galvanized the community around the trash issue by conducting surveys, leading protests, and holding rallies to demand regular citywide trash removal.

"We collected household trash. We even collected roaches that we found in peoples' houses and put them in the bags with the trash. And, we dumped them at City Hall," Earl Thorpe explained to me. "We anticipated going to jail. Sometimes, I had to stay out of jail because I owned properties. I couldn't go to jail all the time. I had to stay out and bail other people out. We were jailed for loitering or disturbing the peace. One of the other Brothers would say to the police, 'We have the right to assembly'. We used our right. We started picketing the mayor, and even going right up to his house."

William Kennedy was a reporter working for The Knickerbocker News at the time. He accompanied The Brothers around the neighborhood and wrote a series on the housing conditions. His articles helped shine a spotlight on the housing and trash issues. Kennedy also offered commentary in a 2006 documentary titled, *The Brothers: The Forgotten Struggle for Civil Rights in Albany*. In the documentary, Thorpe credits The Brothers for the trash removal service that the City of Albany subsequently implemented.

Five Dollar Vote

Machines are a part of our everyday lives. By one definition, a machine is a mechanical structure that uses power to apply forces and control movement to perform an intended action. There was one machine The Brothers fought, but no matter how many times they got knocked down, they kept getting back up. The machine I am referring to is not a small, household appliance or a massive, industrial device. It was an organized body that wielded enormous and long-standing political power – the democratic political machine. A political machine - run by a party boss - hand picks candidates to run for political office and applies forces and control movement to perform an intended action. In the case of the democratic political machine in Albany, the applied force was a five-dollar bribe and the intended action was a vote in return.

The Brothers abhorred this sort of political corruption and the system of patronage it created. Those who were loyal to the machine were rewarded. Those who defied the machine were dealt with accordingly. The machine was in cahoots with the labor unions. The labor unions were in cahoots with Mayor Corning. Mayor Corning was in cahoots with the police department. They used this web of power to control - as Leon Van Dyke puts it - everything from birth to death. They especially applied this power to control black people and used it to keep them abased. Black neighborhoods lacked community resources, jobs, adequate housing, and the quality of life their white counterparts enjoyed. Their communities received nothing in return for their loyal vote, except $5. But, to maintain power, the machine had to ensure their candidates won every election. They needed to influence the vote.

After their weekly meeting inside their office at 170 North Pearl Street where they collectively decided which issues to deal with next, The Brothers agreed to tackle the five-dollar vote issue. They staged protests at South End and Arbor Hill polling sites on Election Day. Lined up like soldiers, they held picket signs that read, "Don't sell your soul for $5." The Brothers tried to counter the lure of Abraham Lincoln on a crisp five-dollar bill, a lure that was hard to resist for poor people trying to make ends meet. Thorpe would ask voters, "That's all you're worth is $5?" He told me a story of a time when his parents were renting from him. "When they went to vote, a committeeman tried to hand them $5, and someone said, 'No no no, don't give it to them. That's Earl Thorpe's dad!" Thorpe's obvious distaste for the practice was well known amongst machine loyalists.

The Brothers even tried to educate residents about the voting process, because some in the community believed the Democratic Party knew how they voted. With access to an actual voting machine through the Awareness Voting Machine Project, they demonstrated to residents how to vote and proved to them that their selection would be anonymous. Not all were convinced, though. There was a polling site on Green Street where residents believed spies were watching them through a hole in the ceiling above the voting machine. They really believed it. This was another way to keep voters in line.

The $5 vote protest was a disruption that did not go unnoticed. As William Kennedy expressed in the documentary, "When you took on the machine, the machine took you on." The machine used its far-reaching muscle to dispatch the police to polling sites. It was a display of that *watchman style* of policing

James Q. Wilson described in his book that I mentioned in Chapter 3. I spoke to Leon Van Dyke recently when he moved back to Albany after some health challenges. As he reminisced about this issue that he considers their most significant contribution in the Civil Rights Movement, he explained to me their Election Day fate.

"That election day afternoon, Gordon Van Ness and others were planning to go out and picket. They didn't want to wait until 5 p.m. when others got off work. A white student wanted to go, so they went. Gordon came back about an hour later and said, 'The police said if we picket, they were going to throw us in jail.' I was a hothead, so I said, 'Let's go back.' We were over on Clinton and Pearl at the polling place. The police said, 'Leon, we're going to throw you in jail.' So, I said, 'Get the van.' There were about eight of us. At that time, we didn't know if they were going to beat us up or what. About an hour later, we saw some Brothers that were also arrested. When they got off work and heard we got arrested, they went home and told their wives they were going to jail. That sealed us. By the time the night was over, every polling place in the city was picketed. Students came from the campuses. We filled the jail with ministers, students, and everyday folks. That moment showed that we, as black men, did something significant. If we made a decision, the other Brothers were going to stick by us. Going to jail didn't mean anything to me. I'd been in jail before. I did four years at Eastern State Penitentiary. To say you were going to put me in the city jail didn't mean anything to me! Democrats still won, but it showed solidarity and destroyed myths," Van Dyke explained gleefully. The charges were eventually dropped, but The Brothers' concerns could not be ignored.

Eventually, Albany County District Attorney John T. Garry 2d opened a grand jury investigation into the long-standing $5 vote buying practices. On the surface, this sounded like a step toward victory for The Brothers. But keep in mind, it was a *democratic* district attorney investigating the Albany *democrats*. Remember I mentioned the web of power? This is another instance where that power is at play. While the DA announced the start of the investigation, there was a caveat. He vowed to arrest anyone in connection with buying votes, but he also vowed to arrest anyone who took the money. Although The Brothers tried to get people to testify that they were offered the bribe, no one was brave enough to come forward. Because the threat of jail scared people away, the grand jury found no evidence of vote buying.

Sometime in the 1970s, people became more astute in election law and worked toward keeping the election process fair and honest. Education was a big part of this, and there was an organized effort to train people on how to become poll watchers. I was one of them. On one memorable Election Day, I was a poll watcher at a polling site on Alexander Street in the South End. This was a time when police officers used to be stationed at every polling place. Officers had a habit of leaning on the machines while people were going in to vote. This was a form of intimidation, especially for those who accepted $5 from the democratic machine. I went up to this brazen police officer that day and admonished him about his actions, letting him know that what he was doing was against the law. I told him he could not lean on the machine while people were voting. He knew I was right, and he reluctantly stopped. Those of us in the trenches were trying to send the message that things had to change, and the police department could not be used as a tool by Mayor Corning's office. It felt empowering to speak truth to power that day at the polling site. My small contribution helped push the needle just a little more toward victory. I credit The Brothers for this. My actions were prompted by the groundwork The Brothers laid when they put their freedom and their bodies on the line for others like me to follow.

Political Candidates

The Brothers recognized that real change happens in an elected seat, so they decided to run candidates for political offices. They were the insurgents trying to unseat the party-backed incumbents. They saw this power play as an opportunity to disrupt the machine and grab a seat at the table of change. Sam McDowell and Robert Gene Dobbs were two of The Brothers who went up against Albany County machine candidates. Although they were unsuccessful, they proved, once again, they were not afraid to take on a power structure that had such a tight grip on Albany.

Stepping out into the political arena took guts. Not only did The Brothers do it, but they laid the foundation for others to courageously follow. Their groundwork paved the way for Homer L. Perkins to become the first black Albany County legislator in 1968, for Nebraska Brace to become the first black alderman in Albany in 1977, and for Keith St. John to become the first openly gay black person in the entire country elected to public office, winning an alderman seat in Albany in 1989.

Legacy

The Brothers disbanded sometime in the 1970s. No one knows the date for sure, and there was no particular event that broke them up. Some say most of them got jobs and started going their separate ways. Others focused on family or moved out of the area. One Brother in particular, Leon Van Dyke, pursued academic excellence and enrolled in SUNY Albany. He climbed the education ladder and received a master's degree before securing a job with the New York State Education Department. One thing I know for sure, The Brothers left a lasting legacy.

In addition to showing us how to look adversity in the face through picketing and running political candidates, they showed us how to control our own narrative when they published their very own weekly newspaper, The Albany Liberator. Peter Pollak was the editor of The Liberator and a strong ally to The Brothers. Reporters from Albany's mainstream newspapers such as William Kennedy and Scott Christianson served as ghost writers, and they showed The Brothers how to perfect their paper. The Liberator was a platform to educate the community about the issues The Brothers were tackling. It not only covered the issues, but it revealed their results. Residents in the community could browse their 10-cent copy of the paper and learn about how The Brothers picketed the office of the John R. Carney Agency – a slum landlord – and read about how they demanded and got results on behalf of poor, black tenants. The newspaper accurately detailed the arrests, trials, acquittals, and guilty verdicts from every entanglement The Brothers experienced with the police. It advised residents of programs like The Brothers' Operation Christmas Basket where they distributed free turkeys and trees to community residents. The Liberator connected readers in Albany to current events outside the Capital Region and the state, giving a glimpse of what the black experience was like across borders as well. And, it even covered details of a sniper attack at The Brothers' headquarters where a shooter fired a gun through the front window, injuring a SUNY student and Knickerbocker News reporter Bill Blando.

There are still a few original members of The Brothers around Albany. Today, 86-year-old Leon Van Dyke hosts a local radio show. He continues to talk about the important issues.

Earl Thorpe retired long ago after working in many fields including the construction industry, but not from the renowned singing group he has long been a part of since 1956. That group, The Fidelitys, was inducted into the Eddies Hall of Fame in 2020. Thorpe actively engages in public speaking where he talks about the civil rights movement. He is an active member of the Metropolitan New Testament Mission Baptist Church where he sings in the choir.

The third Brother, Purcell McDowell, is also still around. He, Van Dyke and Thorpe attended a Dr. King celebration I hosted at my home in 2020. It was a joyous reunion since they had not seen each other in years. We laughed. We sang. We listened to the many stories they shared.

The last time I caught up with Thorpe, I asked him what he thought about the new group of young activists that have come behind him and have participated in protests recently here in Albany and across the globe after George Floyd's murder. He offered this observation, "I think Black Lives Matter is the best thing that ever happened. You have a diverse group. Blacks and whites are together now. You had limited whites before, but now you have an array of people. They [the cops] are particular about who to harass because they don't know who their parents are. These kids come from rich areas, and they are here for a cause. They go and tell their parents this is what they want to do, and their parents support them. Everyone is represented at these protests."

We should all take to heart the lessons The Brothers have taught us and commit to action in some form, addressing the injustices that exist, whether they affect us directly or not. In the words of Dr. Martin Luther King Jr., "Somewhere I read that the greatness of America is the right to protest for right."

Dr. Nathan Wright, SUNY Albany Professor and Founding Chair of the African and Afro-American Studies Department. Public domain image.

6

National Movement, Local Effects: How the Black Power Movement Shaped Albany

1968 – A Year of Turmoil

As I examine the connectivity of police brutality, abuse of powers, social injustice, poverty, racism, and the prison pipeline, one year comes to mind that demonstrates an explosion of events where all these themes collided. No, I am not talking about 2020 – the year that brought the world to its knees, although it, too, would fit the description. Rather, I am referring to 1968. It is a year that has often been described as a year of turmoil and change. It was a huge year for national calamity that has carved out its own place in our history books.

Earlier, I mentioned that The National Advisory Commission on Civil Disorders – also known as the Kerner Commission - released the Kerner Report on February 29, 1968, which it produced at the request of President Johnson to analyze recent protests and uprisings in urban communities. The report found that poverty and institutional racism were driving inner city violence. It reads, "Segregation and poverty have created in the racial ghetto a destructive environment totally unknown to most white Americans. What white Americans have never fully understood – but what the Negro can never forget – is that white society is deeply implicated in the ghetto. White institutions created it, white institutions maintain it, and white society condones it." The report further explains that our nation was so divided that it was poised to fracture into two radically unequal societies—one black, one white.

The highly popular report, published into a best-selling book, was criticized by conservative whites who did not agree with its findings. It backfired on President Johnson who expected his moderate commission members to conclude with some evidence of outside agitation; irresponsible, flame-fanning journalists; or wild conspiracies. Instead, it disagreed with the president's preconceived theories.

According to a 2018 article in the Smithsonian Magazine, "Polls showed 53 percent of white Americans condemned the claim that racism had caused the riots, while 58 percent of black Americans agreed with the findings. Even before the report, white support for civil rights was waning. In 1964, most Northern whites had backed Johnson's civil rights initiatives, but just two years later, polls showed that most Northern whites believed Johnson was pushing too aggressively."

The article continued, "White response to the Kerner Commission helped lay the foundation for the law-and-order campaign that elected Richard Nixon to the presidency later that year. Instead of considering the full weight of white prejudice, Americans endorsed rhetoric that called for arming police officers like soldiers and cracking down on crime in inner cities." Seems like some things never change.

If poverty was keeping blacks in the inner cities and segregated from whites as the Kerner Report suggests, and if white Americans created and condoned this system, then the events that followed a month after the Kerner Report was released should not be surprising. On April 4, 1968, the Rev. Dr. Martin Luther King, Jr. was assassinated in Memphis, Tennessee. Known by everyone as a charismatic leader and civil rights activist whose propensity for non-violence earned him a Noble Peace Prize, right before he was slain, Dr. King was preparing to march in Memphis on behalf of sanitation workers fighting for economic equality. That march was really just a prelude to the revolutionary message he wanted to amplify nationally with his Poor People's Campaign.

Dr. King announced the Poor People's Campaign at a staff retreat for the Southern Christian Leadership Conference in the fall of 1967. He planned for thousands of poor people to descend on Washington, D.C., and camp in tents on the National

Mall. People from southern states and northern cities were to come together to meet with government officials to demand jobs, unemployment insurance, a fair minimum wage, and education for poor adults and children designed to improve their self-image and self-esteem. Dr. King recognized the economic emergency at hand with 35 million poor people in our country at the time. As he so poignantly stated in an interview, "In 1776 the nation signed a huge promissory note. In this campaign, we're coming to get our check."

Those that feared Dr. King's movement knew that if he organized poor people of all races from all over the country, radical change would be inevitable. After all, he and others opposed and protested segregation. The result was federal legislation called the Civil Rights Act of 1964. He and others marched and fought for voting rights. The result was federal legislation called the Voting Rights Act of 1965. Sadly, Dr. King did not make it to Washington D.C. for the Poor People's Campaign. A fatal bullet from a rifle robbed him of that.

On April 4, I left Albany and boarded a Greyhound bus to visit my brother, Ralph, in Washington D.C. He was a college student studying at Maryland State. I broke up the long journey by staying overnight in New York City to time my arrival with his availability to pick me up the next day. Never did I imagine that date would be so infamous. It was there in New York City where I learned of the tragedy that had unfolded in Memphis. The television informed me of the events that left the world in shock. Nonetheless, I pressed on the next morning and boarded the bus to D.C. The anticipation of this young woman from rural upstate New York going to the nation's capital for the first time and seeing a pink sea of cherry blossoms was supposed to be enough to relieve my mind of current events.

I arrived in D.C. in the early afternoon where I was enveloped by smog. It appeared to be smog. The naiveté in me wanted to believe that is what it was. As I stood around in a haze waiting for my brother to locate me, I realized that the translucent cover was actually smoke. Reunited with my brother, he explained to me what was happening in the District. I did not realize there was an enormous reaction in D.C. to Dr. King's death. No one told me. Essentially, I stepped off the bus and walked right into history.

I became fascinated with being in that moment. People were running around carrying all kinds of items from stores. It was a wild scene. As we walked, we saw cars with headlights on in the middle of the day. People were blowing their horns with fierce indignation. There were signs in storefront windows depicting the locations of black-owned businesses. It took us a while to get to my brother's apartment, and I witnessed a flurry of activities all along the way.

Not only did I observe with my eyes, but I was listening to what people were saying in the streets. For instance, I saw people exiting the local dry cleaners with arms filled with clothes saying, "They always over charged us anyway." It was as if they were righting a wrong. They were reacting and angry, yet people felt free. They were free to express themselves in the manor they saw fit. That night, there was still a commotion in the streets. I could hear gun shots. Our mother was back home in New York concerned, as any mother would be who had two of her children away from home and in the middle of chaos. She called us on the phone to check on us. I really did not want to go to bed. My adrenaline was rushing, and I wanted to go back out, but we did not. My over-protective younger brother vetoed that idea.

The next morning, however, we did go back out to walk around and survey the environment. The city had a different atmosphere. By that time, the military had moved in with tanks. It resembled a war zone and was, certainly, amazing to see. Civil rights activist Stokely Carmichael was there as well, trying to promote calm before pushing his Black Power message to the nation.

Being in the moment forced me to think about how people were feeling in the loss of Dr. King. At the time, I was a graduate student from New York who took a weekend trip to see the famed cherry blossoms. But the trip forever shaped my thinking about these types of events. When these things happen, I do not consider them riots. I call them uprisings. People are letting loose their feelings and concerns about being controlled and oppressed. During the uprising after George Floyd's death, I was reminded of this. The D.C. trip was eye opening and forced me to think about what has happened over the years to black people. It helped form my opinion about oppression and reactions to it. I never did see the cherry blossoms that weekend, but I did get a front row seat to witness a movement.

The assassination of Dr. King signaled a major political and social change in America that was also felt in Albany. There was the sense that an era had passed. We all felt the loss of his leadership as we struggled to continue our work for change. Things became more confusing. Presidential candidate and Senator Robert Kennedy, seen as a friend to blacks because of his integrity and devotion to civil rights causes, was also murdered on June 6 of that same year.

In August, we witnessed a Democratic National Convention in Chicago that was probably the most divided in modern-day history. I watched the chaos closely in the streets of Chicago surrounding the convention. Not only was there turmoil inside the convention with several factions looking to be nominated for the presidential seat President Johnson gave up, but outside with pro-war and anti-war demonstrators as well. Police clashed violently with groups and individuals present like the National Mobilization Committee to End the War in Vietnam, the Youth International Party, Students for a Democratic Society, and Black Panther leader Bobby Seale who was arrested and scheduled to go to trial as one of the famous "Chicago 7". They were charged with conspiracy, but that charge against Seale was dropped. He was represented by famed civil rights attorney, William Kunstler, who would appear three years later as negotiator at the Attica

Prison Uprising. In the end, we were left with a defeated Democratic Party while Richard Nixon, who campaigned on a *law and order platform*, became the 37ᵗʰ president of the United States.

On a local level, 1968 was also an important year. The Albany NAACP, with police brutality eradication at the heart of its mission since 1935, developed the Legal Defense Fund to provide legal assistance to the most vulnerable residents who could not afford to defend their human and civil rights. It later transformed into the Legal Redress Committee which focused on criminal justice reform. I was involved closer to the 80s when I became chair of the Legal Redress Committee.

In that same year, the NAACP made a bold move toward attempting to get Albany to act on neighborhood improvements. Headed by Dr. Joseph Cohen at the time, the NAACP strategized and came up with 67 demands that served as a central platform in 1968 to address improvements for housing, public services, education, government, and police. You would think that ridding playgrounds of broken glass where children recreate and creating part-time jobs for teenagers in the Capital District would be obvious services provided by the city. But the lack of these neighborhood essentials and others is what caused the NAACP to act. Seeing what was going on nationally with police relations and being on the frontlines locally with The Brothers, the churches, and other activists, the NAACP's 67 demands included the following which were related to police:

- Human relations course, conducted by trained specialists, be required on a regular basis for all city policemen.
- More black policemen and firemen be recruited and hired.
- Increased salaries for policemen and firemen.
- More police protection and less harassment in the Arbor Hill and South End areas.

- Enforcement of all traffic laws in the city, to promote respect for the law.
- Improvement of police and court procedures for youthful offenders.
- Establishment of a community service officer in Arbor Hill and the South End to deal with police-citizen relationships and to promote understanding between law enforcement men and private citizens. The officer in each area must be acceptable to all neighborhood groups in the area.

The NAACP presented their demands to Albany Mayor Corning who immediately rejected the civil rights groups' terms. Little has changed over the years, especially in hiring black police officers and fire fighters. Back when Peter Pryor was practicing law in Albany, he had a case where he tried to get more fire fighters hired. Even more recently, I had to fight for my nephew to get into Albany's fire department after he was rejected. A police official lied and said my nephew was not truthful during the interview. I retained a lawyer on his behalf, and as we sat with officials, I said, "Can you tell us when this happened?" They said, "We never interviewed him." They were busted for telling a bold-faced lie. How could my nephew lie during the interview if they never interviewed him? They were just not hiring black folks. The NAACP's 67 demands did not yield many results – especially in the area of police – but it did awaken the black community to these disparities.

Following the 10-month uproar of the first nine and a half months of 1968, on October 16, something uplifting and promising happened at the 1968 Olympics held in Mexico City. Two black athletes, Tommie Smith and John Carlos, gave blacks across the country a lift and sense of pride. During the medal ceremony in the Olympic Stadium, they each raised a black-gloved fist while they played the US national anthem, "The Star-Spangled Banner." I was personally exhilarated. To this day,

I have a poster depicting their courageous protest action against racism prominently displayed in my home.

Welfare Rights Convention

When you think about people on public assistance, or welfare as it is commonly called, you probably conjure up images of black people, especially single mothers with multiple children in tow. That is because political and journalistic spin assigned black women to be the face of typical welfare recipients since the 1950s. They have even dubbed them welfare queens and assigned them characteristics of being lazy and unwilling to work. It did not help that Linda Taylor, a black mother who personified this stereotype as she fraudulently collected thousands of dollars through welfare schemes for years, gained notoriety throughout the country as early as the 1970s. While it was easier for the disdain for poverty-stricken families to be hurled at blacks because of women like Taylor, it was, in fact, whites who were and are the largest benefactors of public assistance. Yet, elected officials like President Ronald Reagan and others have used anti-poor resentment as political platforms. They even passed laws to decrease the number of recipients and the amount of welfare payments.

Welfare recipients began organizing in the early 1960s to counter politically motivated attacks against those needing assistance. They gave birth to the National Welfare Rights Organization (NWRO) in 1966 to fight for greater assistance and control over welfare regulations. The organization challenged the negative public image of those on welfare and fought for people to be treated with respect and dignity. Dr. George Wiley, a prominent chemist and former associate director of the Congress of Racial Equality (CORE) became the first executive director of NWRO.

It was at a National Welfare Rights Organization convention in Chicago in 1970 where I met Dr. George Wiley and another one of my heroes, William Kunstler – the same

Kunstler who defended Bobby Seale after the 1968 protests. He was a well-known, radical attorney who took on a lot of high-profile cases. I became enamored with him because of his penchant for civil rights. The work he did on that trial, which began in 1969, was documented in the Netflix show, "The Trial of the Chicago 7."

At the time of the convention, I was working at Trinity Institution where welfare rights were at the top of our agenda. I traveled with one of my social worker colleagues for the weekend-long convention. Trinity had been instrumental in forming a Welfare Rights Organization chapter that was quite active. Catherine Boddie from the South End was the community organizer for NWRO in Albany. I was very interested in going to the convention because I had paid so much attention to what went on in 1968. I was sort of a groupie for Wiley and Kunstler.

It must have been my lucky day. I met a woman in Chicago who introduced me to Kunstler, one of the convention speakers. My brief exchange in the hotel elevator must have impressed him because he grabbed my hand, led me out of the venue door, and escorted me into a waiting taxi. I got to spend the whole day with Bill Kunstler! This was the first time he had been back in Chicago since the infamous trial. After his convention duties were over, he wanted to revisit the courthouse because the time he spent there was a high point in his career and his life. I was along for the ride. It was an exciting moment for me because he was someone I looked up to. I do not know if he was more flattered by my presence - someone who had cheered him on from a distance and stood watch in admiration - or if I was more flattered and elated that he showed enough interest in me to welcome me into his world. Either way, it felt like Christmas morning.

I discovered a great deal of information from Bill Kunstler's session during the National Welfare Rights Organization convention. He did a presentation on the Black Panthers and how the FBI killed Fred Hampton in 1969, chairman of the Illinois chapter of the Black Panther Party and deputy chairman of the national Black Panther Party. He was assassinated in his bed while he slept during a predawn raid. The federal government was out to get rid of the Panthers because they were considered a real threat. When I worked in the prisons, I worked with a lot of the Black Panthers. I learned about the FBI's Counterintelligence Program - or the COINTELPRO - and how they swept people off the streets, jailed them for no reason, or killed them. The COINTELPRO was a covert - and some would say illegal - operation designed to spy on, infiltrate, discredit, assassinate, and disrupt political and other organizations. Things were not always what they seemed. The federal government had an agenda to get rid of the Panthers and other activists they considered radical. Black Panthers and civil rights organizers gave me my real education in criminal justice, and I have so much respect for them.

The National Welfare Rights Organization was dissolved in 1975. But, during its nine year-history, change agents took their message from the local streets of impoverished neighborhoods to the halls of Washington, D.C. Today, the fight continues for a living wage with the *Fight for $15* movement that swept across the country. Many states have already adopted a form of minimum wage gradual increases. Here in New York, a uniform statewide minimum hourly wage was replaced with a minimum wage based on geographic areas and size of the employer in 2016. Upstate cities like Albany will see a minimum of $12.50 an hour on and after December 31, 2020. Thereafter, a wage rate will be set by the Commissioner of Labor, based on economic conditions, up to $15.00. For those able to work, this should help aid them from public assistance to self-reliance.

Dr. Nathan Wright and the Black Power Movement

Albany's black population continued to increase in the 1960s and 70s. Thanks to the community organizing work of organizations like Trinity Institution, The Brothers, NAACP, churches, and block clubs, it was an actively engaged population. Not only were they community-minded, but they were also driven to succeed academically. More and more, they steadily gravitated to higher education as a means for economic advancement. SUNY Albany, my alma mater and the place that helped shape me, was experiencing a surge in black students. Today, 13 percent of its 12,875 students are black.

In response to demands from an increasing black student population, led by the Black Student Alliance, SUNY Albany's president created the Afro-American Studies Department for entry level courses in African American studies. On January 31, 1969, President Collins bypassed normal university channels and formed an Afro-American Studies Department scheduled to offer courses in the fall of 1969. The department was part of the Division of Social and Behavioral Sciences of the College of Arts and Science, which became the College of Social and Behavioral Sciences in 1977.

Prior to the Africana Studies Department forming, SUNY Albany offered courses during the 1960s in the English (Afro-American Literature: Eng 583 was introduced in the fall of 1966), History (History of the Negro in the United States: HY 254 was introduced in the fall of 1966), and Sociology departments (Minority Groups: Soc 150 was introduced in fall of 1964). These courses would eventually form the basis for the interdisciplinary Afro-American Studies Department.

According to the 1969-1970 bulletin of the new department, "The Department of Afro-American Studies was designed...[to] supplement...the intellectual perspectives which have been characteristic of our nation's historically pro-white orientation. This would be accomplished through an investigation of vital disciplines such as political, historical, economic, socio-psychological and derived issues as they relate to the Black experience." Though the primary focus of the new department was studying the black experience in the United

States, from the start the department also included courses relating to African history and culture.

The new department developed rapidly. The 1970 University Bulletin lists 34 courses available to an undergraduate major in Afro-American Studies in the areas of historical issues, economic-political, socio-psychological, or cultural. Since the Fall of 1972, the department has offered a Master of Arts degree. In addition to its strictly academic course offerings, the African and Afro-American Studies Department served as a social support arena. It was and is the only department in which there is a substantial number of black professors, providing students with needed role models in a predominately white environment. I was one of those professors, and I briefly taught a Blacks in Criminal Justice class and a Civil Rights class in the late 80s. The department serves as a home for mentors and those to be mentored. In 1973 the Afro-American Studies Department enlarged its mission to give equal emphasis to the interdisciplinary study of Africa. In recognition of this new emphasis, the Afro-American Department changed its name to the Department of African and Afro-American Studies. In 1990 the department, once again, changed its name to Africana Studies in recognition of a new widening of its intellectual focus - namely the inclusion of courses documenting the whole African diaspora. New areas of concentration included Caribbean and Latin American Studies.

In 1969, the new department needed a capable and bold leader at the helm. SUNY chose Dr. Nathan Wright to become the first permanent chair of the Afro-American Studies Department. My first impression of Dr. Wright was that he was a man way before his time. His Afrocentric style of dress and his pro-black ideologies made him stand out here in Albany. People did not know what to make of this dashiki-wearing scholar who grew up in Ohio. He had the articulation of Dr. King and the mindset of Malcolm X. He had a fire in him like Stokely Carmichael and a calculated approach to black empowerment like the leaders of the Student Nonviolent Coordinating Committee.

Before working in the world of academia, Dr. Wright was an author, penning his first book – "Good Manners for Good People" - at the age of 15. He later went on to write a total of 18 books and more than 300 articles. A well-rounded and educated man, Dr. Wright served in the U.S. Army Medical Administrative Corps during World War II, and holds a doctorate in education and Master of Sacred Theology degree from Harvard University, and another master's degree and a bachelor's of divinity from the Episcopal Theological School. He also added ordained Episcopalian minister to his list of titles and accomplishments.

Dr. Wright was very active in the community. If there was a meeting, he would show up and start talking a whole different language. The Brothers, at the time, were not really talking about topics like black power. We started seeing Dr. Wright come to Trinity to volunteer and tutor the young people. He would show up at meetings, and it was kind of unusual because meeting attendees were usually typically people from the community. He was lively because he came with a radical message.

Dr. Wright became an important figure in the Black Power Movement in Albany. His students loved him and were very impressed by him. Planting seeds of civil rights and black empowerment through self-direction and black leadership, he opened the students' eyes to performing community organizing work. That is when Trinity saw an increase in students getting involved in the community. They were able to take the theories learned in school and apply them in the real world. Trinity was their real world. And we have Dr. Wright to thank for that.

Dr. Wright cut his teeth in civil rights work long before he graced the Capital Region with his presence. In 1946, he protested against random searches by the Cincinnati police. In 1947, he joined the Journey of Reconciliation, traveling with a coalition of blacks and whites on buses and trains throughout the south for the first freedom ride of the civil rights era. They embarked on this journey to test and publicize the 1945 U.S. Supreme Court decision ordering the desegregation of interstate travel. In 1967, he also organized and chaired the first National Conference on Black Power. This major conference, attended by 1,100 delegates from 42 cities and a few hundred black organizations, had key messages focusing on building an economic power base with a *Buy Black* campaign and establishing black national holidays and black universities. It even broached the topic of black separatism.

As a scholar, Dr. Wright wrote about black consciousness and black power from a reformist rather than a revolutionary point-of-view. His plea for cooperation among races and within the black community, "Let's Work Together," was published in 1968 and nominated for a Pulitzer Prize. He was of the mindset of group solidarity. This thinking was a shift in the civil rights movement which often focused on individual rights.

I knew Dr. Wright and certainly knew of all his accomplishments, but I did not work as closely with him as others like my friend Leon Van Dyke. As I recalled memories of Dr. Wright while speaking with Leon recently, he said to me, "He [Dr. Nathan Wright] was saying stuff that I didn't fully understand until later. He published nine books at that time. He was so advanced that he scared everybody. We interviewed him for 'The Liberator,' and he said that the Afro-American Studies Department should be in every department. He was talking about this in 1969. At that time, I had a 10th grade education. I never thought about going to college. But this guy Nathan, who had a master's degree and a bachelor's degree in divinity and a doctorate in education, embraced a young man like me as if we were equals. He didn't look down on us. He made The Brothers feel good about ourselves. He lived in a big house outside of Albany. He would invite us over to hang out. He influenced a lot of students."

Dr. Wright retired first to Riverdale, New York, and then to East Stroudsburg, Pennsylvania, where he died of kidney failure from complications of diabetes on February 22, 2005. He was 81 years old. Before his transition, Dr. Wright was instrumental in using a national platform like the Black Power Movement to shape our city. From the church, to the community, and to the classroom, he left a lasting legacy during his season in Albany and the United States.

Boji Jordan and fellow South African in 1992.
Boji was a revolutionary political activist
against racism and apartheid.

Challenging the Political Status Quo Locally and Abroad

Theresa Cooke

Many people have challenged Albany Mayor Corning during his 41-year, strong grip he had on the city from 1942-1983. I have mentioned some of the individuals, groups, and neighborhood associations already. Although some have caused a ripple in his political ocean, I would argue that no one was more successful at single-handedly creating a tsunami in his career like Theresa Cooke. Cooke was a tough, Irish woman who looked corruption and injustice square in the eye. Her intolerance for the political shenanigans of Dan O'Connell's Democratic machine and his sidekick in City Hall, Mayor Corning, gave her the bravery she needed to help reform the systems in Albany.

Theresa Cooke was not an Albany insider. She was born in White Plains, New York, and reared in Pleasantville, New York. Even though this Albany Tulip Queen first runner-up came to the Capital Region for school in the 1950s where she earned her bachelor's and master's degrees from SUNY Albany, she did not move back to Albany until 1970 at the age of 34 when she relocated here with her husband and children. So, she had nothing to lose when she began to speak out. As a mother active in her children's education, Cooke began asking questions about school district policies. Officials ignored her, but she would not let it rest. She accused the school board of conducting illegal meetings, among other things.

The school board was not her only target. Cooke quickly turned her attention to Mayor Corning's budgets and how the city was spending taxpayer dollars. As president of the Albany Taxpayers Association, she spent thousands of hours researching how municipal governments should work and spend money, according to a Times Union article from 2017 that recapped her activism.

"At a press conference in front of the mayor's house, Cooke once declared that Corning didn't understand the workings of democracy. She was proven right, perhaps, when the city subsequently raised the assessment on the Cooke home by 250 percent," the article read.

Many people privately supported Cooke and her criticisms of Mayor Corning. Some were scared to support her publicly because they were crippled with fear of the Corning administration. Cooke even considered running against Corning for mayor in 1973 but decided not to when businessman Carl Touhey entered the race. Little did I know, that same Touhey would later become my father-in-law. Theresa collaborated with Carl during his run for mayor. His campaign called for "a clean sweep." That meant destroying the democratic machine and its many forms of corruption that cost the taxpayers dearly. I recall Times Union political cartoonist Hy Rosen's cartoon of Carl with a broom and Theresa with a mop in hand. In it, Carl suggested that he would sweep, and Theresa could mop the city clean of the O'Connell Machine. Even though his attempt to unseat Corning was unsuccessful, the race was very close – 3,500 votes close - and some attribute his near victory to Corning's weakened political influence because of the Theresa Cooke affect. Others claimed Corning and the Democratic Machine stole votes.

Cooke scored a victory the following year when she ran as a Republican for county treasurer. In a blow to the Democratic machine, she pursued rich, political donors who evaded paying taxes. She also investigated discrepancies in city assessment records. That investigation went up in smoke when a fire at City Hall destroyed the records.

The City of Albany's spending did not go unnoticed. The State Commission of Investigation commenced a year-long investigation into Albany's municipal purchasing practices. It concluded in 1972 that the local Democratic political machine wielded control in Albany that cost taxpayers millions of dollars.

"It would appear that the [Albany County Democratic] committee is the well-recognized overriding power that controls hiring, firing, raises, promotions, contracts, purchases and prices and probably every other activity in the operations of the city of Albany," the New York Times reported. "Such 'paralyzing outside influences and control' resulted in serious laxity, incompetence and mismanagement in connection with purchasing and in incomparable gouging and overcharging and the waste of public funds."

Some of the unethical practices outlined by the commission included city workers getting paid for time they did not work, party officials showing up at City Hall to collect donations from political appointees, and businesses receiving public contracts without bidding or scrutiny from municipal auditors. According to the hearing testimonies during the investigation, one company - North End Contracting Corporation - bought a jeep for $800 and charged the city an hourly rate for using it at a municipal landfill—for a total of $23,208.

The State Commission on Investigation referred its findings for possible criminal indictments to a Republican district attorney. The Albany Taxpayers Association had collected enough documentation of municipal irregularities to persuade the commission to open its inquiry. We have Theresa Cooke to thank for that.

I was both in awe of Cooke whom I met around 1972 and inspired by her commitment to work to change a system that she believed was corrupt, unjust, and harmful to democracy, the city, and social justice. "Where did this gentle, middle-class, white woman get the courage to take on a powerful political machine?" I wondered. Fortunately, I got close enough to her to watch and observe her community action approach. I became part of a group of progressive Albanians who were willing to support her efforts to change how Albany did business. They included Dr. Larry Sturman, my father-in-law Carl Touhey, and his son and my husband, Charles Touhey. I was part of a small group of people who worked hard on all her campaigns, whether civil or political.

We watched how she used the media to get her message of change across to the public. They followed her closely as she showed up at public sites and meetings to challenge or denounce some practices she wanted to call attention to and ultimately change. She always came prepared with laws, city ordinances, court decisions, and official reports as she took on Corning and the machine face-to-face. But, she was always so professional and calm in her approach. This demeanor gained her respect from both sides of the fence. It seems weird now that she was always referred to as Mrs. Cooke.

Cooke certainly influenced me in my approach to community organizing for change. Among other things, I learned that you not only had to be compassionate, but well prepared with good accurate information that supports your claims. I learned that you could be more effective by operating in a professional, yet staunch, manner that allows one to remain true to his or her cause. I learned not to fear or be intimidated by those with significant economic and political power, for *people power* can be even stronger. Most importantly, I learned that mainstream media can be a powerful educator of the public who can then lend support to your cause.

Using my newly acquired lessons from Theresa Cooke on activism and challenging the status quo, I strengthened my resolve to fight racism in Albany, but first I joined in the growing global struggle against apartheid in Africa.

Local Fight Against Apartheid

As a child, I thought a lot about Africa and thought of it as a dark, backward, and unreachable jungle, thanks to the racist portrayals of the continent. Unfortunately, my introduction to Africa was through films. There were "King Kong," "King Solomon's Mine," "Mogambo," a couple featuring my idol, Sidney Poitier, and, of course, the flood of "Tarzan" movies. They all painted a demeaning and disturbing picture of Africa, the *dark continent*, and its native peoples pictured as stupid, animal-like creatures whose only purpose was to serve every need of the white missionaries and colonists who exploited them. Later images of Africa turned more political, showing and denouncing black resisters to their colonization. They were fighting against apartheid, a system of legalized and institutionalized racial segregation in South Africa. This system, set up by the National Party in 1948, was designed to ensure the white South Africans – who were in the minority – dominated politically, economically and socially.

Under apartheid, South Africans were ranked based on race. Whites enjoyed the privilege of having the highest status, followed by Asians - those who were descendants of indentured laborers and migrants who arrived from India in the late 1800s and early 1900s. Next on the social stratification were coloureds – those who were of mixed races. Lastly, at the bottom rung of the racial hierarchy were blacks. This is important to know because, based on which one of the four races South Africans belonged to, they were relegated to second-class citizens or elevated to prosperity. Those who would suffer the most under this rule – black South Africans – endured this injustice for nearly 50 years.

My first trips to Africa were in the 1990s, giving me a more accurate picture of the continent. I visited western Africa on several trips, then Egypt nearly 10 years ago. South Africa became more of an interest to me after meeting Boji Jordan, a

Xhosa-speaking Albany resident who introduced me and others to an international struggle in Africa that I would become involved in locally. Their struggle was related to the black struggle for justice in America and Albany.

Boji was a native South African and comrade of Nelson Mandela, the persecuted freedom fighter who took on apartheid and finally defeated it from his prison cell. Boji became an influential member of the community as an educator, anti-apartheid and civil rights activist, and promoter of South African culture, language and history. He taught me much about his native country, Mandela, and the African National Congress' (ANC) long struggle for freedom. Through his tales, he convinced me that we had to go to South Africa together.

Unfortunately, that never happened. But, I was determined to get there somehow. It was not until 2011 that I got the opportunity to travel to South Africa and visit places that Boji had talked to me about, especially Cape Town and the townships. I particularly enjoyed meeting brilliant, loving, friendly, and overall amazing residents of the nearby township of Gugulethu where I saw great poverty but wonderfully engaging, musical, and friendly people. But the visit to Robben Island, I must admit, was one of the most emotional and satisfying highlights of my life. I deeply felt Nelson Mandela's presence when I gazed into the cell he had once occupied and the rock quarry where he and so many other black African freedom fighters had labored for so long.

I later visited Durban, South Africa, and found it to be the hottest and most humid place I had ever experienced on Earth. Yet, I was still able to learn much about South African history by visiting museums and talking to people I met. And, I learned of the peoples' deep love and respect for Mandela who was ill with a respiratory condition at the time I was there. My taxi driver warned me that when Mandela dies, South Africans will mourn so deeply that it will shake the world. He was right.

In Albany, I celebrated the life of Mandela with Boji in front of the Capital District African American Cultural Center shortly after his death on December 5, 2013. Many others joined us, including Vera Michelson, who - with Merton Simpson and Boji - founded the Capital District Coalition Against Apartheid and Racism (CD-CAAR). Mike, as she was lovingly known, led efforts to isolate the apartheid regime by organizing demonstrations and local participation in numerous cultural boycotts. She also promoted the divestment of New York State of public pension funds from corporations that supported apartheid. Mike attended an African National Congress Conference in Zambia and traveled to other African countries including South Africa, Namibia, and Mozambique, in conjunction with her anti-apartheid work which supported southern Africa liberation struggles.

Football is the most popular spectator sport amongst many fans in the United States, but around the world, rugby is quite popular. Rugby is a sport like football, and South Africa's revered rugby team is called the Springboks. In September 1981, the Springboks tour was bearing down on Albany for a scheduled match at Bleecker Stadium in the West Hill section of the city. Mike and others were outraged that Mayor Corning was planning to allow the team to play in Albany. There was international scrutiny because of South Africa's system of Apartheid, and many other nations showed disapproval by boycotting sporting events, divesting funds, withdrawing military aid, calling for economic sanctions, and condemning the policies of that country, etc. Our local, grassroots activists regarded Mayor Corning's decision as an affront to humankind. After all, other major cities in the U.S. were canceling their planned games including New York City, Chicago, Los Angeles, and Rochester, for fear of widespread violence. But not Albany.

The Capital District Coalition Against Apartheid (They added Racism to the name a year later) organized for the purpose of building opposition and protesting against the planned

115

Springbok match. Strong opposition to Mayor Corning was building. Newspapers and religious organizations came forth to call upon Corning to cancel the event. Even the Catholic Bishop Howard Hubbard and Episcopal Bishop Wilbur Hogg issued strong statements condemning Mayor Corning's stand, claiming that welcoming the Springboks was tantamount to the city associating with racism and rejecting the religious teachings of residents.

A New York City-based anti-apartheid organization – Stop the Apartheid Rugby Tour (SART) – helped organize a protest here in Albany. It represented 100 civil rights, religious, political, and sports organizations. The group was originally going to protest in New York City but decided to change cities because of Mayor Corning's stance. Richard Lapchick, a spokesperson for the group, was quoted in the Knickerbocker News as saying, "We will fully mobilize for Albany. Since the mayor in Albany has made a decision to go ahead with the match there at a public facility and the people in Albany organized against it, we feel this is the most appropriate site."

The controversy surrounding the rugby match reached Governor Hugh Carey's office. He weighed in and decided to cancel the match, but a judge ruled to overturn the governor's decision.

As a doctoral student at the time, I was not deeply involved in what was happening around me. But, I did lend my voice in opposition to the Springboks and the mayor' stance. Claiming the team had a First Amendment right to play was hypocritical at best. After all, Mayor Corning had vigorously prohibited the appearance of famous singer and actor, Paul Robeson, at a concert in Albany in 1947 because he was labeled a Communist sympathizer. Where was *his* First Amendment right?

After being on the frontlines of the protests to prevent the Springboks from playing in Albany, Mike and the CD-CAAR would later join with the Center for Law and Justice and other civil rights groups in the fight against racism in policing in Albany. They were not successful at stopping the South Africa Springboks against the United States Eastern Rugby Union match on September 22, 1981, but they were highly successful in mobilizing the community in solidarity to support the oppressed people of South Africa. By adding the word racism to its name, the Capital District Coalition Against Apartheid *and* Racism created a link between apartheid in South Africa and racial injustice in the United States. The group continued to organize for 15 years until South Africa held its first democratic election where Mandela became president.

Theresa Cooke, Albany County treasurer and president of the Albany Taxpayers Association, and unidentified gentleman.

Reverend Henry Johnson, Alice, and Vera Michelson at a news conference.

Protest at Albany City Hall against the South African rugby
team, the Springboks

Albany protestors march in the rain against Apartheid in South Africa.

Part 3

The Center for Law and Justice

Alice joins Jessie Davis' family and family attorney Lewis Oliver
for a news conference.

8

The Jessie Davis Killing

On Monday, July 9, 1984, I sat weary eyed in my small New York Civil Liberties Union (NYCLU) office at 90 State Street in Albany wondering how to respond to a pile of requests for legal assistance from community residents. They included complaints of illegal dismissals by employers. Others were desperately seeking a pro bono attorney to file lawsuits for a variety of reasons. It was my job to read each request and assess whether there was an acceptable civil liberties issue, that is, a violation of the bill of rights, inherent in each request that might serve as a precedent-setting case that the New York City office attorneys might be interested in addressing. Then I would either provide useful information to address the problem or report the unfortunate news that the NYCLU would not be able to provide legal assistance.

I was also the Legal Redress Committee chair for the NAACP where I handled requests for assistance from Albany area residents claiming racial discrimination from several sources. These complaints provided a little more latitude for action. I could use my discretion to decide which cases warranted my attention and involvement, precedent-setting or not.

The phone rang as I sat there contemplating possible responses to my pile of requests for help. The caller informed me of a police shooting death of a young, black man on Clinton Avenue the previous morning. The caller was furious and wanted me to do something about it. In rapid succession, calls flooded my office from community members expressing their anger over the police killing of the young man known by many as Jessie Davis. They wanted action. No more could the police be allowed to kill blacks. I knew there needed to be a community response and quick. Several of us started making calls to local activists simultaneously, and we expeditiously set up a meeting to discuss the situation.

It would not be the last meeting. Several were held over the following weeks. We tossed Ideas and thoughts around, but community members reached no consensus on a plan of action. I sought advice from local attorneys and others and dwelled for days over what course of action we should take that would hold the Albany Police Department and the officers involved accountable.

Over the next few weeks, we learned more about Jessie Davis from his family members and neighbors. Jessie was only 35 years old and had been treated for mental health problems. He was well known by the police department because his ranting and raving on the streets had previously caught their attention, but everyone knew he was harmless.

The police department did its usual internal investigation as District Attorney Sol Greenberg prepared to submit the case to the grand jury. The official story was that Jessie had run into his apartment, locked the door, and was making noise. At least six police officers approached the apartment begging Jessie to open the door. Jessie refused, so the officers went to the roof and attempted to enter the apartment from a rear window. Jessie saw them and police claimed he approached them with a knife and long fork. Police claimed they felt threatened and shot Jessie to death.

Over the following months, a grieving and outraged community engaged in a series of marches and rallies and was determined to make significant changes in the department and how it related to residents, particularly those of color. Residents formed the Albany Coalition Against Police Abuse to tackle this daunting issue. With pressure from the community, public statements by groups of white and black clergy, the district attorney was forced to present this case to a grand jury. Meanwhile, the NAACP drafted proposed legislation to create a civilian review board, and 18 community groups came together to form the Albany Alliance for a Civilian Review Board.

While I participated in many of these actions, for days on end, I sat alone in my office contemplating what our next step should be. Then it came to me. Believing there would never be an indictment of the involved officers, I prepared a letter from the NAACP to Mr. Greenberg requesting that the grand jury issue a report of its findings in the case. He complied, but to no avail. The report basically stated they found no reason to prosecute the officers. The officers were cleared of all wrongdoing. We were left with no recourse other than filing a civil rights lawsuit. Local attorney Lewis B. Oliver took the case, and I agreed to help support the initiative by finding some financial support and garnering community involvement. Jessie's sister, Louise, seemed in need of someone she could trust. It turned out to be me. I became her personal advocate, providing her guidance, transportation and information about how the legal and political systems worked.

It took over 10 years for the case to go to court and for Jessie's family to obtain a small piece of justice for him. The police department was forced to make some changes in its policing policy due to continued advocacy by many community groups and individuals. One example was changing the procedures for handling mental health cases. A mental health mobile crisis unit was created and is dispatched to support police when a mental health crisis occurs. Yet nothing of a transformative nature occurred.

Because the police were never charged or prosecuted and officers were cleared, many people in the community were dissatisfied and determined to keep the case alive and continue to work for significant changes and reforms in the city police department. I stayed with the case until the very end. Jessie's sister and other family members sought advice and moral support from me and others. As a result, I came to know Jessie's sister quite well. I also worked closely with the family's attorney,

Lew Oliver over the years. But, other individuals and groups supported the effort in varied ways, including helping to raise legal funds. Community media organizations stayed close to the case as well, reporting on all aspects of it, especially the advocacy work we were doing.

Our community action work paid off in several respects. When it became known that Jessie suffered from mental health problems, community action efforts led to the development of a mobile crisis unit that could be called upon to support police and others who found themselves dealing with people suffering from a mental health crisis. They were dispatched from the Capital District Psychiatric Center. It also led to changes in police training on how to deal with mental health crises.

Community leaders then pushed for the police department to develop a civilian complaint review board – an independent body that would investigate police brutality and killings - but the city would have none of that. Mayor Thomas Whalen III was opposed to that idea. According to a Times Union article from May 22, 1985, he would not consider a civilian complaint review board because "it would abrogate the authority granted both to the Legislature and to this [the mayor's] office. He also questioned whether such a board would conflict with provisions of the Civil Service Law, the Taylor Law and the collective bargaining contract between the city and the police union."

Instead, Mayor Whalen put forth a new proposal to create a citizen advisory council to monitor the relationship between the black community and the police department. It would be comprised of local religious groups, the state university, the police department, and the black community. Because it would not have a policy-making role or serve as a complaint review board focusing on complaints of police misconduct or brutality, the black community opposed the mayor's plan. I was vocal about my opposition. Speaking to the Times Union in 1985 as a member of the Albany Alliance for a Civilian Review Board –

one of my many hats - I expressed that unless Mayor Whalen conceded to the wishes of the community and incorporate a civilian review board that would hold officers accountable for their actions, everything we had done would have been in vain.

Jessie's killing caused a rift between the Albany Police Department and Mayor Whalen. Police Chief Thomas Burke opted to retire, along with other high-ranking officers, including Sgt. Norman Warrell, whose unit included officers involved in Jessie's killing. This created the opportunity for John Dale to become assistant chief, while John Reid took Burke's place as chief of police.

In 1986, we had to settle for a community/police relations board comprised of representatives from a broad spectrum of community organizations and groups, high-ranking police officials and city administration staff. Its ostensible purpose was to improve poor community/police relations thought to be a major factor leading to police abuse and killings. But its real function was to keep the group powerless. I was a charter member of the Board, representing the Albany NAACP. We met monthly to discuss problems of concern, but not to resolve any issues. Then, in 1990, after much haggling, we proposed a new community police review board to replace the community relations board. It was our intention to establish a more powerful body that could deal with police accountability. Convinced that a stronger body with investigatory and subpoena powers would be imperative, that did not come to fruition then.

In the following years, Lewis Oliver worked tirelessly on preparing Jessie's lawsuit. I was in frequent contact and assisted where I could. Funding was the biggest obstacle. Among other things, they needed expert witnesses, and they usually commanded a handsome fee. Then something amazing happened. During Lewis' discovery, he came upon a photograph taken at the scene in Jessie's apartment as he lay dying. It was taken by a police officer who rushed to the scene of the shooting. The photo showed a dying Jessie Davis lying on the floor with a key chain and toy truck in his hands and bleeding from a bullet wound to his head. There was no knife or fork. That photo had been placed in a file at the Albany Police Department. Dumbfounded and angry, I discussed the situation with Lew. How should we use the photo? First, Lew needed money to enhance and copy the photo. So, I got the job done.

Soon, the case was ready for trial. I kept the family apprised of the case and what to expect. However, we did not expect the city attorney to show up and offer the family $12,500 to settle the case out of court. The family sought my advice. They had grown tired and weary. Although it is my practice never to offer advice - only information - I convinced them that the city's offer was an insult. They agreed and prepared to go to court in June 1995.

This was the day we had waited for so long. The trial was scheduled to be heard in Utica. I picked up Jessie's sister and half-sister and drove them there. We arrived in plenty of time to position ourselves in the best seats to observe and hear all that would take place during the proceedings. However, it was difficult to determine exactly what was happening. Lawyers were fluttering around, thumbing through stacked papers on the front tables, and whispering to each other. Then, the judge motioned them to approach the bench. Although we could hear nothing that was being said, we sensed that something important was happening. A spectator sitting just behind us interpreted the scene for me and informed me that a deal had been struck and that there would be no trial. I relayed the message to my two companions with my interpretation. "You have won something and lost something. The city will pay you $500,000 instead of the $12,500 they offered you a couple of days ago. But, you lost the opportunity to have a trial that would force the truth to be told and hold Jessie's killers accountable." They understood but wanted to think of it as a victory in a war they had waged and fought for 10 years. We made our way back to Albany in silence, stunned by what had just happened. When we arrived, the media wanted to talk to us, so, we arranged an impromptu news conference.

Long before Jessie Davis' killing, I longed to be free to work with the local community to help identify and solve problems presented to the community by law enforcement and the criminal justice system. Of particular importance was my belief that policing, the entry point of the system, short of being owned and controlled by community people, needed to be monitored and held accountable for its actions by the community it is mandated to serve. In addition, a true democracy requires that people are treated equitably and fairly throughout the system to secure and maintain the public safety. For me, Jessie Davis' shooting and law enforcement handling of the case provided the strongest incentive for me to develop a way to work for change in policing and the criminal justice system. A community-based organization just might be the way to go, I thought. So, I started one.

I did not see any local organization solely focused on policing. Sure, there was the NAACP where I chaired a committee. And, as I mentioned, I worked for the New York Civil Liberties Union, the defenders of civil liberties and civil rights. The types of legal issues we tackled varied and were limited in number as we focused on those precedent-setting cases. Offering free legal services, we had to be selective.

Jessie Davis' case influenced me to create what is now known as The Center for Law and Justice a year after he was slain. It started out as the Criminal Justice Center, but I changed it a few years later because the name was very similar to an organization operating in Schenectady. In the name, I wanted to get across the message that the law was important, but we wanted it to be carried out in an equitable fashion. Above all, I knew that to be effective, we had to be independent. I wanted an organization that could not be controlled by politicians or funders. So, I had to figure out how to get money, yet remain free to do that which

I believed was necessary and morally right. That has proven to be the most important feature of the Center – no one owns us.

It took a little while for people to learn what we were all about. I was already known, to some extent, because of the other community work I did prior, including my roles at Trinity. But, I had to distinguish myself for people to recognize this new organization I was affiliated with. There were many abuse cases out there. Davis was not the only one. I realized we had to look deeply at the criminal justice system itself, and the start of it was policing. I wanted to focus on the front end, rather than the back end. This new organization gave me the opportunity to work with individuals who were in crisis because of policing and brutality. I liked the challenge of trying to get some justice for them. I wanted to be an organization for people who were not being heard or were being treated unjustly. The Center gave them a place to start. I saw myself and the Center as providing a voice for those treated unfairly. I wanted them to have someone they trusted.

Then, I started seeing myself as a change agent. I wanted to see how we could promote justice for all and effectively address the oppression of the poor and people of color in particular. By identifying policies and practices that were oppressive, it did not take long for me to be on the radar of the Albany Police Department. Because I was very critical of the department and the DA's office, I was labeled as someone who did not like the police, but I worked with Assistant Chief John Dale to establish a good relationship with APD. Chief Reid used Dale to connect with the black community through a community policing unit. Dale was someone I had known since I was a teenager, and I had considered him a friend. He even took me to see Chief Reid once, and to my surprise, the chief seemed to be hiding behind his office door trying to avoid me. My first impression was, "This guy is scared of me!" This let me know the Center might be shaking up the establishment.

WE WHO BELIEVE IN FREEDOM

Alice joins members of Green Haven Correctional Facility's
Political Action Committee.

Prison Work – Advocacy from Within

Two years before Jessie's murder, I received a doctoral degree in criminal justice and took the director's position of the New York Civil Liberties Union in the Albany office. This provided me the opportunity to accept invitations to visit prisoner groups throughout the state. I gained a strong interest in examining the issues of what was going on inside the facilities.

I accepted an invitation to go to Green Haven Correctional Facility – a maximum security prison in Dutchess County - to attend a prisoner conference on criminal justice. I accepted based on the belief that I would be able to teach those imprisoned about the system and the causes of criminal behavior that I had learned over the past several years.

I entered the tightly, white-controlled fortress with heavy banging doors that controlled the movements of its young black male occupants who acknowledged my presence with warm smiles and majestic greetings as I moved through the cold corridors. I was ushered by two accompanying guards into a bare room containing a long table with six black men sitting around it and clothed in dark green jumpsuits. An empty chair at the head of the table was reserved for me, so I was told by the guards. After I took my seat, the guards left me alone with the imprisoned men. They then relaxed and welcomed me with gracious smiles while expressing their appreciation for my presence.

The men at the other end of the table identified themselves as members of the Political Action Committee. Larry White was the group's president. Larry, a thin, intense, middle-aged man with salt and pepper hair and a warm and easy smile that let you know he had been around for a while, then introduced Eddie Ellis, the co-chair, and the other four members of the committee. Eddie, a little shorter in stature than Larry, appeared more quiet, serene, thoughtful and analytical, which would prove to be the case later.

They distributed an agenda for the meeting, which included an introduction of me. Then, Larry and Eddie took control of the meeting. They opened the dialogue by explaining the big picture of the criminal justice system, the history and goals of the group, their current program activities, their hopes for educating the outside community about the real purpose of prisons and the need for change, and their own plans to bring about that change. Their key philosophical approach and element of their program for change was what they called, *The Non-traditional Approach to Crime and Criminal Justice* that included their definition and explanation of the disproportionate incarceration of African American and Latinx in America.

How incredibly fortunate to be in the company of these men – most of whom had been in Attica during the 1971 uprising. Following the Attica Uprising, the state relocated many of the imprisoned men thought to be political radicals. Many of them ended up in Green Haven where they formed a think tank to explore black history, enslavement and its legacy for blacks and Latinx, the status of the relationship between communities of color and prisons, and the role of communities of color to those incarcerated in prisons and how to relate to them.

I was awe struck of the greatest magnitude as I listened and hung onto their every word. Their Afrocentric approach to understanding black history and American criminal justice was earthshattering for me. There I was with a doctorate in criminal justice, feeling inferior to these men who had a firm grasp on understanding the system. They knew why and how it became the oppressive and racist tool for white supremacy and the corresponding racist policies that characterized the current criminal justice system that, in turn, supports mass incarceration.

Over the next 30 plus years, I would come to know them and many other persons imprisoned and those released from the state's prisons; intimately bond with many; become close friends and partners in activities of social change; visit many of the state's prisons in response to invitations from prisoner groups and organizations and a few from prison staff members to discuss issues of racism, incarceration, black history, and proposed state legislation of mutual concern.

While Eddie was imprisoned, he penned a three-part series for The Scene newspaper in 1991 on the relationship between prisons and communities of color. In the third part, he presented the need for non-traditional solutions to the problems of crime, imprisonment and racism. Eddie was such an awesome writer and researcher. To fully grasp his idea of incorporating non-traditional solutions, I have detailed his article below in its entirety:

The Non-Traditional Approach

"Our Non-Traditional Approach begins as it must, with truthtelling. This is the starting point. The truth as we see it will differ from the general or traditional assumptions about truth. It will also differ from 'truth' as seen from some other non-Afro-Latino perspective which is why developing our own perspective is so important.

"The Non-Traditional Approach says that race and class distinctions have created a special place in society for blacks and Latinos such that all educational efforts, whether in prison or in the community, must address this reality. Racism and classism have locked most of us out of the economic mainstream, hence our education must have a unique dual role. It must offer us the tools needed to address these specific problems and it must also empower the student of color to cope with two separate worlds: one in the general society and another in his or her own community. This dual approach mandates that we reassess the entire system to determine what the new needs of our people are and how curriculum can be structured to best meet those needs. General education is not enough, which is why the schools and

prisons are failing. Education must be community specific and Afro-Latino centric.

"The difference between general and community specific is that general makes the individual fit the policy, where community specific makes the policy fit the individual. Taken one step further, our approach proposes that because of the 'direct relationship,' all areas of the community's life and the institutions erected to serve it must be re-examined with the idea in mind of the community taking control. This should be the goal of the socially conscious activist prisoner as well as the community representatives with whom he or she works. The first steps toward this goal should be efforts directed at allowing the black and Latino community a greater voice in the decisions which relate to prisons. This makes sense because prisons are institutions which serve our communities almost exclusively.

Future Projections

"The destiny of the black and Latino community is ultimately tied to that of the prisons by virtue of the back and forth movement of tens of thousands of prisoners per year. Our analysis through the historical perspective, direct relationship and the non-traditional approach establishes another direction for both the prisoner and their home communities which is Afro-Latino centric and community specific. Our analysis demonstrates that prisons traditionally and currently are operated on the basic assumption that the individual's behavior was wrong and thus seeks to change or correct that behavior. This theory of rehabilitation attempts to correct the individual such that it returns him or her to the condition or state that they were in previous to the objectionable behavior, hence 're' (to do over) habilitate. With blacks and Latinos, their condition previous to the objectionable (criminal, anti-social, deviant) behavior was one of a disadvantaged, second class citizen, in relationship to full access to the benefits, rewards and power in society. This directly contributed to the objectionable behavior. Our Non-Traditional Approach says that the goal should not be to rehabilitate a

prisoner but instead to empower him or her. Empowerment, in non-traditional terms, means to transform; to equip the prisoner with the ability to transform themselves from what they have become, into what they can be. Empowerment means taking control of ones life and the circumstances of their environment such that he or she has a voice in the decisions that impact or relate to the mind. The Non-Traditional Approach seeks to create that empowerment in the prisoners, in the prisons and outside in the community such that African American and Latino people can acquire the capacity to realize their will even with opposition from others. Working collectively, prisoner with community, such a goal is not only realistic but attainable.

Attica Remembered

"September marked the twentieth anniversary of the tragic Attica Prison Rebellion that ended with the death of 43 people. State troopers killed 31 prisoners and nine hostages. Prisoners who took part in the rebellion were demanding reforms in prison conditions. They seized control of the prison and took 37 hostages. After four days, Governor Nelson Rockefeller supported the storming of the facility. State troopers who numbered about 1,500 indiscriminately fired into the prison yard, not only killing 40 people but severely wounding 89 people. Soon their civil suit against New York State will go to trial.

"A commemorative symposium was held in Buffalo on September 12 and 13. It was sponsored by the New York State Coalition for Criminal Justice, the Center for Justice Education, and the SUNY/Buffalo Graduate Group on Justice in Democracy.

"At the University of Buffalo, Alice Green, director of the Center for Law and Justice in Albany, addressed the gathering on the topic of 'Young Black Men in the Criminal Justice System.' She expressed her belief that significant change in the criminal justice policy of over-reliance upon the imprisonment of people of color, would not take place until three major obstacles to such change are effectively addressed. Those obstacles are racism, abstractionism (the tendency to reduce prisoners to statistical

and subhuman entities) and community inaction and passivity. She added that in order to fully understand current criminal justice policy and its intent, we must look to the history of the relationship that has existed between white racism, the American criminal justice system, and blacks. She said that, 'Historically, racism – the promotion of white supremacy – has always been the major factor underlying this nation's criminal justice policy. The fact is grounded in the history of black presence in this country. Black communities were born from the conditions of slavery and the experience of racism, particularly its role in shaping the American criminal justice system. Following emancipation, there was increased reliance upon the criminal justice system to both re-enslave black men and to promote and maintain the principle of white supremacy.'"

Eddie's own words signified the depth of his knowledge and passion for this topic; he was ahead of his time. This amazing person had a great influence on me. He and Larry both were two intellectuals and educators, and I focused a huge amount of my time with them. They wanted to get the community into the prisons to shine a spotlight on the inner workings of prison life and the circumstances that led them there in the first place. They saw the connection in what was going on in the community and how it would eventually define what prisons looked like. Their vast research showed a cycle. You could look at people with poor housing, education, healthcare, etc. and it would define what their life would look like forever.

Eddie, Larry and others initially formed the Political Action Committee (PAC) where they conducted annual conferences and invited other groups like Quakers, community organizations, etc. Subsequently, it became heavily focused on the Legislative Conference which brought in legislators, especially the elected officials within the New York State Black and Puerto Rican Caucus. We did this on an annual basis. The Center for Law and Justice played a major role in organizing the conferences and lending support to the PAC and other organized people behind bars at Green Haven and elsewhere. New York

State Assemblyman Arthur O. Eve was a key player, and I got the opportunity to work with him on prison reform initiatives. His interest went as far back as the 1971 Attica uprising, where he spearheaded a committee of public officials who attempted to resolve the conflict between the prison guards and the incarcerated population.

The imprisoned men proposed legislation and helped stakeholders understand the concept of the *prison-industrial complex*. This term describes the rapid expansion of prisons throughout the U.S. and the jobs created across several industries to supply goods and services to the prisons. Industries such as construction, surveillance technology, food services, private probation companies, and more greatly benefited – and still do - every time someone went to prison. Unfortunately, the "someone" is disproportionately blacks and Latinx.

We have the Rockefeller Drug Laws in the 1970s to thank for the sudden influx of persons going to prison. Then New York Governor Nelson Rockefeller, swayed by the political mood at the time, decided to take a tough stance on those committing drug crimes by instituting harsh prison terms for possession or sale of relatively small amounts of drugs. He imposed mandatory prison sentences of 15 years to life for drug dealers and addicts — even those caught with small amounts of marijuana, cocaine or heroin. Most people incarcerated under these draconian laws were convicted of low-level, nonviolent, first-time offenses.

It was not hard to see how the Rockefeller Drug Laws caused racial disparities and inequities in New York's criminal justice system. According to drugpolicy.org and many other reputable resources, "Rates of addiction, illicit drug use and sales are approximately equal between racial groups. But while black and Latinx people make up only 33 percent of New York State's population, they comprise nearly 90 percent of those currently incarcerated for drug felonies."

When I look at how prisons were being filled with black folks and the amount of money spent on imprisonment, I thought those dollars could have been best spent on education, rehabilitation, employment, healthcare, affordable housing, and other resources in the community. That is when I knew it was important for me to try to find ways to stop this trend somehow. Eddie and Larry were very helpful. They had the research on this. They educated me on statistics germane to the areas where the imprisoned men came from. Unfortunately, 75 percent of the state's prison population at the time came from New York State's *"Seven Neighborhoods"* where unemployment, arrest, and death rates were the state's highest. Those neighborhoods included areas in New York City, Buffalo, Syracuse, Rochester, Mid-Hudson, and Albany. Larry once said in an interview, "I used to wonder, how come every time I come to jail, I know all these guys? And then I began to realize, wait a minute—if we are a minority in the street, less than 15 percent of the population in the street, how the hell are we a majority in prison? How did that come about?"

Since I did not see any other organization tackling these issues head on, I wanted to be a change agent. I wanted to make sure the community understood how the whole system was designed to pull people into the prison system.

Eddie and Larry took advantage of educational opportunities provided to them in prison. They earned degrees while there and worked with the younger guys to foster activism in them so that they would become advocates when they were released. Because of their mentorship, they were highly respected by those they served with, as well as the staff.

Eddie's activism started long before he entered Attica or Green Haven. In the 1960s, he was an activist in Harlem and was a Black Panthers leader. The FBI's COINTELPRO, which we now know targeted black and Latinx activists, pursued Eddie. Just like all the other pro-black and "woke" civil rights organizers at that time, he was considered a threat. Law enforcement accused him of killing a person he had never even seen before. For this, he spent 25 years in prison.

Once he was released in 1994, Eddie returned to community activism where he was involved with the Neighborhood Defender Association, an organization known nationally and internationally for its innovative, community-based, holistic public defense practice. He appeared on the Phil Donahue Show in 1995 with other formally incarcerated men to talk about life in prison. One of his major contributions was the establishment of the Center for NuLeadership on Urban Solutions at Medgar Evers College to train formerly incarcerated people as community leaders, do research, and publish criminal justice papers. After a few name iterations, today it is called the Center for NuLeadership on Human Justice and Healing and provides an interdisciplinary forum for policy makers, legal practitioners, law enforcement, civil society leaders, clergy and previously incarcerated academic professionals seeking to elevate Human Justice and transform the criminal punishment system. Much of the educational and research materials Eddie and Larry developed would later be used by legislators and college educators.

Larry White was incredibly serious about effecting social and criminal justice change that could come about through the development of a strong partnership between incarcerated people, community groups, and legislators. He spoke and wrote with deep passion about this goal. After all, he had spent most of his life behind bars by the time we met. He entered the system at an early age, was free for a while, then was back in the system in 1976. Larry was always pushing for more community involvement in the prisons. He collaborated in the founding of the first prison chapter of the NAACP in New York State at Auburn Prison in 1970. He was a good organizer, planner and communicator, especially through his writing.

Larry continued his work drawing in and developing other leaders, even after his long-time friend, Eddie Ellis, was released. However, in the mid-1990s, he was transferred to Shawangunk Correctional Facility in Wallkill. But, he did not skip a beat. He continued his social justice work, mainly drawing attention to the needs of lifers and long-termers in the system. Larry grew fearful that he would die in prison, the great fear of so many incarcerated people.

To improve prison conditions for the older population and prepare them for their parole boards and eventual release, Larry became a key leader and organizer of the Shawangunk Lifers and Long-Termers Organization and served on the editorial board of the organization's official quarterly newsletter, The Lifer's Call. As well, he organized the group's annual conference.

Larry wrote that the mission of the organization "...is to establish linkage with community-based organizations in an effort to jointly develop programs and approaches that reverse criminal behavior in state prisoners and improve their opportunities for release. Reversing criminal behavior involves a holistic approach that requires not only efforts directed toward changing the individual offender, but which enlists and empowers the offender to play a participatory role in the crime reduction efforts of their community." (May 8, 1999).

Larry asked for my assistance with promoting their Spring 1999 conference in a March 3, 1999 letter to me. He sent me an agenda packet and asked me to make copies of the materials and distribute them to community individuals and organizations. He noted that the prison had expanded the number of community guests who would be allowed to attend the conference to 50. I attended the well-organized and informative conference at the prison. Although the organizers and speakers were concerned about programming and services for an older prison population, they felt it important to focus on the growing incarceration of people of color and its debilitating impact on the families and communities of the incarcerated.

Their intent was to broaden community dialogue on criminal justice to include young and older people and their families, as well as their communities, and strategize about how to affect public policy.

Larry was finally paroled in 2007 at the age of 72, and like Eddie, immediately got involved with working in the community on a host of criminal justice issues. He became recognized as an expert of aging and imprisonment. I attended a lecture he gave at Albany Law School about 10 years ago. He also worked with us at the Center for Law and Justice when we did community programs on incarceration.

There were so many amazingly heroic people incarcerated in our prison system. Another one worth mentioning is Joseph "Jazz" Hayden. I corresponded with him for years while he was imprisoned, but I did not meet him in any of the prisons I visited. Jazz was consumed with winning the right to vote for the incarcerated felons in prison. He argued that their disenfranchisement violated the Voting Rights Act because blacks were disproportionately incarcerated which diluted the voting strength of black communities. He also claimed that it violated the 14th Amendment equal protection clause by denying the vote to individuals based on differences in enfranchisement laws in different states, that is, some states allowed imprisoned felons to vote while others did not and probationers in some states were allowed to vote while in others the right was denied. He pointed out other inequities in the system.

On September 13, 2000, in Hayden v Pataki, Jazz filed a pro se lawsuit pursuant to 42 U.S.C. Sec. 1983 in the U.S. District Court for the Southern District of New York, challenging a state law prohibiting him from voting solely on account of his felony conviction and incarceration. He received research support from students and faculty of the Yale Law School. Unfortunately, his efforts were not successful. But he never gave up the challenge, even after his release.

While attending a prison reform conference in Washington, D.C., I walked in late to a session on felon disenfranchisement and missed the introduction of the panelists who were considered experts on the topic. One of them caught my special attention. Could this be Joseph Hayden? When the panel ended, that panelist ran to me and gave me the biggest hug I had ever received. He sensed that I must be Alice Green with whom he had corresponded with over the years. We continued our association over the years while we worked to educate our communities about the importance of allowing felons the right to vote.

Prison work became a large part of my life. I was a known figure amongst the population at correctional facilities throughout the state. For some, I was all they had. Literally. I realized this when an imprisoned, Muslim gentleman named James Johnson listed me as his next of kin. Fishkill Prison in Beacon, New York contacted me when he died on September 8, 2002. They wanted me to take his body. The one thing he feared was dying in prison and being buried there. So, when he died, I decided to treat him like a family member. I had a memorial service, and I contacted the Veteran's Administration. It was able to provide a burial since Mr. Johnson was a World War II veteran. I enlisted the help of a known leader in the Islamic community, Brother Yusuf Burgess, to ensure a proper Muslim burial.

Fortunately, I was able to put together an obituary because he wrote me letters over the years, and I paid for it to run in the Times Union. This gentleman maintained his innocence until the end, and I wanted to make sure I added this declaration in the obituary. The Times Union did not want to print this information, but it was important that I included it. I had to reach higher up at the newspaper to get it printed. The Capital City Lodge #78 here in Albany funded the memorial service. Robert Jones and Worshipful Master Dorsey Whitehead, two lodge members, presented me with their generous donation during the memorial service, and it was an awesome display of support. Not one person who attended the memorial service knew who Mr. Johnson was. It was amazing how people felt a connection to him and did not even know him.

In 1985, Governor Mario Cuomo appointed me to the Citizens Policy and Complaint Review Council. It was a position that required Senate approval. I was surprised he appointed me because I was a known reform advocate, as well as a prison abolitionist. When the Rockefeller Drug Laws went into effect in 1973, the NYS prison population was 12,500. It quickly started taking off. I started following the stats and the prison population moved rapidly toward 55,000 in 1990. By the time George Pataki became governor, the number was around 72,000. The governor started using floating barges as jail cells and using available prison cells up near the Canadian border. Those being jailed were sent by airplane to available spaces upstate. That really bothered me. Never had a county used state facilities and those outside of their geographical boundaries to house people. The Council gave me the authority to visit jails across the state, including Rikers Island and the floating barges. I also got to meet with many sheriffs and deputies in jails and at conferences.

No sooner had I settled into the Council when I was summoned to the governor's office to discuss taking on the position of deputy director of the New York State Division of Probation and Correctional Alternative. His office expressed some concern that I might cause trouble for the administration because of my activism work. Our beloved late Congressman John Lewis would call that *good trouble!* I had my own concerns. I was not sure how I might function as a bureaucrat. I had always enjoyed the freedom to speak as I wished and to do what I thought needed to be done. But, on the other hand, I became convinced that I would be in a key position to institute change and push for the use of more alternatives to imprisonment. Some inside the system pushed me to accept the position, but deep inside of me, I knew that it was not the place for me. After agonizing over the offer, I decided to give it a try.

From day one, it was an uncomfortable position for me to be in. Some of the staff expressed surprise that I had a doctorate in criminal justice. They were sure that I was an unqualified affirmative action appointee. This angered me. But, I soon learned that I was indeed *not* a bureaucrat. I was chastised by higher ups for taking a position on an issue that conflicted with that of the administration. I felt lost with little to offer the organization, and I was not happy in the position. Activism was in my blood, not bureaucracy.

After three years, I decided to leave the position to devote more of my time to the Center for Law and Justice. Unfortunately, I was offered the position of legislative director of the New York Civil Liberties Union, another position that I knew I should have turned down. When I worked for the Civil Liberties Union's Albany office earlier, I had the opportunity to work with and observe real, professional lobbyists, particularly Barbara Shack and Thomas Stoddard. Barbara was a savvy wealthy New Yorker who knew numerous key state legislators as friends. Thomas was a brilliant, young lawyer who knew the legislative process well. They both became my very close friends, and I adored them. But, I knew that I did not possess their savvy and was certainly not socially connected to legislators whom I came to resent. I found most of them arrogant, egotistical and hungry for power. Most were from New York City, while I came from rural Upstate New York. How could I possibly relate to these New York City dwellers or persuade them on anything, as Barbara and Thomas had done? I knowingly took on a job that I was unprepared for. It lasted for almost a year. I then knew I had to do that which I was cut out to do. I was a political activist and community organizer, not a lobbyist. I decided to run the Center for Law and Justice full time. After all, it was what I enjoyed doing. I was determined to be good at the work I was meant to do - work that those imprisoned were grateful for. In fact, one of them wrote me this poem long ago that sums up my advocacy, and I hold it close to my heart:

ODE TO ALICE
Alice Green is her name
Her actions the coward will blame

They took him and shook him
And beat him right to the ground
They called him some names
They make up some claims
And later revealed what they found

Resisting arrest
To that they attest
But tell us what's the first charge?
Was it looking suspicious?
Or looking too dark?
Or was it cops just igniting a spark?

Questions abound
The stories astound
Come forward
Let's get the truth

But who do I tell
When I am going through hell
And I feel like my head's in a noose

Her handle is green
She's tiny and lean
And she never retreats from the scene

Her eye on the prize
Always strong always wise
She seems not to run out of steam

She is a thorn in their side
And we say that with pride
'Cause try as they might

WE WHO BELIEVE IN FREEDOM

They can't break her fight

In times of confusion
In these times of pain
It's a sense of balance
We try to maintain

We find this in Alice
As she perseveres,
We are proud to be known as her peers

We are looking for heroes
The old story goes
And we found this under their nose

She's a gem
She's a jewel
She's the one they can't fool
And she can't be bought with a smile

Alice
You're the one that we love
We cherish and treasure
We'll be with you all of the while

Alice at Green Haven Correctional Facility with members of
the Political Action Committee.

Eddie Ellis attends Center for Law and Justice Community Conference on Crime and Criminal Justice.

(Left to right) Joseph "Jazz" Hayden, Alice, and Larry White.

Exterior of the Center for Law and Justice,
220 Green Street, Albany. Photo courtesy of Marco Flagg.

10

The Center For Law and Justice – Community Lifeline

Malcolm X once said during a speech, "I for one believe that if you give people a thorough understanding of what confronts them and the basic causes that produce it, they'll create their own program, and when the people create a program, you get action."

In 1985, I took action. I created the Center for Law and Justice because I, too, believe in giving people a thorough understanding of what confronts them and the causes that produce it. The Center gives marginalized Albanians a thorough understanding of the social justice issues that intersect with their daily lives. What I have birthed and nurtured for 36 years is a civil rights organization that provides community education on civil and criminal justice, legal guidance and advocacy, crisis intervention, and community planning and organizing around criminal justice, civil rights and civil liberties issues of particular concern to poor communities and those of color.

Starting a community-based organization was as natural for me as tulips in the spring. My work at Trinity, the NAACP, and the New York Civil Liberties Union - as well as my academic foundation – prepared me for such a time as this. However, the reality of having no funding jolted me at the onset. I decided to start small. I found a tiny office that was available at Orange Motors and received permission from the company to work there until I found something more suitable and that would be located closer to the heart of the city. A short time later, I learned that businessman Richard Gerrity owned the Arcade Building at 488 Broadway, which was situated almost mid-way between Arbor Hill and the South End. I had met him earlier and thought that I

151

might be able to talk him into donating office space for my project.

The Arcade Building had been prime office and commercial space during most of the 20th Century. Located near the railroad station and a short distance down the hill from the State Capitol, it was valuable space. But, the huge building was, then, in disrepair and practically empty of tenants. The future of the building was uncertain, but there was speculation that Gerrity intended to sell it as soon as he found a buyer. The uncertainty did not bother me. I needed space and was willing to be a temporary tenant if needed. Gerrity agreed to donate the space to me, and I happily accepted it. The small, dark office was equipped with a single-line rotary phone and my old manual typewriter my mother purchased for me when I was a college freshman. She paid for it on an installment plan, using funds she could ill afford. These two relics are unheard of for 90s babies and beyond. But back then, they were essential tools of the office. Slowly, word got around town that I was no longer with the NAACP or the New York Civil Liberties Union. This was pre-social media, so the popular mechanism for disseminating information was word of mouth. Clients started to call me with their criminal justice-related issues. I was back in business.

To my great relief, a recent high school graduate named Floyd stopped by the office. The young, black male appeared shy and quiet. He wore horned rimmed-glasses and presented himself with an infectious smile. In a meek voice he told me of his interest in pursuing a business career and related that he had computer skills. We chatted for a while about his aspirations, and I told him of mine regarding the new organization. Then, he asked if he could volunteer to help me in the office. Much to my amazement and relief, my first staff member started immediately. He began answering the phone and typing letters. With Floyd taking care of the office, I started working on recruiting board members so that we could apply for 501(c)(3) tax exempt status, which would allow me to aggressively seek funding.

Soon, letters started arriving from people incarcerated in the local jails and prisons across the state. Most were seeking pro bono attorneys or wishing to file complaints about their treatment behind bars. Floyd and I handled some of the complaints directly. We referred others to Prisoners Legal Services or a state agency with oversight responsibilities. Floyd introduced the idea of using a computer to help with our growing case load. We were able to get a used one donated. My computer skills bordered on next to nothing, so Floyd took on additional work using our new office tool.

The AIDS List

One of our first major issues to tackle was AIDS. The 1980s was a decade that introduced us to HIV, a virus that attacks the immune system and can lead to AIDS if untreated. Long before concerns of COVID-19 deaths, AIDS was the deadly virus everyone was scared to catch. While sporadic cases of AIDS were documented prior to 1970, available data suggests the current epidemic started in the mid to late 1970s. But this dreaded virus, undoubtedly, became a household name in the 80s.

The City of Albany's police and fire departments began compiling AIDS lists in the 80s. These lists contained names and addresses of individuals they suspected of having the virus. This did not sit well with me and many others in the community. As a member of the Albany Police Community Relations Board, I proposed a resolution demanding that Albany police discontinue its practice at both Division One and Division Two police headquarters. To me, this was just another means of possible discrimination against people of color in the South End and Arbor Hill, the two areas assigned to Division's One and Two.

As I told the Times Union in July 1987, I did not believe these lists provided protection to police officers. To me, it was nothing more than a false sense of security. AIDS victims that did not know they had the virus posed more of a risk to them as they could not warn the officers. The AIDS Council of Northeastern New York shared the same objections and concerns. In addition to dumping the lists that were in file cabinets and posted on headquarter walls, the resolution also called for adopting standardized health precautions for dealing with all people in situations in which there is a chance of virus transmission.

The police union justified its use of the list. Officers feared they were going to encounter someone who had AIDS. It was basically ignorance about how AIDS was transmitted. There was a stigma around this virus. If you had AIDS, no one wanted to come near you. This was alarming as it related to law enforcement and the community, and it potentially affected what was going to happen, particularly in black neighborhoods. If residents in those neighborhoods had an issue where they needed the police to respond, they may not have been treated like they were humans.

After putting much pressure on APD and the fire department, they discontinued keeping the AIDS lists a month after we discovered them. As the head of The Center and a member of the NAACP, I, along with other groups such as the New York Civil Liberties Union and Lamdba Legal Defense and Education Fund, was instrumental in getting them to cease their actions. We sent a letter to Mayor Whalen and filed a Freedom of Information Law (FOIL) request to obtain all city records pertaining to the lists. We needed clarity on the city's policy on compiling and maintaining these lists, especially after we heard contradictory information on whether the fire department kept lists or not. High-ranking officials confirmed they maintained a list, however, the fire chief disputed this claim and denied having one. Was this a cover up?

Police Misconduct

Albany's police department has been historically and overwhelmingly white, so in 1985, it was no surprise that Albany only had eight black officers – less than three percent of the police force. Blacks accounted for 16 percent of the total population in Albany. When Mayor Whalen appointed John Dale as the department's first black police chief in 1989, Dale increased the number of people of color and women on the force, but Mayor Whalen's changes failed to significantly improve what some saw as a deteriorating relationship between the police and communities of color. There were increased charges of police harassment, mistreatment, and abuse of black and Latinx residents.

Local criminal defense attorney bent on taking Albany police officers to task for their blatant abuse of power against people of color was the infamous Terence Kindlon, known for his high-profile cases. In 1989, he acted to expose racist police actions reported by his clients, those of the Center for Law and Justice, and others. Reportedly, nearly all black and Latino males were being indiscriminately and illegally stopped and strip searched at the Albany Bus Terminal. We needed more concrete evidence that this was happening. Kindlon hired a private investigator to secretly monitor police activity at the station. The investigator followed up with what he had found in a written report. We were all shocked when he reported that not a single white person was stopped and not one black or Latino had gotten through the bus station without being stopped. Some of them were stripped searched. The investigator's findings infuriated many in the community. It confirmed what we already knew about the treatment of people of color by the police.

Police brutality incidents persisted during the 1990s. In 1994, Capital District Citizen Action called for the creation of an independent civilian review board, and the Capital District chapter of the New York Civil Liberties Union (NYCLU) issued a report, "The City of Albany: The Need for All-Civilian Review of

Police Misconduct to Ensure Accountability and Fair Law Enforcement." In the report, NYCLU called for – as the name suggests - an all-civilian review of police misconduct to replace the existing internal investigations unit of the Albany Police Department.

Also in 1994, Alderman Keith St. John introduced legislation to establish a citizen review board with subpoena powers. After his measure was defeated by two votes, several widely publicized police encounters with black men contributed to increased community-police tensions and prompted new calls for a citizen review board. In one case, three young black men, 19-year-old Adrian Moore; 16-year-old Jason Moore; and 19-year-old Radcliff Angus, were arrested by police during a street disorder outside the Albany Domino Club. The men maintained their stance that police hurled racial slurs, beat them, and unleashed a police dog on them outside the club. After community members held several protest marches, the police department began an internal investigation into the officers' actions.

Later that year, a young, black college basketball star, Jermaine Henderson, was arrested after an alleged altercation in an Albany bar with two off-duty police officers, William Bonnanni and Sean McKenna. Henderson, while handcuffed, was allegedly beaten by the two white officers in the police station garage. A deputy police chief took the unprecedented steps of suspending the officers for 30 days without pay and filing assault charges against them. Then Mayor Jerry Jennings ordered the release of what some called damaging evidence that suggested a cover-up attempt by fellow officers.

Rank-and-file police officers and the Albany Police Officers Union were strongly critical of these APD actions. Several officers suggested that some of their fellow officers were protesting the arrests of Bonnanni and McKenna by making fewer arrests. An estimated 100 officers marched in front of City Hall in open protest to the official handling of the matter.

The NAACP and other black groups raised concerns about the continuing strength and influence of the Albany Police Officers Union, a group that many contended had historically dominated and unduly influenced policies governing the relationship between the police department and the black community.

Several well-publicized lawsuits during the late 80s and early 90s added to residents' mistrust of the police. I collaborated on several police abuse cases with defense and civil rights attorneys including Mark Mishler, and others. They defended clients that included Greg Baity, Daniel Amslaw, Ronald Grier, James White, and James Lunday. During that time, the City of Albany paid out nearly $1 million, either in out-of-court settlements or by court order, for violating these plaintiffs' civil rights.

A young, tall, black man walked into my office one day to seek help because he claimed to have been brutalized by police. His name was Robert Butler. I can never erase the look of deep sadness on his beautiful brown face as he sat down in front of my desk to tell me his story. In a quiet manner, he proceeded to speak about the nightmare he had experienced in the South End police station. He slowly spoke about riding his bicycle from Arbor Hill to the South End to visit his young son. For some unexplained reason, he was stopped by two police officers and taken to the station. Evidently, they thought he was delivering drugs. Robert was interrogated for hours at the station, but he had done nothing wrong, so he had no information to share. Another officer entered the interrogation room to take over. According to Robert, the new officer took out a baseball bat from the corner of the room and used it to beat him. As he proceeded to share his story of the beating, tears started running down his face. I was so touched and angered as he spoke that I started to weep along with him. His story touched me deeply. Robert and I filed a complaint with internal affairs. How could this terrible thing have happened? There were some who seriously doubted that it had.

Not too long after Robert told me his story, another young man came to my office. He told me that he was traveling to Rochester by bus with a brief stop in Albany. He claimed that he was picked up by police and taken to a police station for questioning. He reported that one of the officers took out a baseball bat and proceeded to beat him with it. That was it! Two men came to me with very similar stories. Someone inside the department was beating black men. I enlisted the aid and assistance of the Coalition Against Apartheid and Racism. They were drawn into our spat with the police and soon engaged in an effort to organize the community to expose "Batman" as they labeled police Detective Kenneth W. Sutton.

Detective Sutton was also involved in a brutality case against a 36-year-old black man named James Lunday. Lunday was waiting for take-out food when four white officers mistook him for a drug dealer. He said Detective Sutton slammed him on the hood of a car, handcuffed, kicked, beat, insulted, and terrorized him while the other officers watched. Detective Sutton contended that Lunday punched him, therefore he had to restrain him. Officer Mathia Sidoti, a former officer granted immunity in exchange for her testimony, said Sutton's story was concocted to cover up police misconduct. Lunday's only brush with the law was a traffic violation that happened several years prior to the incident.

We held rallies and protests demanding that Detective Sutton be removed from the police force. But, that did not happen. However, Lunday did file a $7.3 million police brutality lawsuit against Detective Sutton. Claiming that the lawsuit had no effect on his decision, Sutton retired from the department in 1990. Lunday was awarded a mere $35,000 for the physical and emotional pain Sutton caused.

1991 – One of the Center's Busiest Years

I started working at the Center full time in 1991. What a busy year that was. We had just ushered in the new year, and while some still had tinsel and lights hung from the Christmas holiday, Division 2 lockup had a different kind of hanging. On January 3, 1991, police found 21-year-old Corey Sheldon - suspected of robbery a few weeks earlier - hanging from his cell in an apparent suicide. I remember his father calling me at the Center. He just found out his son died. I went to the station to try to find out whatever I could for him. Corey's father did not believe he committed suicide. Neither did many of us in the community. Til this day, Doreen Sheldon, Corey's mother who has long left the area, believes her son was the victim of police misconduct. With so much mistrust, it was hard for people to accept information coming from the police department. The community supported this family who grieved their black son's suspicious death.

A week after Sheldon's death, community stakeholders held a meeting at the Arbor Hill Community Center to discuss Sheldon's tragedy and other recent complaints of police brutality in the black community. This meeting, led by the Capital District Coalition Against Apartheid and Racism and with support from the Center, was also training grounds for how to properly file complaints against the police. There were about 100 people in attendance, including several of Sheldon's family members.

Concerned that we were not doing enough, one of Sheldon's cousins said, "Let's go to the mayor's house." That is exactly what we did. Meeting attendees piled into cars to carry out the plan for a pop-up demonstration in front of Mayor Whalen's house on South Pine Avenue. It was peaceful, but he did not appreciate the frustrated, loud crowd being out in front of his house. We might have been out there for about a half hour. We sang in January's bitter chill and chanted in unison, "What happened to Corey Sheldon?" and "Where is Whalen?"

There was no sighting of the mayor. His house went dark as soon as we arrived. Because of my reputation for calling out police misconduct and going toe-to-toe with the mayor on these issues, Mayor Whalen accused me of organizing the protest in front of his house. I did not. I was definitely there, however. I even brought with me a copy of the Constitution of the United States. The Albany Police Department did not seem to believe it existed for black people. Mayor Whalen and my friend Chief Dale were upset with me. The mayor called the protest, "Vintage Alice Green". I supposed that was meant to be an insult. But I took his slogan, wore it like a badge of honor, and added it to a poster I carried during one of the Dr. King Memorial Observance parades where I marched alongside Harry Belafonte.

We were encouraged that there might be some major changes at the police department. With John Dale in charge, he developed a form of, what has become known as community policing, by decentralizing functions of the department in hopes that the approach would improve community/police relations. Police substations were soon located in the Arbor Hill, West Hill and South End neighborhoods, bringing specially trained officers closer to the population. Arbor Hill residents were particularly delighted. Dale had grown up and lived in the area, and everyone knew him on a first name basis.

One of the important issues I worked on at the Center was changing how individuals reported police brutality. We had complaint forms in our office for community residents to use, as we wanted to be a part of the process. The problem was in the practice of going to the police station to file a complaint by yourself. People had to because that was the protocol. To me, this practice needed to change. Since I had an amicable relationship with Chief Dale, I met with him on this matter. I pointed out how some people feared going to the police without having someone accompany them. I could not understand why it was not allowed. Whether black or white, I thought people should be free to have a companion with them while putting on

160

a cloak of bravery to meet face-to-face with individuals in the very same system that caused them trauma in the first place. Believing that the time was right, I convinced Chief Dale that he should change police policy and allow people who filed police abuse complaints with internal affairs to be accompanied by a person of their choosing. The Center became a clearinghouse for complaints against the police. The Center's staff attorney and I helped people file complaints, and we even accompanied complainants when they were questioned by police.

Nineteen-ninety-one was also the year the Center launched what would become the Annual Capital District Conference on Crime and Criminal Justice, based heavily on the perspectives of the "Non-traditional Approach to Crime and Criminal Justice" and the theorized direct relationship between prisons and communities of color pushed by Political Action Committee members Larry White, Eddie Ellis, and others. I was motivated and inspired by both our prison work and emerging changes in city policing.

Two related events also competed for my time. Along with all that was going on, I worked with the Capital District Coalition Against Apartheid and Racism to help the community raise needed funds to support the Jessie Davis lawsuit, which was in its sixth year. There was a push in the community to erect a Dr. Martin Luther King, Jr. statue in Lincoln Park several years after the King Holiday was approved. There was some controversy over who would design such a statue. Many of us were not pleased when a white woman was selected. Funds had to be raised to support the project. Some suggested that any funds raised should be shared with the Jessie Davis Legal Fund to support the continued lawsuit against the city.

In 1993, the committee for the Dr. King statue planned a large fundraiser dinner at the Omni Hotel in downtown Albany. Several of us, including Merton Simpson from the Coalition Against Apartheid and Racism, decided to demonstrate in front of the hotel so that we could approach guests as they arrived and left. We wanted to get across the message that the funds from the dinner should be shared with the Jessie Davis Legal Fund. It was to be an overnight sit-in or sleep-in and fast. We informed the hotel about our plans but were told it would not be allowed. Hotel policy stated you had to be a guest of the hotel to be on hotel property. Once the managers knew our plans, they refused to allow us to register as guests.

Not to be outdone, I came up with this brilliant idea. I remembered Howard Kahn of Urback, Kahn, and Werlin - the most prominent certified public accountant firm in the area - was a member of the Center for Law and Justice's board of directors. He was also a board member of the Omni Hotel. I presented my problem to him. We wanted to stay overnight on the sidewalk in front of the hotel, but at least one of us needed to be a registered guest. Howard was such a wonderful man. He agreed to register himself and me as guests of the hotel. His only concern was, "I hope my wife Bonnie doesn't learn that I registered at this hotel with Alice Green." We laughed about it a lot.

We sent out a news release to the media announcing our plans for a 24-hour fast and sleep-in in front of the Omni Hotel. Our news conference was set for 6 p.m. Channel 6 news sent a crew out and planned to go live with our demonstration. At the allotted time, the camera was set to go. Then, something disruptive happened. A flash lightning and rainstorm came and blew the camera off the tripod, leaving us all in the dark. Channel 6 was unable to go live. Sadly, we received no television coverage. But, we were not deterred. The storm subsided and a Times Union reporter showed up. Soon, the guests started arriving and we confronted each of them to support our efforts to convince the MLK fund to share its resources with the Jessie Davis Legal Fund. We lost. But, we continued to fast and sleep in our bed rolls until dawn. It would not be the last time that I would do a sleep-in in Albany.

The other issue competing for my time was women and the criminal justice system. Due to the Rockefeller Drug Laws, the number of women charged with being drug mules was increasing significantly, and women were fighting back against abusers and being charged with killing their spouse or boyfriend. As a result, we started visiting incarcerated women at Bedford Hill Correctional Facility to learn more about their unique situations. It was astonishing to learn almost 90 percent of them had minor children they had to leave behind.

As a result of my growing knowledge and interest in incarcerated women, I was invited to attend a major conference in Oklahoma City in late October 1991. There, I delivered two speeches on the topic and engaged in informative workshops. I left the conference convinced that the female incarceration rate would soon increase at a higher rate than that of males, and sure enough, that is exactly what happened.

To assist men and women in prison connect with their communities and to share more information with the Capital District community about what was happening in prisons - which were closed institutions - The Center started publishing a quarterly newsletter called The Advocate. We encouraged both populations to share information, thoughts, ideas, opinions and calendars. We also discovered great writers who were imprisoned.

The Center published The Advocate for nearly 10 years. It was a major, labor-intensive, and expensive job to mail the publication to imprisoned people across the state and sometime beyond. The work had to be done by hand and addressed to individual people inside the prison system. My childhood friend, Margaret Sharrow Sim, devoted herself to getting the big job done each issue.

The Advocate became extremely popular inside the prisons. It was especially useful as a vehicle to spread information from The Center's Annual Capital District Conference on Crime and Criminal Justice to the prisons and to community residents. The Political Action Committee (PAC) at Green Haven received a great deal of coverage at the conference. Details of the PAC's work have been included in The Advocate. Readers could pick up any issue and learn about the latest police brutality cases, issues in juvenile justice, drugs and prisons, death penalty, mental health in the criminal justice system, etc. It included localized issues, as well as national debates. One of The Advocate's most read and impactful stories was the one written on the death of Raymond Stallings. I devoted space in a previous chapter about this young, black husband and father who died tragically from a heart attack after police cars followed him from Delmar to Albany for no reason. Raymond was frightened to death.

The Center's 2nd Annual Conference was a huge hit. Now out of prison, we invited Eddie Ellis to speak at the event. Across the state, people rejoiced at the news that he had been released. As his biggest fan, no one was more delighted than I was. He was also one of The Center's board members, so it was great to welcome him to Albany.

More than 50 community organizations and well over 200 people attended the conference. Prior to the conference, I learned that several Albany police officers were actively engaged in attempting to intimidate some residents who had registered for the conference which planned to focus on policing. I was so infuriated that I filed a formal complaint with the police department, but to no avail.

The Center's annual conference and The Advocate gave us an avenue to express our perspective on major criminal justice issues and provided an effective way to get many in the community to connect to each other. It was especially useful in linking incarcerated people to their communities, which, to some extent, opened the closed prison system.

Vickie Smith, Mark Mishler, Alice, and others from the Coalition Against Apartheid and Racism gather to protest police brutality.

Robert Butler, one of many black men claiming to have been beaten with a bat by Albany Police Detective Kenneth W. Sutton.

Alice marches behind actor Harry Belafonte and the late
Gov. Mario M. Cuomo.

WE WHO BELIEVE IN FREEDOM

Alice clashes with a NYS trooper during former Gov. George
Pataki's speech.

The Cost of Prison Reform Advocacy

MLK Day Observances

One of the Center's program and community action agenda items was to promote social and criminal justice change. The year 1986 marked the first national holiday devoted to celebrating the life of Dr. Martin Luther King, Jr. The Center participated in the Albany celebration which was organized by the state. The celebration included a ritual that would be followed on the third Monday of January for many years to come. The event would start with a gathering at State and Pearl streets for a march led by the governor and other state and local dignitaries to the Empire State Plaza Convention Center. The program there would include music and a speech by an invited guest. Following this formal program, the large audience would be treated to cake served on the concourse. Folks then gathered on Madison Avenue in front of the Plaza to march to Lincoln Park and gather around the statue of Dr. King for more speeches and the laying of the wreath.

The Center decided that the entire event provided a most propitious opportunity to spread its message of the need for major reforms in our criminal justice system, from arrest to sentencing, incarceration, parole, and the death penalty. The system disproportionately incarcerated black and brown people destroying individuals and their communities. So, each year, starting in 1987, we planned and executed a set of activities, demonstrations, and protests to call attention to this major crisis that was not recognized as such by most people. Over the years, we were able to garner media attention to promote these issues. Some of our protest actions are quite memorable and were carried out primarily during Governor George Pataki's administration. We were especially disturbed by Governor Pataki's conservative approach to criminal justice. During his initial campaign, he gave strong support for passage of a death penalty bill that we had fought against for years. Even though his predecessor - Governor Mario Cuomo - built more prisons during his tenure, he was admired for his strong stance against the death penalty which kept New York without a death penalty law while he was in office.

My anger toward and resentment of Governor Pataki must have been what prompted me to confront him when he showed up shortly after his first inauguration to lead the Dr. King Day march that formed on State and Pearl streets as it had since 1986 with Governor Cuomo and Harry Belafonte in the lead. About 50 anti-death penalty protesters planned to join the march displaying their signs of opposition.

As I prepared to line up and join the 1995 march, I stood there on the sidewalk watching Pataki, who had vowed to bring the death penalty back to New York State, position himself as our new governor, preparing to lead the march named in honor of Dr. King, the leader of non-violence. I could not be silent. So, without thinking, I walked over to him and asked him not to lead the march because he had proposed that a very violent act be legalized which would be an affront to Dr. King. My exact words were, "Mr. Pataki, my name is Alice Green. I am respectfully requesting that you not lead the march in light of your position on the death penalty." Since he was new and unsure of himself, he obeyed me and moved from the leadership position which I took over. I was later accused of misrepresenting my role in the march, but that was not the case. When he asked me if I was with the march, I thought he meant was I a part of the march, not an official.

The next year, Pataki sent his Lt. Governor, Betsy McCaughey Ross, to the MLK celebration at the convention center to deliver a speech on his planned budget that the Center thought harmful to the poor and communities of color. My response was to interrupt her speech to register my concerns. The Record newspaper reported, "For the second time in as many years, Green, executive director of the Albany-based Center for Law and Justice, disrupted the celebration of King's birthday yesterday in the Empire State Plaza Convention Center, engaging in a shouting match with McCaughey Ross during her remarks...The battle in the convention center compelled the lieutenant governor to invite Green to share the podium and microphone to address the crowd..."

Some in the community started to raise questions about the propriety or correctness of celebrating the Martin Luther King Holiday. Was it offensive and inappropriate to demonstrate at celebrations honoring him? The head of the Martin Luther King Commission voiced his opposition to such behavior. One community member, Geralyn McDowell praised our actions. She wrote the following op-ed which appeared in The Sunday Gazette in January 1996:

"It was winter, mid-1980s, and a crowd of non-violent activists gathered at Doane Stuart School in Albany, attracted by the promise that New York State was planning to establish an office to promote non-violence based on the work of Dr. Martin Luther King, Jr. The introductions were lengthy, as each person noted every cause he had worked on, each organization he belonged to, until it was Thoreau Raymond's turn. The Quaker elder stood and was spare with her words. 'The state and non-violence,' she intoned, and paused briefly before going on: 'I was intrigued by the connection between these two words.'

"This is my clearest memory of that day. The promise of the event proved empty as far as support for grassroots organizing was concerned. I would later work at the Mohawk territory of Akwesasne in association with the state's Martin Luther King, Jr. Institute for Non-violence and find out that, in a crisis, toeing the party line of the powers that be was the institute's real concern. I thought of Thoreau Raymond's words then, as I did again when I heard the news of Dr. Alice Green's courageous witness at the Martin Luther King Day observances in Albany.

"My information is from news reports. I had spent the holiday at the new Mohawk settlement in Montgomery County, where, over cups of coffee, an elder and I discussed living in community. I had long ago decided that I could not stomach the state-controlled observance at the Capitol, where politicians posture while the folks who do the daily work of non-violence and social justice are relegated to the audience.

"So it was a surprise to turn on the television and watch Lt. Gov. Betsy McCaughey Ross wrestling a microphone from Alice Green, executive director of the Center for Law and Justice, admonishing her that 'this is a day to work with us and pray with us,' while others in the background proclaimed that Green's actions were not 'in the spirit of Martin Luther King.'

"Ross' audacity in assuming that she has the right to tell Alice Green what this day is about speaks for itself. And I will refrain from putting words into Martin's mouth or interpreting his intentions; there are many others all too ready to do that. The larger question that we need to ask is: Are we celebrating saint or prophet?

"Saints are safely ensconced in history. We can choose our memories and romanticize their legacies. How often do we hear the 'spirit of Martin Luther King' invoked as if it were some benevolent godfather hovering over us one day a year when we should all be nice before going back to business as usual?

"Give me a prophet over a saint any day. As Martin's friend Rabbi Abraham Heschel reminds us, the prophet, by definition, 'interferes.' The prophet speaks in a loud voice that challenges the status quo and the false semblance of civility. The

172

prophet does not agree to work with a system that is basically unjust. The prophet rejects co-optation for what it is. The prophet wreaks havoc with the plans of the power brokers.

"And, perhaps because we see so few, people do not know how to respond to the prophet. We observe this in the media response to Green: The local news anchors who interviewed her that night seemed most concerned that her actions could be interpreted as being 'rude'. These are the same people who regularly report on the Pataki budget, with its lethal cuts in such basic human services as food for hungry children and medical care for sick people; its inhumane treatment of juvenile offenders; its slashing of the Tuition Assistance Program and educational opportunity programs – they report this without questioning the civility of such a selfish agenda.

"Times of crisis call for a different ethic. A person passing a burning building who breaks the door down to save the lives of the people within can hardly be called rude for not ringing the doorbell.

"And there can be no praying with people who, as Green said in an interview, 'are preying upon fears and promoting stereotypes, causing further divisiveness. Civil rights foremother Fannie Lou Hamer said, 'You can pray until you faint, but if you don't get up and try to do something, God is not going to put it in your lap.' Alice Green got up and did what she was called to do: strategic, effective, non-violent, direct action complete with the key elements of surprise, determination, and speaking truth to power.

"Newspaper photos showed Green carrying 'A Testament of Hope,' Martin Luther King's collected writings, and I opened my copy, randomly choosing a page to see what he might say. I found an essay written for the Saturday Evening Post in 1964 that analyzed the response of the white leadership to the civil rights movement: 'They failed to perceive that non-violence can exist only within a context of justice...The simple fact is that there cannot be non-violence and tranquility without significant reform of the evils that endangered the peace in the first place. It is the effort of the power structure to benefit from non-violence without yielding meaningful change that is responsible for the rise of elements who would discredit it.'

"The state and non-violence. The governor's office called the events of the day 'unfortunate and sad.' I disagree. The prophet turns the tables. It is most fortunate that people, especially the children in attendance, had the opportunity to see non-violence – Martin's tactic, Martin's creed, Martin's legacy – in action. Celebrate the Prophet Martin, rejoice in the Prophet Alice. We are all fortunate to have in our midst a woman who, as Daniel Berrigan wrote of Dorothy Day, is 'living as though the truth were true.'"

Following this event, the lieutenant governor and I engaged in civil conversation establishing what McCaughey Ross described as "grounds of mutual respect." I invited her to come to the Albany Housing Authority community room and meet some of the kids who would be harmed by the governor's proposed budget. To my surprise, she did just that. The kids were thrilled!

The next year, I was told I needed a permit to be in the park near the Dr. King statue and site of the ceremony following the march. I applied and received a city permit. It was our plan to set up a table and distribute literature opposed to incarceration. But, when time came for us to distribute materials, police officers came and moved us out of Lincoln Park, table and all. I protested, but it fell on deaf ears.

During 1997, the Center focused increased attention on prison conditions and the mounting incarceration numbers filling those prisons. Once again, we decided to use the Martin Luther King, Jr. celebration to increase pressure on Governor Pataki to address prison issues, hoping he might be more receptive to our message during this election year. When the Center staff and I learned that Pataki would return to speak at the 1998 Martin Luther King celebration, we thought it would provide us a great opportunity to call attention to the problem of our growing state prison industry that was incarcerating blacks at a rate eight times that of whites.

We also knew state troopers would be watching my every move when I entered the Empire State Plaza. The fear was that I would again disrupt the governor's speech, and they were instructed to prevent it. While I was seated in the audience, state troopers kept approaching me and warning me not to disturb the governor's speech. Our plan was to silently unfurl a large banner that read, "No More Prisons" when the governor got up to speak. I did exactly as I had planned. And, when I did, six state troopers - including one identified as actor Sidney Poitier's nephew - seized the banner and forcefully carried me out of the convention center while I screamed, "NO MORE PRISONS!" After being held for nearly 30 minutes, state troopers offered to take me anywhere I wanted to go except the convention center. I refused and was then taken to the police station to be formally arrested. That charge was later dismissed by Albany City Court Judge John Egan. In so doing, he ruled that my actions were neither criminal nor disorderly. My actions were protected speech under the First Amendment of the United States Constitution. I am convinced I would have won the civil rights lawsuit. The state had illegally kidnapped me and used prior restraint by verbally prohibiting me from taking action.

Attorney Jonathan Gradess, who headed the New York State Defenders Association that trained and educated indigent defense attorneys, was outraged by the state's violation of my rights. He had become a good friend who I admired and respected deeply. He encouraged me to file a civil right lawsuit, which I did, but later dropped because it required too much of my time and energy that I felt was best used to work for change in the criminal justice system and direct the work of the Center. In carrying out my mission, I would develop a closer relationship to Jonathan and work with him at the Defenders Association and in the community on numerous criminal justice issues, particularly anti-death penalty, prison reform, and improved indigent defense services. I also learned so much from him. He was so knowledgeable about the law and the most compassionate advocate for social equity and justice. He deeply hated racism. I was heartbroken when he died in 2019. I lost a good friend and the best advocate for social justice I knew.

At this point, I realized my advocacy work was not enough. I needed to do more to educate more people about the evils of the criminal justice system. My protests against Governor Pataki caught the imagination of those in the Green Party. Soon, I was approached by party official Mark Dunlea, and he asked me to consider running for governor of the State of New York. I laughed hysterically but promised him I would think about it. After turning the idea over in my mind for days, I realized that, among other things, it would be too time consuming and take me away from my work at the Center.

I rejected the offer noting that I was not a politician and never thought about becoming one. Then, I received a call from the actor, Al Lewis – yes, the same Al Lewis who played Grandpa on the television show, The Munsters, in the 1960s! He informed me that he had been approached by the Green Party to run for governor and would run if I ran for lieutenant governor. He and Mark reasoned that running for a statewide office would give me a powerful platform to discuss all the criminal justice issues that I was so compassionate about. They also offered me a chance to help write and promote their criminal justice platform which would get wide attention across the state. I gave the offer a great deal of thought. Running would indeed allow me to promote my agenda and help the Green Party win enough votes to be placed on the ballot without going through the tedious process of collecting signatures. I succumbed and agreed to run with no pressure to win, just promote the criminal justice platform that included all the issues I cared about. I completed my mission and the Green Party received more than enough votes to be placed on the ballot. An added bonus was getting to travel with and learn more about Al "Grandpa" Lewis, a delightful man that I enjoyed tremendously. When he died in 2006, I was asked to speak at his memorial service conducted at the Riverside Church in Harlem, along with folks such as journalist Amy Goodman.

The campaign taught me how to be more effective in conducting news conferences to get my message across. Taking advantage of improved skills, the Center started holding media events to call attention to numerous issues and causes. We started holding news conferences on the Concourse to take advantage of the large cadre of media personnel who came to cover the performances and speeches scheduled for the convention center before the march to Lincoln Park.

At one of the yearly events, which did not go as planned, I took the opportunity to demonstrate a horrible form of punishment adopted by the New York State Department of Corrections. Those incarcerated, who violated prison rules repeatedly, were placed on a bread, raw cabbage, and water diet. Our office received many complaints about the bread diet called "the loaf" used to punish them. So, to demonstrate to the media how horrendous the punishment was, I stayed up most of the night before the 2003 King celebration, baking loaves of this "horrible" bread that I would share with the media so they could bear witness to this atrocity. State officials refused to release the recipe. To get the bread recipe, I was forced to file a Freedom of Information Law request. Unfortunately, the recipe I finally received was for 50 loaves of the bread. My math was not good enough for me to calculate the measured ingredients needed for two or three loaves of the disgusting bread. The task took me most of the night, but I persevered.

The bread was still warm when I arrived at the allotted spot to demonstrate by taste to the media how horrible the punishment was that was being carried out in our state prisons. I wanted them to have a first-hand experience of what it was like. Everything was set up for the demonstration. I cut the first piece of bread and decided to taste the bread as I talked to the cameras. As I started to chew, I suddenly realized that in changing the measurements of the ingredients, I had created a delicious loaf of bread, perhaps the best that I had ever tasted! There was no way I could go ahead and serve the media this wonderfully, delicious bread and then call for a stop of this dietary punishment. So, I grimaced in pain and kept talking about the "horrible loaf" incarcerated people were forced to eat as punishment without offering the media a taste of the bread as planned.

Center Staffing and Allies

Ruby Dee and Ossie Davis had always been two of my favorite actors and social activists. After all, they were staunch supporters of Malcolm X. They were true activists who wanted to use their name and prestige to assist small organizations and individuals working for change. When we planned a fundraiser to recognize immigrants and black and brown Americans for their contributions to this country, we came up with what we thought would be a far-fetched idea - get the two actors to personally support our effort.

Somehow, we obtained their telephone number. Nervous, I dialed it, expecting to get a maid or other assistant who would brush me off or discourage me from pursuing this bold request. I almost stopped breathing when I recognized the voice on the other end of the line who greeted me with a warm hello. It was Ossie Davis. After gaining my composure and commenced breathing again, I introduced myself and asked him to support our project. Without any hesitation, he and Ruby Dee agreed to work with us. It was not the last time that I would meet up with him. Years later, he showed up at a church in Elizabethtown, New York in the Adirondacks to support a progressive program sponsored by the civil rights and education program, John Brown Lives. Again, he was extremely gracious and led a conversation on race, history and reparations owed to black Americans.

Our work started attracting numerous people who wanted to be a part of the Center's social justice movement. Many were young, undergraduates, recent college graduates, formerly incarcerated people, and members of the area's progressive community, including professional lawyers and social workers. Several students became extremely interested and committed to the work we were doing that after completing their internship, refused to leave the Center. They wanted to serve and learn more about criminal justice, law, poverty, and community organizing. Many went on to do social justice work and community organizing for change.

There were formerly incarcerated people like Charles LaCourt, Brother Yusef Salaam, Jay Coleman, David Howard, Richard Jackson, Richard Smith, Lafonso Bonner, Darryl Johnson and many more who were determined to improve their life situation and make significant contributions to the community. Several members of this group of formerly incarcerated men met at one of the Center's community meetings and decided on the spot to form a support and community organizing project to help fellow re-entry people find jobs, lobby for prisoner and parolee rights, and support each other to successfully deal with their unique problems while doing constructive work in the community. They named their group ROOTS. The Center eventually hired several of them. Vera Michelson, who had her hands in many community pots, decided to work closely with ROOTS and provided needed support until she died in 2019. Others who joined us in our work included Robin Busch, Katie Agar, and attorneys Daniel Salvin, Annie Rody-Wright, and Kalimah Jenkins. All of them, including many others, went on to do impressive and meaningful social justice work in communities and held a variety of professional jobs.

The Prison Ban

The world was about to embark on a new millennium. A great deal of hype and excitement filled the air around the globe. Several coordinated events – including fireworks and cultural activities - were planned to celebrate the end of 1999 and the arrival of 2000. Even Prince proclaimed in 1982 that he wanted to party like it's 1999. Many were sensing a new birth of freedom.

The coming year resonated very differently inside our prisons. It caused many to seriously reflect on their lives, their surroundings, and their future. While those on the outside commemorated the changing of the calendar in a celebratory fashion, those behind the wall could only hope for a new era which would end the separation from their families and their suffering in institutions that never seemed to change, but only got worse. Those imprisoned did not feel the same joy as others did.

While recognizing the increased feeling of despair at this time, I was planning the 9th Annual Legislative Conference at Green Haven Correctional Facility. Major issues on the agenda included a moratorium on prison construction, repeal of the Rockefeller Drug Laws, and the need for higher education programs in prison.

As in other years, the Green Haven Political Action Committee brought together those who were imprisoned, prison administrators, legislators, and representatives from community groups across the state. Its goal was to develop stronger linkages between the incarcerated, their families, and the communities from which they came and to which they will eventually return.

That year, the conference planning was overshadowed by expressions of hopelessness permeating the air. An increasing number of those imprisoned in other facilities across the state started writing to the Center about their despair. This prompted me to increase my prison visits. With concern and frustration in their voices, they talked to me about being dissatisfied with their condition. There was increasing dialogue about continuing prison construction under Governor Pataki, the growing prison industrial complex, and the decrease in parole release, among others.

Rumors started flying around the state that those imprisoned were planning to express their frustrations through some kind of demonstration on January 1, 2000 – the arrival of the new millennium. I did not know if this was true or not, but during one of my prison visits, I let the men know that whatever was being planned, if anything, the Center would seek out pro bono attorneys to help them, should they need one. Soon, prisoners started writing down their complaints and preparing lists of demands for change in their condition. Their grievances and demands asked for - what they called - *truth in rehabilitation*. This means, they did not want to return to their communities unrehabilitated and subject to a return to prison. They understood that the recidivism rate was 40 percent to 50 percent within three years. So, they asked for such programs as viable vocational training, academic training, substance abuse treatment, viable violence therapeutic programs, and sex offender treatment programs.

At one prison, those incarcerated penned their grievances, demands, and criticisms of prison policies, programs, and procedures in a well-written, but barely legible four-page pamphlet titled, WAKE UP!!! The document was sent to the Center with the request for us to copy and distribute it to their family members and others. I agreed to carry out their request. Since it was not a very legible document, I instructed a student intern in my office to retype and make it more attractive for reading. No words were changed, just the format and an added graphic. This action would come back to haunt me in 2000.

181

When the clock struck midnight on the year 2000, the millennium was here, but the great disturbance that the state feared and prepared for never happened. There were no hunger strikes, work stoppages, and other protests or demonstrations of note reported, although prison guards in high numbers were alert and ready to tackle any lawlessness they may have encountered. Relieved, the state administration set out to identify and punish prisoner advocates and volunteers thought to have supported some kind of prisoner action against the system, even though none occurred. Guess who was at the top of their list? Me, of course!

My brother filled in to receive an award given to me by imprisoned men at Green Haven. I was not able to make that engagement for some reason, so I asked him to go since he lived near Green Haven. He misspoke, suggesting I would support them in the event of a strike to protest their grievances. This statement got the attention of the media and the authorities. Surely, I would be under a microscope as a result.

In 1998, I accepted an invitation from a prisoner group at Attica. I had not been to Attica before and was quite anxious to visit the place that was the scene of the infamous Attica Prison Uprising in 1971. On the day I was preparing to leave, I called the prison again to confirm my visit. Let's face it. Attica is not around the corner. Before I made the four-hour trek to Wyoming County, I wanted to double check, especially since I had been hearing murmurings through the grapevine of dissatisfaction with my advocacy.

I talked to a gentleman on the phone who identified himself as Zoh, program manager. In an angry tone, he told me that I would not be allowed in the prison because I was a radical and the prison was conservative. Furthermore, he said, "You caused a prison disturbance at Dannemora Correctional Facility." I was shocked since my one and only visit to that prison had been with the New York Correctional Association as an authorized volunteer prison observer. That visit was uneventful.

The Attica visit rejection signaled the coming of a larger action. Sure enough, in May 2000, I received a letter from NYS Department of Correctional Services (DOCS) Commissioner Glenn Goord informing me that the Center and I posed a threat to the safety and security of all New York State's 72,000 inmates and the entire state prison staff. I was accused of inspiring a system-wide inmate action for merely helping to disseminate that pamphlet to people on the outside.

"...I have directed each superintendent to deny all visitation access by you and any member of your organization. I have taken this action because you and the members of your organization, if permitted to be present in any correctional facility, pose a clear threat to the safety and security of correctional employees and inmates. In this regard, I note in particular the role of you and members of your organization in encouraging an illegal systemwide inmate action on January 1, 2000. Thanks to the professionalism, vigilance and dedication of department employees, the action was averted, albeit at a cost to taxpayers of millions of dollars," said Commissioner Goord in a letter dated May 9, 2000.

According to DOCS, it considered the pamphlet to be contraband. In it, unidentified authors called on all state inmates to engage in a form of protest by ceasing their work activities and rehabilitative programs. The imprisoned people argued that they were not released at their minimum sentences, no matter what program they completed. The 16-member parole board, mostly appointed by Governor Pataki, did not properly consider their productivity and improvements during parole hearings.

"Right now, it does not make a difference if we program, if we work hard to maintain DOCS, or if we behave. We are not released at our minimums... We are not saying we should not be placed in prison if we commit a crime. All that we are asking for is justice. DOCS is violating the most fundamental principle which is the sacred foundation of civilization: justice," the pamphlet read.

I attempted to appeal Commissioner Goord's decision but was unsuccessful. I have even appealed to the office of several governors over the years, as well as State Senator Neil Breslin, but no relief has come. Desperate for action, I also enlisted the help of a law office out of Chicago to help me get on the Rev. Jesse Jackson's radar. As a prominent, civil rights activist who commands a large audience, I knew he would be the right person to help me shine a light on this injustice. That road was also a dead end. However, the prison ban attracted state and national media attention. Several media outlets reported on the matter, including The New York Times, and The Associated Press. I also appeared on Bill O'Reilly's national talk show.

As I expected, many incarcerated people were angry about the ban. Their letters to the Center increased significantly, and I felt angry and sad that I would no longer be allowed to visit with groups of incarcerated people after doing so for 20 years. I was leaving behind so many of them who were torn from their families and communities but saw a glimmer of hope as we had talked about their hopes, dreams and freedom. I loved being a part of their lives and doing whatever I could to supply a little bit of optimism and sense of belonging to the society that shaped their lives. For more than 21 years, I have been banned from New York State prisons. For now, I remain blacklisted; shut out of the system I tried so hard to get in to help as many people as possible.

Another Clash with Pataki

My final, direct contact with Governor Pataki was in Arbor Hill. He chose the neighborhood community center to announce his new urban initiative which centered on sending state police into urban communities to help local police fight crime. He announced his initiative outside the Arbor Hill Community Center at a well-attended news conference that drew not only the media, but community residents who gathered to see what was going on.

How telling, I thought - announcing a punitive measure in front of a children's recreational center in one of the poorest and blackest neighborhoods in the city. What a message he was sending to the residents of that community! "We have come up with a new way to oppress and imprison you," was the message I heard. I responded by attempting to pose a question to Governor Pataki during the news conference. He tried to ignore me. He refused to acknowledge my presence. By now, you should understand I am not one to back down from a challenge or allow someone to dismiss me. I pushed forward until he was no longer able to ignore my presence and my question about the negative impact of his initiative. His response was simply to reiterate his punitive message.

Highly offended and angered, I wore my indignation openly as I left Albany for a weekend trip to Essex in the Adirondacks. I invited two of my Albany-area friends, activist Vera (Mike) Michelson and attorney Sarah Birn, to join me there. As luck would have it, Governor Pataki arrived in Essex that weekend as well. He purchased a summer home just down the road from mine, as if by design to aggravate me further. Sarah came up with the idea of stopping by his house unannounced to broker a truce between me and the man who became my nemesis.

As we drove past his house, she announced that the meeting should take place here and now. Although I thought the idea was useless, we drove into his driveway and noticed his wife, Libby, was seated on the porch of the big, white house overlooking Lake Champlain. She came off the porch and slowly walked toward our car as Sarah walked toward her. Vera and I witnessed this strange encounter with uncontrollable laughter, knowing what the result would be. Sarah naively presented her proposal for Governor Pataki to meet with me. She said that Libby listened for a moment and then exploded with an angry response. "Alice Green is an angry black woman, and George will not meet with her!" Sarah turned around - stunned by the rejection - and quietly entered the car amid our continued laughter as we drove away.

It was no secret that one of the most powerful men in the State of New York and I did not play in the sandbox together nicely. The media was well-informed of our acrimonious relationship. So, when a reporter asked me one day what I thought about my new neighbor, I flippantly responded, "Well there goes the neighborhood."

Alice is surrounded by NYS troopers as she protests against building new prisons.

Alice is released from State Police custody after being arrested for protesting.

Jonathan E. Gradess, executive director of the NYS Defenders Association and anti-death penalty advocate.

Alice models a shirt designed to bring awareness to former Gov. George Pataki's plan to build more prisons.

Center for Law and Justice's Dr. Martin Luther King Jr.
demonstration in Lincoln Park in 2002.

Alice and Former Albany Police Chief
Steve Krokoff

Policing Problems and Selection of New Police Chief

There are so many names I wish I did not know. Tamir Rice, Botham Jean, Michael Brown, Antwon Rose, Stephon Clark, Eric Garner, Laquan McDonald, Alton Sterling. So many videos I wish I could unsee. The only reason why I do know their names is because of their single commonality. They were all unarmed black males who died at the hands of police officers in America.

Before they became household names in recent history, we were introduced to Amadou Diallo in February 1999. He was a 23-year-old immigrant from Guinea who was gunned down by four Street Crimes Unit police officers in the Bronx, right in front of his apartment building. He, too, was unarmed, and when stopped by the plain clothes officers, Diallo reached for his wallet. This fatal move cost him his life. The officers mercilessly emptied their semi-automatic pistols, releasing 41 rounds – of which 19 bullets pierced Diallo's body. How could officers empty their clips into human flesh, and according to one eyewitness, continue shooting even after Diallo was already down? Their racial profiling cost this young man his life.

The four officers were charged with second-degree murder, among other charges, in this unforgettable tragedy. Because of the publicity surrounding the case, the court ordered a change of venue for the trial. The spotlight was now on Albany at that point, the chosen location. I believe the defendants thought they would have a better chance upstate where they were likely to get an all-white or predominately white jury. Sadly, those who cut Diallo's life short were acquitted of the charges in February 2000. Of course, protests ensued. Rightfully so. At least 15 protestors were arrested in Albany, along with many others downstate.

191

I was right in the middle of it all. National and local media were stationed to cover every aspect of this high-profile trial. I conducted several interviews with TV crews well into the rainy night. When I heard a lot of protestors had been arrested, I rushed down to the South Station. Undeterred by the possible fate they could encounter, other protestors crowded around the police station on the outside. They verbalized their objection to the arrests that added fuel to the fire that was already ablaze from the disappointing trail results.

The police were not quite sure what to do. Protestors on the inside behind bars. Protestors on the outside crying injustice. Albany outsiders in town to observe it all. And the media capturing every moment. Police Chief Nielson, whom I had a good relationship with, sought my counsel on what to do to calm the situation that had unfolded. He was scared to death at the possibility of something bad happening on his watch. I told him to release the people. The chief needed to make it appear as if they were doing their law enforcement due diligence, so he devised a plan to first question each individual protestor who was locked up, one by one.

After the first detainee was questioned, I led him out by the arm and escorted him outside where he was free. We were met by cheers from a relieved crowd. I pivoted my body to walk back into the station to do it all over again until each protestor was free.

The Albany-based trial of the police officers charged with killing Diallo and the prison ban pushed the Center to focus increasing attention in the early 2000s on policing reform, citizen oversight, racial profiling community policing, public defense, and mass incarceration issues. We worked with the New York Civil Liberties Union that released a report which called, again, for a stronger Citizens' Police Review Board, one that would have subpoena power and could do independent investigations.

Meanwhile, racial profiling by police was gaining attention and raising concerns across the country, and Albany was not left out of the mix. Police data presented at a Review Board meeting heightened those concerns over stop and frisk practices in the city. Several community criminal justice advocates, including the Center, called upon Police Chief John C. Nielsen to develop - with resident input - a policy against racial profiling. He agreed and arranged a series of meetings for us to work on developing such a policy. We also pressed for the chief to publicly release the policy we completed sometime in late August 2001. Unfortunately, the terror attack on September 11, 2001, renewed efforts across the country to profile Muslims. Our local policy was also filed away and has never been released publicly as planned by the department.

The push to get adequate, state-funded, public defense service became another issue of major concern. Jonathan Gradess of the New York State Defenders Association provided leadership on this. Jonathan reached out to the Center encouraging us to become more involved in his vision of how to address the expansive public defense clients' needs and involve them in the process. It was Jonathan who brought the idea of a client advisory group together. He made us even more aware how much the Center's clients were dependent upon and should have a voice in how public defense services should be delivered. Jonathan's highly compassionate involvement in this issue was impossible for anyone to ignore. Alongside Jonathan, we also drew the connection between the lack of adequate public defense for our clients and the growing mass incarceration decimating communities of color.

Johnathan and I developed a strong, loving, and close relationship built on mutual respect. This great champion fighter for peace and the rights of the downtrodden and I bonded over the public defense services issue. He hated racism and injustice with the deepest passion, and he always wore it on his sleeve for all to see. I learned about his passing while in London and wanted to leave the country immediately to return home and grieve over this great loss to me and so many others across New York State and the nation.

All these issues were heavily influenced by President Bill Clinton's disastrous crime bill legislation of 1994, which significantly increased on-the-street policing, led to greater numbers of stops and frisks and arrests of black and brown people, and caused mass incarceration to jump sky-high. The resulting disproportionate incarceration of this population helped to sap their communities of young men, fathers, mothers, partners, sons, and daughters and destroy families much in the way that enslavement had done.

By 2001, the Center was hit with so many important peace and justice issues that we had to work night and day to keep up. Some of the increase may have been attributed to the increased popularity of The Advocate. It was growing with more community and incarcerated people reading it and responding with comments and requests for help on so many fronts. Also, we had gotten national exposure due to the Amadou Diallo case (Court TV), the prison ban (The Bill O'Reilly Show), and my run for lieutenant governor with Al Lewis (Good Morning America). Fortunately, several progressive professionals came to us looking to help, and we were delighted to have them join us.

A few years after the terrorist attack on 9/11, we focused much of our attention on the treatment and entrapment efforts by the federal government. In 2004, two leaders of an Albany mosque, Mohammed Hossain and Yassin Aref, were entrapped in a government sting operation carried out by the FBI. Acting on a tip from a convicted felon who was secretly cooperating with federal prosecutors – allegedly to reduce his own prison sentence – the FBI charged the men with conspiracy and treason. They were convicted and sentenced to 15 years in prison, even though the prosecutors never proved their case. But, because of the events from 2001, prosecutors were anxious to convict

Muslims. Many in the community were outraged and protested their conviction and sentencing and provided financial and legal support throughout their period of imprisonment.

The Center stayed involved as well. I was a daily fixture in the court room, watching every development as it unfolded. I cried when I heard the guilty verdict. We all knew they did not do what they were accused of doing. These men, known throughout the community, had children at home they would leave behind.

The arrest raised concerns about personal freedom and the federal government's increased powers of surveillance upon its citizens after the Patriot Act was enacted. I spoke to a reporter for The Final Call at the time and expressed how we had a racial profiling problem in Albany, and the media was not helping because it portrayed those who may look different as the enemy. I was fortunate to be able to keep in contact with Yassin Aref. We corresponded with each other until his release and deportation to Iraqi Kurdistan in 2018.

Still banned from New York State prisons, we stepped up our efforts to call attention to the devastation the Rockefeller Drug Laws were unleashing on black and brown communities. Many reports, including that of the New York Correctional Association, showed that 94 percent of those in the state's prisons convicted of drug-related crimes were people of color. We knew that something had to be done and joined forces with protesters from New York City and across the state in our effort to be heard on our cry for change. Family members of those incarcerated, joined by Al Lewis, my old gubernatorial running mate, came to Albany frequently to protest the state's drug policy and echoed our call for change.

We found another way to call attention to the evils of the Rockefeller Drug Laws - through New Yorker staff writer Jennifer Gonnerman's book titled, "Life on the Outside: The Prison Odyssey of Elaine Bartlett," published in 2004. Elaine, a mother of four children, agreed to carry a small package of cocaine from New York City to Albany to earn money she desperately needed to buy Thanksgiving dinner for her family. Due to New York's drug laws, this first-time offender was arrested in Albany and sentenced to 20 years in prison. She did 16.

Elaine's story is about her life in prison and the struggle to rebuild her life with family when she was released on parole. It is also an indictment of the Rockefeller Drug Laws that imposed extremely harsh sentences for crimes involving the possession and sale of even a small amount of narcotics. The book was powerful. I was so moved by her story that I contacted her, and we got to know each other. The famous actor, Charles Grodin (who recently died), was also moved by her ordeal and gave her a great deal of moral support. He joined her at an event sponsored by the Center to simultaneously promote the book about her life and educate the public on the evils of New York's drug laws.

Increasingly concerned about New York's other harsh sentencing laws, the Center joined others in pushing for an end to the death penalty. Our collaborators included local and state organizations such as the New York State Defenders Association and the New York Coalition Against the Death Penalty. We were aided by David Kaczynski, brother of the "Unabomber" Ted Kaczynski. David was a strong anti-death penalty advocate. Among his arguments against the practice, he postured that his brother could have been executed which would have been a miscarriage of justice because his brother was mentally unstable. Locally, the Center organized and joined in many protests and demonstrations against the death penalty and the need for New York State to remove it from its books. Not only did we protest on the streets, but inside the Capitol and courthouse lobbies as well. I believe our combined advocacy efforts is the reason why the death penalty in New York has died.

In March 2003, I got an opportunity to visit Cuba and jumped at the chance to learn more about its culture, history, and its educational and criminal justice systems. While there, the news came across the television that the United States, along with some coalition forces, initiated war on Iraq claiming that Iraq, under Saddam Hussein, had or was about to have the capacity to build weapons of mass destruction that would endanger the United States.

I knew that many in our community would be upset over the news of America's aggression and that the Center would be expected to join with anti-war individuals and groups in the Capital District. After all, during the Civil Rights Movement, Dr. King highlighted the impact of war on communities of color. This nation was spending resources that could have gone to aid our most vulnerable populations. The Center has always taken an anti-war stance.   We joined and organized peaceful demonstrations and protests against U.S. actions in Iraq, fearful that an all-out-war could break out.

Buoyed by a small, but deeply committed staff and volunteers, the Center took on a variety of important issues, often clashing with the Albany Police Department – as you know by now. Another one of my points of contention was the position that, as a citizen of Albany, I should have had standing to file a complaint with the Citizens Police Review Board regarding the police killing of David Scaringe, a 24-year-old resident of Albany. He was a bystander walking home when police fatally shot him on New Year's Eve 2003. They were chasing a traffic violation suspect by car, all the while firing at the suspect. Not one of the eight bullets hit their target, but one lone bullet pierced Scaringe's chest. I thought the best thing to do would be to file a complaint with the Citizens Police Review Board with the hope of it triggering a possible independent investigation with the Common Council. I thought an independent investigation would get rid of mistrust that exists when the police are policing themselves.

The officers claimed they believed their lives were in danger during the chase. Sounded like the standard talking points to me. This incident went before a grand jury, and the grand jury decided not to bring charges against the officers who killed Scaringe. It also did not make any policy recommendations. I lost my claim of legal standing to file a complaint about the shooting.

To make matters worse, the police chief at the time – Chief James Turley – said he did not believe the department's policies were flawed. He also stated, "These two officers have gone through an emotional nightmare and will have that with them for the rest of their lives." I, on the other hand, was more concerned about the emotional nightmare Scaringe's family and friends would have to live through for the rest of their lives. They will forever have that empty seat at the holiday dinner table – all because of a traffic violation he had nothing to do with.

Unlike a trained boxer, I never stay down after a knockout. I get back up and get back into the ring of social justice. We started a program in 2004 called Street Smart where we taught young people about their rights if they were ever stopped by police on the street or arrested. We developed a curriculum and had a lawyer on staff who would talk to students, particularly those at Albany High School where we established a good relationship. We took this information and turned it into a brochure and plastic card. The card was a handy tool we would tell students to keep in their wallets so they could pull it out and refer to it when stopped. Eventually, we phased out the card because we did not want the students to reach for it in front of a nervous or trigger-happy cop. The killing of Amadou Diallo gave us a grave example of how that could turn out.

We invited police officers to be a part of the Street Smart program as well. People who were formally incarcerated also stepped in to assist with education efforts, but that began to sound and feel like a "scared straight" program, which is not what we wanted. The Center still conducts the Street Smart program, mostly in the summer.

In addition, the Center focused efforts on female prisoners as well. We used the film, "What I Want My Words to Do to You" by Judith Katz, as a backdrop for our focus. The film documents Bedford Hills Correctional Facility inmates and their personal journeys to find the words that tell their own stories, and the power of those words to move the outside world. I had met and befriended Judith at a Lake Placid film festival. With this film, we were trying to get the community to understand the unique position women who were incarcerated were in. Most of our previous work had focused on men who were imprisoned, but we wanted to get people more involved in the issues affecting women. A Siena College professor started using "What I Want My Words to Do to You" to educate students.

In January 2004, the Center hosted famed civil rights fighter Joseph Lowery, who was in town to serve as the keynote speaker for the annual King Day celebration. Anytime I was in the company of a civil rights icon, I was always blown away. Lowery was no exception. These leaders were people I looked up to. To be in their presence was wonderful to me. It was very inspirational to see someone I had read about, especially someone such as Lowery who was in the trenches with Dr. King.

We also fought against proposals to bring back black-and-white striped uniforms for those in jail - you know, the wide horizontal stripes that are reminiscent of chain gangs. They had made a comeback in places like Warren County and Chautauqua County jails. How backwards, I thought. This was a dehumanizing and demeaning change. Instead, I believed the correctional facilities should have been putting energy and resources into rehabilitating people to make sure they were able to reconnect with society once they were released from jail.

In 2004, I was a guardian for a black senior at Albany High School. He had been enrolled in school in New York City for the previous three years and was a serious truant. Shortly after enrolling at Albany High, he attempted to return to his old ways – being late and skipping an occasional class. But this time it did not work.

Whenever he failed to show up for class on time, I received a call from school officials. This allowed me to respond quickly, and to work with school staff. It worked. My young man stayed in school, graduated that June, and went on to college.

If law enforcement officers had been involved, I believe things would have turned out differently. This student and his family had a history of negative contacts with police that included parental arrests and police abuse. The student mistrusted the police because he had already experienced a long history of police stops and abusive treatment before his 15th birthday.

Yet, in 2004, Albany Mayor Jerry Jennings rolled out a plan where city police officers patrolled the streets looking for students 16-years-old and younger who should have been in school. They put the truant students in the back of their police cars, a spot reserved for those accused of committing crimes. The officers transported the students to the city's detention center - some in handcuffs - and awaited their parents to pick them up to whisk them off to school.

Yes, it was the law for students 16-years-old and younger to be in school. And yes, truancy may have been a factor in low reading scores and high school dropout rates. While I admit truancy was a problem, I do not believe it was a problem for law enforcement to handle. At the time, Albany's school population was two-thirds black. And in 2003, nearly 80 percent of youths arrested were black and Latinx. With the police conducting these types of sweeps, they could have easily escalated to brutality, arrest or worse, especially in a community that historically mistrusts the police.

The truancy plan also did not address the underlying social, economic and political factors involved. Any program designed simply to pick up school skippers and return them to class without a strong and serious commitment to alleviating the forces that make life difficult for our children is deceptive. We needed strong families in which parents could earn a decent wage and in which family members live in adequate housing, receive proper health care, gain access to good, nurturing schools with strong educational programs, and be treated fairly and equitably in all aspects of their lives.

Mayor Jennings did not take too kindly to me objecting to his truancy program. He fired back at me in the media. "I'd like to see her step up to the plate with a program to help reduce truancy," he said to reporters.

I became increasingly disenchanted with Mayor Jennings and his influence on policing. He hired James Tuffey to head the department in 2005. Tuffey had been president of the police union and had a reputation in the black community for being a racist bully. As chief of police, he had written vicious articles about me and incorrectly denounced me, a longtime resident, as an outsider. Chief Tuffey and Mayor Jennings were personal friends. Upon becoming chief, he immediately cut back on community policing efforts and closed community outreach offices that had been championed by Chief Dale.

Seeing Tuffey as a threat to the community and concerned about all the issues on the Center's agenda, I decided to run for mayor when approached by the Green Party. Becoming mayor was certainly not my goal. I thought that it would be an effective way of getting attention on all the issues the Center was struggling with. And, being realistic, I knew it would be impossible to defeat a democrat in the City of Albany. But, I took on the challenge anyway.

My campaign manager, Mark Dunlea, scheduled me to do news conferences at various sites around the city to get media coverage and promote public discussion on a variety of issues. My theme, "It is all about families," was selected to spark conversations about education, healthcare, poverty, housing, policing and public safety, and more. And since these are the types of issues families generally discuss around their kitchen tables, my team and I used the concept of table talking to strategize and discuss issues of concern on a weekly basis. I also spent a great deal of time on the street and knocking on doors to sell my message and encourage people to vote. My campaign was aided by two famous endorsers – presidential candidate Ralph Nader and Peter Yarrow of the Peter, Paul, and Mary musical group. They both came to town to endorse me in news conferences. Peter was already a good friend of mine; we had met several years earlier.

It was ironic that I should run for mayor. As I mentioned before, my father-in-law Carl Touhey ran a serious campaign against Mayor Erastus Corning in 1973 and came close to winning on the Republican ticket. Many still claim he had the most votes, but Corning managed to steal the election. Carl's son, Charles - my husband - ran against Corning in the mayor's final race after serving as mayor for a record 42 years. Corning handily beat Charles. I had a respectable showing, receiving about 25 percent of the votes cast and spending only about $6,000 compared to Jennings' expenditures of more than $200,000. To me, I was a winner.

With the campaign behind me, I jumped into many hot, community issues around policing, juvenile justice, and community education on criminal justice matters. Chief Tuffey actively promoted his new policing plan that included the closing of neighborhood station units. The community was not pleased. I gave testimony at the Common Council seriously questioning his plan. I also called attention to some of the community complaints the police department was withholding from the Review Board.

Gang violence became an issue of concern by many. Community meetings and discussions were called to discuss and find solutions to what was seen as a growing and menacing problem. One of those suggestions that caught on to some extent was a legislative proposal that encouraged the development of dress codes that could be used to curb violence. During this growing and heated discussion, 16-year-old Jermayne Greer was arrested for recklessly handling a gun causing the death of Kathina Thomas. The case caused a great uproar throughout the city. Marches and meetings were held with residents calling for long-term imprisonment for children while giving support to the family. The Center was involved in the case, trying to protect the rights of this juvenile who was allowed to talk to the police without legal representation.

The celebrated case of Tracy Grady returned in 2007 when he sought a new trial. In 1999, Mr. Grady was arrested on charges of shooting and wounding two police officers in Arbor Hill, who he claimed were threatening his life after a traffic stop incident. Following the shooting incident, Grady allegedly stole a car, drove to a friend's house in Troy, and then disappeared. A nationwide manhunt commenced, and he was listed on America's Most Wanted fugitive list. In the meantime, an elite SWAT-type force created havoc in Arbor Hill. They tore the area apart searching for Grady. I, along with other community leaders, cried out for help, and many made it known they deeply resented the police tactics used. Others were too frightened to complain. Mistrust between the police and the community deepened and there were renewed calls for a more powerful police review board. But, the department could not listen to the voices of community residents because Grady was accused of shooting police, and all the stops were pulled out. Police were in a mindset that allowed their anger to rule while they visited great harm on residents in the area.

The manhunt lasted several weeks. Grady, who had been living on the street and in homeless shelters, was finally caught and arrested on January 18, 2000, in Atlanta by Albany's black Detective Kenneth Wilcox, Detective Sgt. Charles Arsenault, and federal officers. When he arrived at the Albany County Jail, he made it clear he would not speak to anyone before he had an opportunity to speak with me. I went to visit him at the jail. He seemed so tired.

As expected, many police officers saw Grady's attack as both a personal one and an attack on all of law enforcement generally. The police union reportedly issued a statement that read in part:

"We're encouraging our officers to come and support their brothers, Tom and Stosh (Nadoraski's nickname), because what Tracy Grady did in November 1999 was not only an attack on the two of them but an attack on the Albany Police Department and an attack on law enforcement in general. We are the people who put a uniform on and go out every day and serve the citizens of Albany."

There was widespread interest in the start of the June 19, 2001 trial which I attended with a large number of police officers. Some expressed resentment at my presence. I was seated in what they considered the police and their families' section in the public courtroom. But, I maintained my space.

Grady was represented by two super attorneys - Isaiah "Skip" Gant from Missouri who spent much of his professional life working to save accused murderers from the death penalty; and Kathryn Kase, an Albany resident who I knew and admired greatly. Law school students showed up at the trial in hopes of observing how these two masterful attorneys would defend Mr. Grady. Cheryl Coleman was the special prosecutor in the case. Both officers recovered from their wounds, received promotions, and returned to work after six months. Grady was sentenced to 25 years and lost his appeal on May 31, 2007.

Still seeking ways to focus the community's attention on these major social and criminal justice issues of concern, I agreed to write a blog at the request of Michael Huber from the Times Union. I managed to do it for about a year but found it unbearable. When given anonymity, many of the horrible racists and white supremacists come out of the woodwork to spew their vitriolic messages of hate and anger. I had always taken pride in what I referred to as my thick skin. Criticisms, especially constructive ones, I was able to listen to and accept those I thought helpful and could learn from. But the blog messages coming through were sickening. It brought me back to a reality I had experienced growing up in a rural white town in the Adirondacks, a politically conservative area with few residents of color. Many of the respondents to my blog messages expressed anger, hate, racism, white supremacy, and desires to use violence against me and others. I decided that it was too emotionally draining.

Police Chief Selection

Things seemed to be heating up inside the Albany Police Department in 2008 and 2009. I started receiving anonymous letters from police officers discouraged by the racism they saw within the department. The letters urged me to do something about the problem. They did not seem to understand I was powerless to act on unsigned letters. Undeterred, these anonymous letters were now being sent to government officials, the Times Union newspaper, and other leaders in the community. Supposedly, things were becoming increasingly tense inside the department to the point that a group of concerned officers formed a Coalition Against Racism and Bigotry.

Meanwhile, groups of community residents started demanding a return to community policing due in large measure to Police Chief James Tuffey cutting back on neighborhood police units and wanting a more punitive approach to law enforcement. He had been president of the police union and was seen in the community as brutal, lacking compassion, embracing racism, and unwilling to listen to the community.

The letters from inside the police department kept coming. At one point, they alleged that Tuffey, while in a stairwell at police headquarters, told an assistant chief, "This was not just some spook that was killed," a reference to the October slaying of Richard Bailey, a white University at Albany student in the Pine Hills neighborhood of Albany. As soon as the public learned about the reported incident, Tuffey abruptly resigned, then issued a news release to that effect. He had been chief for almost four years.

Neighborhood groups and policing experts at the School of Criminal Justice, University at Albany, engaged in increased conversations about community policing. This became a key topic as they began focusing on who should succeed Chief Tuffey. They were adamant about finding someone who supported community policing.
The City of Albany underwent charter revisions that required the mayor's new police chief appointment to be approved by the Albany Common Council. For years,

chiefs were appointed by the mayor. The charter revision did away with that.

Well Mayor Jennings must have thought he was above the rules when, reportedly, he promised John Pikus - a head official at the local FBI office - the job. He would have been allowed to do this in days gone by. There was a loud community call for a search committee that would recommend a candidate to Mayor Jennings. So, the mayor eventually heeded to his obligation to appoint the members of a selection committee. I was one of his appointees. Surprised, yet honored to be at the table, I agreed to be a part of the committee.

When the selection committee of eight met for the first time to get our instructions from Committee Chair Judge Larry Rosen, I asked how we would make decisions. I was told it would be by majority vote. Ever inquisitive, I then asked what would happen if there was a tie vote, a likely scenario with eight committee members. Judge Rosen responded, "There will never be a tie vote." That response exposed the committee as a farce. Mayor Jennings chose committee members who could be counted on to follow the lead of Rosen who would be steering the committee in whatever direction the mayor wanted. And, it became clear that I was appointed to the committee to make it appear legitimate. Years later, my suspicion seemed to be confirmed by Rosen. But, once I realized what was supposed to happen, I became determined to undermine it all by reporting to the community the truth about the charade. I did everything I could to keep the process honest. I even testified before the Common Council about what I thought was going on and kept the community informed through meetings. We ended up with some credible candidates that included Steven Krokoff, a police officer who was a strong supporter of community policing.

In February 2010, after months of battling, the selection committee had set the date for a key meeting, one that would ensure Deputy Chief Steve Krokoff was considered for the top position. That meeting was on a Monday. A few days before, however, I left town with members of my family to travel to Atlanta to celebrate the birthday of a childhood friend of ours. As luck would have it, a huge snowstorm hit the northeast disrupting train and airline travel. We found ourselves stuck in Greenville, South Carolina on the Sunday before the big meeting, with no public transportation to return to Albany. I was desperate. Some of us decided the only way out of South Carolina was to rent a car and drive through the storm. I left part of my family in South Carolina and took to the road with my brother, husband and sister-in-law. I knew I had to return to Albany for the deciding vote on the short list of potential police chiefs. After more than 12 hours of driving, we arrived in Albany. Exhausted, but thrilled to be back in town, I attended the meeting and was able to make my voice heard, a voice in solidarity with the community's wishes. My goal was to steer them toward Steve Krokoff.

The committee had a total of three community forums, as well as public comment sessions before the Albany Common Council and its Public Safety Committee. The last committee meeting, held on April 6, 2010, was just nerve-racking. We choose and gave the mayor four, unranked candidates to select from. But it was like pulling teeth to get my fellow committee members to do the right thing. This last meeting was characterized by:

- A refusal to generate minutes of the committee's discussion of candidates, even with names excluded

- A refusal to develop clear criteria for evaluating candidates
- A general discussion of each candidate and a majority vote to determine which names would be forwarded to the mayor
- A refusal to rank candidates based on their strengths and qualifications
- A refusal to provide any substantive information to the mayor about the candidates and why they were selected
- A refusal to provide, with the forwarded names, a recommendation that the mayor consider providing the person selected with a contract

Because I was so vocal about the search committee process from the beginning, Judge Rosen had tried to appease me by promising me the opportunity to issue a minority opinion statement. This was an opposing take on what transpired during the police chief search. He never thought I would issue a 34-page report on the work of the selection committee titled, "The Albany Police Chief Advisory Selection Committee: A Companion Report." In the report, I thoroughly detailed how the selection process was fraught from the outset with considerable problems related to time, transparency, structure and thoroughness.

At that point, it was in Mayor Jennings hands. It was up to him to make a final recommendation to be approved by the Common Council. Would he ignore the will of the people who were vocal about finding someone who believed in community policing? Would he give a nod to one of the four whom he thought he could control with puppet strings? We waited with bated breath. In July 2010, the wait was over. My top choice, Steve Krokoff, was appointed chief of police. We had won the hard-fought battle to bring community policing to the city of Albany.

Many in the community celebrated our victory. People were happy we identified a new chief who was a proponent of community policing. My friend Vera (Mike) Michelson organized a congratulatory/appreciation dinner party. We knew our work for real change had just begun. But, we now had great hope. Being a part of the search committee for a new chief, fighting for the best candidate for the community, and keeping the process honest and transparent is one of the Center's highest achievements.

Alice speaks at a rally in Albany after the
four officers who were on trial for
second-degree murder of Amadou Diallo
were acquitted.

Alice opens her home to raise funds for her Albany
mayoral campaign. From left to right – Alice,
unidentified gentleman, singer Peter Yarrow, and
Alice's granddaughter Olivia.

Alice signs memorandum of understanding on April 1, 2016, with other community and government partners to bring the LEAD program to Albany.

13

The Center For Law and Justice Clients and Programs

Unjustifiable Police Killings

Having a new chief take the reins of the police department was refreshing and hopeful. Steve Krokoff was young, educated, articulate and personable. Most of all, he was committed to community policing and police department transparency. We connected immediately. I started to trust the department with Krokoff and his new deputy chief, Brendan Cox, at the helm. However, things were not without incident.

We were sidetracked by a couple of law enforcement shootings in the area. Albany County Deputy Sheriff Vincent Igoe shot and killed Marcos DeJesus Alvarez on March 19, 2010, an undocumented Mexican immigrant who did odd jobs to make money to send to his wife, Agustina, and their six children. Reportedly, Mr. Alvarez was walking after midnight on a road near the Albany Airport when Deputy Sheriff Igoe pulled over and asked him what he was doing there. Police claimed Mr. Alvarez threw a piece of concrete and lunged at Deputy Sheriff Igoe, who then shot him twice. Igoe was cleared of all charges.

We were not satisfied with this explanation, wondering why the officer had stopped Mr. Alvarez in the first place and why it was necessary to shoot this unarmed man. I continued to question the shooting. When Sheriff Craig Apple came into office, we were still raising concerns, and I requested a meeting with the new sheriff. He graciously agreed to meet with me and go over the details regarding the shooting that caused Mr. Alvarez to bleed to death. To this day, I cannot accept the killing as justifiable. Mr. Alvarez posed no threat and was unarmed. An autopsy showed no evidence of alcohol or drugs in his system at the time of his death.

The second police shooting was the killing of 19-year-old Nah-Cream Moore on December 29, 2011. I introduced you to this young man in Chapter 1 who was shot by Albany police on South Pearl Street. Reportedly, Moore was a passenger inside a Range Rover, and the police recognized the driver as a relative of Moore. Police reported Moore was armed with a loaded handgun and said he attempted to lift it during a tussle with police.

Newly appointed Chief Krokoff was anxious to be transparent about the killing, so he called a news conference that included community leaders such as Willie White, Vivian Kornegay, me, and others. It turned out to be a bad decision. Emotions ran high, and Krokoff did not have answers yet to the many questions the community raised. Although many criticized Chief Krokoff's handling of the case, I tried to remain optimistic since the chief promised us there would be an extensive, internal investigation. I hoped to get satisfying answers so that the progress we made would not be erased.

In an opinion editorial featured in the Times Union, which I often wrote after these types of incidents, I noted, "Albany finds itself at a critical juncture. Will we pursue a path of renewed commitment to forging a mutually respectful and meaningful partnership between our citizens and the police? Or will our undeniable grief and outrage condemn us to the loss of significant progress made in the battle for justice for people of color? ...Those responsible for this tragedy must be held accountable. At the same time, however, the citizens of Albany must seize this opportunity to build upon recent progress in police/community relations to ensure that we never again lose one of our own at the hands of law enforcement."

Sadly, a grand jury concluded the killing of Nah-Cream Moore was justified. District Attorney David Soares seemed determined to convince the community that the officers did nothing wrong in this case. He put a premeditated plan in place. Prior to announcing his decision to the public, Soares summoned about six or seven community leaders, including me, to his office. He shared information about the case with us and laid out evidence in favor of the officers. Oh, he was convincing.

As I was still trying to process the information, Soares hurriedly whisked us into another room where the media awaited an announcement. Television cameras and reporters were set up for a news conference, one that I was not informed would be taking place. He wanted our presence at the news conference to provide legitimacy for his decision.

As the city's veteran advocate on criminal justice matters, of course, the reporters wanted to know what I had to say. When one of them asked me if the police had acted responsibly, I answered, "From what I know, yes." What I meant was, if the information provided to us was accurate, and officers truly believed their lives were in danger, it would have been appropriate. It did not come out that way during the news conference, but I further clarified my position at a meeting in the South End later, because I felt my words to the media were misconstrued. Make no mistake, my concerns lingered.

As I look back, I now realize how Soares used us. He wanted us to support his efforts to ensure the general community would accept a no bill indictment of the officers involved in the shooting. To this day, I am still left with questions. As I recall, the police claimed they knew Nah-Cream had a gun in his possession when they followed him earlier. That car was later seen parked on the street with Moore and a driver inside. What was never explained to my satisfaction was why they approached his stopped car without caution if they suspected a gun was in there? How did all the commotion take place outside of camera range if the officers had a camera, especially if they anticipated an encounter with a gunman? Why was there no audio recorded on the camera? My conclusion is Nah-Cream was murdered, and the police officers involved were not held accountable by the district attorney.

Drug Laws Affecting the Black Community

The Rockefeller Drug Laws, which allowed for extremely harsh prison sentences for drug offenses, resulted in a 2000% increase in drug crime incarceration from 1970 to 2000. Modest reforms to these drug laws showed signs of improvement in 2009, and in August 2010, President Barack Obama signed the Fair Sentencing Act of 2010. This reduced the statutory penalties for crack cocaine offenses and eliminated the mandatory minimum sentence for simple possession of crack cocaine, while increasing statutory fines.

Conservative officials on the federal, state and local levels had to come up with new government tools to continue the practice of mass incarceration. Using the federal Racketeer Influenced and Corrupt Organization (RICO) Statute of 1970 and the New York State Organized Crime Control Act (OCCA) of 1986 - both designed to address large-scale corrupt organizations such as the Mafia - the federal and state governments started imprisoning Albany's young black and brown males for as much as a third of their lives for "conspiracy" and "enterprise corruption."

To accomplish this destructive feat, Capital Region law enforcement officers conducted four, Albany drug sweeps under the federal and state statutes that prohibit "racketeering," a catch-all phrase for associating with an organization to profit from illegal activity. Under the statutes, the respective governments can *further* penalize individuals for prior *and* current convictions for distinct crimes that already carry their own severe sentences. For example, an individual's prior convictions for two state felonies can serve as "predicate" acts for a federal RICO charge. If a federal prosecutor can demonstrate that the two state felony convictions - for which the individual may have already served state time - were committed as part of a pattern of racketeering activity to maintain an interest in an "enterprise," the individual faces another 20 years of federal time for a RICO conspiracy conviction.

Proclaiming to be "making the City of Albany a safe place for our citizens" by arresting individuals who "preyed upon our community," at the time, these sweeps sent scores of Albany's young black men to prison for more than 600 years combined for non-violent offenses. Though the sweeps apprehended only a few individuals convicted of the more serious crimes alleged by officials, most of those arrested were sentenced for the single federal offense of "RICO conspiracy" or the single state crime of "enterprise corruption." In essence, many of Albany's black men were sentenced to serve a third of their young lives behind bars for merely having associated in one way or another - either through a phone call, by enjoying similar music, by attending the same social function, or through some other seemingly innocuous connection - with those suspected of criminal activity.

Much of the affected communities were terrified. Mothers and fathers flooded the Center with phone calls begging for information, answers and assistance. Community confusion abounded. "How," they wondered, "could our sons commit a crime in the community while in prison?" The Center and other groups held community discussions to help explain what was going on. We watched the courts hand out harsh sentences to defendants who were taken out of prisons, ushered to a courtroom, and re-arrested for crimes they had already done time for. Young men were led into court and given stiff 15 to 25-year prison sentences after being pressured to plead guilty or face a much stiffer sentence.

The drug sweeps resulting in mass incarceration of the city's young, black men helped preserve Albany's dubious distinction as having one of the most racially disparate drug incarceration rates in the state, and according to at least one study, in the entire nation. We had already tried to alert Albany and other Capital District communities about the seriousness of the problem in a February 2012 report titled, "The Disproportionate Impact of the Criminal Justice System on People of Color in the Capital Region." In that report, I detailed Albany's history of disproportionately incarcerating people of color, particularly for drug offenses. Unfortunately, that racial disparity continues today.

I did a series of reports to alert the community to the problem and used them to promote community meetings and discussion about it. Later, I prepared a report on the treatment of juveniles in the juvenile justice system which paralleled that of the adult system.

To encourage change and examine the state of community policing as a promising way of addressing our criminal justice problems, I published, "Pathway to Change: African Americans and Community Policing in Albany." The community was growing increasingly despondent and angry over the criminal justice system, flamed by the 2013 "not guilty" verdict when Trayvon Martin was killed in Florida in 2012. The community held vigils and marches with demonstrators singing, "We who believe in freedom cannot rest, we who believe in freedom cannot rest until it comes."

The Center continued to produce surveys and reports on policing and the criminal justice system throughout the decade. Aside from prompting community discussions, they are currently being used for study in colleges and criminal justice programs and among social justice advocates across the country.

By 2007, Albany County had gained a national reputation for it high rate of incarceration for drugs and the racial disparity between blacks and whites. The Justice Policy Institute published "The Vortex: the Concentrated Racial Impact of Drug Imprisonment and the Characteristics of Punitive Counties." I could see it unfolding, but still I was astonished to learn from that report that of 198 counties studied nationwide, Albany ranked 48th in the rate of prison admissions for drug offenses, 11th in the rate at which blacks were sent to prison for those offenses, and 5th in the nation of black to white drug admission rates.

My concerns grew over this alarming disparity. I started searching everywhere hoping to find answers to combat this terrible disease brought on by the War on Drugs and the continued and growing use of mass incarceration to address the problem of drugs. Obama's Fair Sentencing Act did not seem to be resulting in the change I had hoped for. There was some hope when his Affordable Care Act bill was signed. I thought the new legislation would improve health care for the poor in our community, decrease the possibilities of their incarceration, provide better health care for those incarcerated, and hopefully, reduce recidivism rates. It appeared the Act would give incarcerated people - a population at high-risk for lacking adequate health care - the opportunity to have continuous access to health care for the first time.

When given the opportunity to attend a small round table in New York City with President Obama, I took it, hoping to shine a light on the problem. I lost no time posing the question of prisoner health care directly to the president before anyone else had a chance to get his attention. I was impressed because he was so thoughtful in his response to me which took at least 15 minutes. Our paths would cross again at the Waldorf Astoria United Nations celebration. He remembered me, much to my delight, and characterized our earlier talk as a "good conversation" on the topic of prisoner health care and the Affordable Care Act. Our paths would cross several more times at The White House. However, prison health care, although improved, continues to be of great concern, especially during this period of the COVID-19 pandemic.

My next major step to address the drug war and incarceration rate was to join forces with the New York Drug Policy Alliance. Gabriel Sayegh, an incredible staffer there, asked me to help organize a community meeting to listen to residents' concerns about the city's drug enforcement policies and access to drug treatment. He was working with the New York Academy of Medicine, which was carrying out a large study on drug policies and their impact on communities. Its study culminated in a report titled, "Blueprint for a Public Health and Safety Approach to Drug Policy," which was published nearly 40 years after Governor Rockefeller signed his drug laws. In the report, the Academy maintained that the criminalization-based approach to drug policy was inappropriate, ineffective, and not based on evidence. The Academy called for a change in policy to one that was a public health approach based on the four pillars of prevention, treatment, harm reduction, and public safety.

The Academy's report came just in time to affect changes in Albany's law enforcement policies. Kathy Sheehan became Albany's first female mayor in 2014. She was seen as progressive and committed to criminal justice reform. Therefore, I was delighted to accept her invitation to serve on her transition team as co-chair of the public safety committee, alongside Steve Krokoff. Our major suggestion dealt with adopting the Academy's recommendation for drug policy change. I urged that we adopt the policy of treating drug use as a health issue rather than a law enforcement issue. Mayor Sheehan adopted and put in place this policy recommendation that would guide the police department.

LEAD Program

That research and the Report's recommendations led to major changes, not only in Albany, but across the country, most notably in Seattle, Washington. Under a consent decree, Seattle looked for ways to address racial disparity in drug arrests and incarceration. It developed a program called Law Enforcement Assisted Diversion (LEAD). Then, they went around the country promoting this new program designed to divert persons involved in low-level drug and other offenses from prosecution. Instead, they were referred to case management services and housing.

After receiving an invitation to attend a lecture on LEAD in D.C., I invited Police Chief Krokoff and his deputy, Brendan Cox. Impressed, they brought the idea back to Albany and proceeded to work on developing a program for our city, with the Center's involvement. To observe the Seattle program, a group from Albany and I went there for a week. The group consisted of police officials, social service organization members, and community residents.

We officially launched the Albany LEAD program on April 1, 2016, with a ceremony at the Center. Eight of us signed Memorandums of Understanding, committing our organizations and agencies to work on developing a strong and effective program that would eventually reduce mass incarceration and reduce Albany's racial disparities in diversions and arrests. The signers included: the mayor, Albany police chief, Albany county executive, Albany county district attorney, Albany county sheriff, the Business Improvement District, the Center for Law and Justice, and Katal, an organization that played a major role in helping develop and manage Albany's LEAD program. The KATAL Center for Equity, Health, and Justice was New York City-based and had no vote on the newly formed LEAD Policy Coordinating Group that would direct the work of the Albany LEAD.

Recognizing the need to be more holistic in our approach to delivering effective services and changing social policy, I developed collaborative relationships with other community service providers. We became particularly interested in working closer with people who had been imprisoned. Michelle Alexander, through her seminal work, "The New Jim Crow," made us even more aware of the plight of this population and the impact of mass incarceration in communities of color. Her book caught my attention immediately upon its release. She seemed to be all about criminal justice reform activities. We all knew the problem of incarceration and the relationship between prisons and those communities. Incarcerated people like my mentors - Eddie Ellis, Larry White, and many others - had already taught us the lessons about incarceration. We knew the history of enslavement and its lasting legacy of oppressions. We knew about the Jim Crow practice of convict leasing. But, no one articulated it better than Alexander. She told the world mass incarceration constitutes a racial caste system for people of color in America.

I was so moved by her book, published in 2010, I started doing community reviews and discussions around it. There was a hunger for this information, and one group encouraged me to keep the book discussion going. We started meeting in the South End once a month for 10 years but stopped in 2020 when the COVID-19 pandemic hit. Members of the group continue to contact me, eager to start meeting again to talk about racism and criminal justice, which became worse during the spring of 2020 with more police killings coming to light.

H.E.A.L. Program

Guided by Michelle Alexander's book and community discussions, I developed a new approach to services offered at the Center and involved some key organizations in our work. The new approach was called H.E.A.L., spelling out our umbrella program offers of – **Health** services, **Education** services on a range of social justice issues, **Advocacy** to assist clients in getting goods and service they needed, and **LEAD**, our attempt to divert more people, particularly people of color, from the criminal justice system. To do the necessary work, we developed working relationships with Albany Medical College in a service- learning project for medical students and physicians; the School of Pharmacy and Sciences; the Legal Aid Society; LEAD, and its involved governmental entities and others; volunteer attorneys; financial experts; college students; and high school students. With such support, the Center has been able to assist thousands of Capital Region residents. Several became high-profile cases. One of the most memorable one was that of Thomas Smith.

Thomas - a thin, dark-skinned, black man in his early 50s - walked into our office one summer afternoon in 2016 asking for help. For 15 years, he had been incarcerated for bank robbery. Upon his release from prison, he was able to move into a homeless shelter. He managed to get a job at Walmart in Guilderland, about five miles from the homeless shelter where he resided. Many times, he walked to work, determined to get there. Thomas' duties included returning shopping carts to the store left in the parking lot by customers.

A customer left empty soda cans and bottles in a shopping cart one day, Thomas explained. No one claimed the abandoned returnables, so he deposited them for cash. For this, Walmart fired him. This seemed like a great injustice. I called officials at the store and complained profusely. The media got wind of the story, and his situation caught the attention of people nationwide and across Europe. I did an interview for the British media. People continued to express their outrage at Walmart, not only for how it treated Thomas, but for all the non-union workers of the company across the country. We joined forces with many throughout the nation, calling for a boycott of the chain while demonstrating at several of its stores. The entire Center staff worked tirelessly to support Thomas in so many ways. Local legislators joined in the struggle to get justice for

Thomas. A GoFundMe account raised more than $20,000 for him. I tried to help him manage the money because I saw a pattern of reckless spending, but he refused my help. He expressed great interest in sharing some of the money with his teenaged son for his education.

The Center helped Thomas find another job as a dishwasher. Relieved, he had an apartment and a car. We believed he was on his way to success, and our work with him had paid off. He even stopped by our office on occasion to treat us to pizza. On one of his planned stops to bring us food, I heard a commotion outside our Green Street office. There were police cars and residents drawn to something happening in the street. News cameras were on the scene, and one Channel 13 reporter chatted with me outside my office as we awaited news on what was unfolding. Coincidently, she was asking me how Thomas was doing, since she and everyone else knew how heavily involved the Center was in his case. I bragged about how well he was doing like a proud mother touting the accomplishments of her honor roll student.

Soon, I saw the figure of a man from a distance lying in the street with police officers hovering around. Fearing that someone was being brutalized by officers, I made my way to the site of the action and the man lying in the street, but police halted my movement. Rumors started flying from street spectators that police had just shot a man in his car. I learned later that the man at the center of attention was Thomas. Although police shot through his car window, miraculously, Thomas was not hit.

Sadly, Thomas returned to robbing banks after he depleted his funds. We learned he was a serial bank robber. During the summer months, Thomas robbed the First Niagara on State Street in Albany, the Citizens Bank on Washington Avenue, the First Niagara on Western Avenue, and then back to the First Niagara on State Street for a second time. Evidently, the police tried to stop Thomas after the last robbery. They followed him to a spot near our office where he planned to deliver food to us. The police claimed Thomas backed his car into them when they caught up to him, and they shot at him through his car window.

The Center staff and I were heartbroken and devastated. Upon his arrest, I visited him at the Albany County Jail. He was a broken man, and I felt so powerless to help him after our nearly two-year association. He looked at me and called me Doctor Mom, a name he affectionately called me. Thomas maintained his innocence, but the video footage from the robberies told a different story.

After all the publicity died down, community residents and criminal justice advocates expressed their sympathy for me. I was perplexed by their expressions of sorrow for *me*. Their feelings were so misplaced. They should have felt bad for Thomas. We all let Thomas down. He was the product of a home and a community without love and support for him as he struggled with depression and drug addiction. Thomas was a heroin addict, and we did not clearly see it. Those who did, failed to get him the treatment he so desperately needed. Our society failed him again by imprisoning him for 15 to 17 more years. We lost and failed the man who came to our office in 2016 looking for help.

More High-Profile Cases

Around the same time Thomas sought our help, three black female students from the University at Albany claimed they had suffered racist slurs and an attack by 10 or more male and female students on a city bus. This case received national attention. One of the students, with a parent, contacted our office for assistance with their claim. We were able to provide legal guidance and refer them to an attorney.

I was on campus the day students held a rally on behalf of the young women. They had a community of supporters and were regarded as heroes for fighting back against what seemed like the worst kind of bullies – racist ones. The college president and I were having dinner during the rally with the Little Rock Nine, civil rights icons who were in town for an event. Gaining notoriety in 1957 for challenging racist segregation policies in school, they knew all too well what it felt like to be a student and experience the sort of hate that was reported.

The case had an ugly turn of events when the Albany County District Attorney charged the young students with assault and misleading police about the alleged incident. Once again, District Attorney David Soares called in a group of community leaders, including me, to view videotapes and support his charges against the three students. The videos we watched provided no clarity to what actually happened on the bus. Again, I felt used by District Attorney Soares. He seems to have developed a knack for inviting residents in on controversial cases in hopes of providing legitimacy to his claims for prosecution.

After a hearing, the students were expelled from the University of Albany. The DA charged them with falsely reporting a racially motivated attack, assault and harassment. One of them pled guilty to disorderly conduct and the other two went to trial, which I attended with many observers watching. The trial drew many spectators including a large contingent of their family members.

The young women were eventually found guilty of falsely reporting a crime but were acquitted of assault and harassment charges. Although those watching this case closely were blind-sided by the turn of events, we were pleased the women found competent attorneys to represent them. Mark Mishler was one of those attorneys, and Frederick Brewington, a well-known and respected attorney, was the other. In the courtroom, following the trial, family members greeted me and thanked me for suggesting Mishler as their attorney. Mishler criticized DA Soares for the indictments which he said were not necessary. He asserted the charges were blown up into the "crime of the century."

Less than a year later, I got involved with another high-profile case. Remember Ellazar Williams? I teased his story to you in Chapter 1. He is the young, black man who police detectives shot in the back in August 2018, after responding to reports of a black man in a hoodie with a gun. Two shots from the detective rang out with one hitting then 19-year-old Ellazar in his upper left back area. The detectives did not find a gun, but they recovered a knife in the area near the chase. Ellazar was taken to Albany Medical Center with the bullet still lodged in his spine. The doctors reported he was permanently paralyzed from the chest down.

The first account from the Albany Police Department was Ellazar had been shot in the left shoulder, and police responded with a lethal weapon because they feared for their lives. Several days later, I told the acting police chief I wanted to see Ellazar, so he took me to the hospital where I visited with the victim. After examining his body, I was stunned by a bullet injury to his upper back.

Many community voices called for transparency and an official report on the shooting. An unwritten report came about a week and a half later. I was summoned to the police station with a few other community members to listen to the department's report of the shooting. The new police chief, Eric Hawkins, was on the job for a mere 24 hours. He presided over the meeting and made it known he supported the report's findings and its conclusions. I was extremely angered by the report and its conclusion that the shooting was justified. None of the officials could satisfactorily explain the necessity for the shooting and the department's claim Ellazar had been shot in the neck and shoulder area. I challenged the police department's account of the shooting by expressing my concerns at a Common

Council meeting and publishing my own response which pointed out many discrepancies in the unwritten police report.

For example, APD's arrest report, made without an arresting officer's signature, and the unwritten investigation report provided contradictory information. The arrest report stated Ellazar was displaying a knife and refused to drop it when ordered to do so by Detective Olsen. It then stated Ellazar ran *in the direction* of Detective Olsen with a knife, causing him to shoot Ellazar. Commander Michael Basile, in his oral presentation, said Ellazar was running *away* from Detective Olsen when he fell and dropped a knife. When he attempted to "rearm" himself with the knife, Detective Olsen, who was approximately eight to 10 feet from Ellazar, shot him in fear for his life. So, which one of these accounts is accurate?

Other than the lawyers seeking to be selected to file a civil rights lawsuit, Ellazar and his girlfriend were abandoned by all those responsible for his paralyzed condition. We, at the Center, took up Ellazar's cry for help. Due to Times Union reporter Paul Grondahl's interest and reporting on his situation, a GoFundMe campaign brought in several thousands of dollars. It was only the beginning of a long journey, taken on by the Center, to find help for his every need – housing, physical and mental health, financial support, therapy, food, medication, and so much more. Service-learning students and staff from the Albany Medical College have courageously pitched in to support Ellazar and the Center as we care for him.

The battle for his life and well-being continues as we provide for his ongoing need for support. While activists and supporters in the community continue to remind the city administration that the matter is not over, no city officials have offered to help Ellazar, acknowledge his injuries, or apologize, claiming his lawsuit prevents any discussions or actions on their part.

Alice and Ellazar Williams.
Photo courtesy of Paul Grondahl.

President Barack Obama greets Alice at a
New York City intimate gathering.

Alice and author Michelle Alexander in Harlem.

Protestors take to the streets after George Floyd was murdered on May 25, 2020. Photo courtesy of Persist Print.

14

The Time for Reckoning

The Center for Law and Justice Reports

In 2010, a new book splashed on the scene and captivated the attention of much of the country, especially we activists who had been working almost a half century to call attention to the problem of the disproportionate incarceration of black and brown people in America. The problem and its calamitous impact on blacks hit me hard during the time of the Attica uprising in 1971 and my subsequent involvement inside our state prisons and jails.

I introduced this book earlier - Michelle Alexander's "The New Jim Crow: Mass Incarceration in the Age of Colorblindness" – and it is thought to be one of the most influential books of the past 20 years. For many, it was shocking to be still talking about Jim Crow in what was now deemed a post-racial society, two years after Barack Obama was elected as the first black president in this country. So here was this black woman eloquently speaking out about and condemning the nation's entire criminal justice system and, as Ibram X. Kendi describes it in his review of the book, "...exposing discrimination from lawmaking to policing to the denial of voting rights to ex-prisoners." He went on to claim, "'The New Jim Crow' transformed forever the way thinkers and *activists* view the phenomenon of mass incarceration." He was so right. But, I had already learned the lessons Michelle Alexander taught by working with incarcerated people for more than 30 years.

She was much more articulate and able to speak directly to America and, particularly, other activists involved long before me. Her book prompted me to start discussing the book throughout the community and with a special group that organized and met in the South End for 10 years, as I have already mentioned.

I took every opportunity I could to hear Michelle speak in public. She spoke so eloquently with great passion and resolve. I learned directly from her that she had also been heavily influenced by some of the same formerly incarcerated people I knew and worked with. They included men like Eddie Ellis and Jazz Hayden.

Not only did we talk about the book, but it influenced the Center's programming, research, writing and activism. I joined with former prisoners and community groups such as the Prison Project housed at the Riverside Church in Harlem. I met there many times, sometimes with fellow activists, including Michelle Alexander and my long-time heroine and prison abolitionist, Angela Davis.

"The New Jim Crow" inspired me to dig deeper into the problem of mass incarceration and its effect on Albany and the Capital District in hopes that community members would learn more about the impact of the justice system on people of color in our own community. In early 2012, I started preparing a series of research reports to educate the community and, hopefully, get more residents involved in efforts to change criminal justice policy. The first report in the series was titled, "The Disproportionate Impact of the Criminal Justice System on People of Color in the Capital Region." That report was published and discussed throughout Capital District communities that year. By invitation, law enforcement officials – police and prosecution - joined me in responding to my report at several of these events. We certainly did not see eye to eye on many issues, but I felt the discussion was important.

This first report examined some of the specific impacts federal, state, and local criminal justice system practices had on people of color in the region, detailing the overrepresentation of these groups among Capital Region arrests, convictions and sentencing to state prison. I chronicled the devastating impact the criminal justice system has on individuals and communities of color. Furthermore, I examined the disproportionate incarceration statistics in the context of "The New Jim Crow" movement which asserted that mass incarceration serves to maintain a racial caste system that denies education, employment, housing, and voting rights to those who carry the label *felon*, in much the same way the post-Civil War Jim Crow laws denied rights to blacks. After presenting my examination of the problem, I provided recommendations for change which included completing and attaching racial impact statements to any proposed changes to policing, prosecution, public defense, and sentencing statutes and policies.

By October 2012, I was able to complete a second report in which I examine the fate of local youth in our juvenile justice system. It is titled, "The Disproportionate Impact of the Juvenile Justice System on Children of Color in the Capital Region." Among other things, I describe the state of the system, the need for change and, most importantly, what I saw and the devastating consequences of involvement with the system. This included the possibility of juveniles placed in one of the state's secure confinement facilities, which have been found to foster brutal results. What I found most troublesome is how much more likely it is for children of color to become enmeshed in the juvenile justice system through such avenues as the 'school to prison pipeline. Children who are incarcerated as minors are those most likely to be incarcerated as adults.

In the third report, I set out to answer, particularly for affected families how their youth were being brought into the justice system and the resulting devastation it wrought, especially through drug sweeps conducted in Albany's communities of color by federal, state, and local authorities, employing racketeering statutes to carry out the assault on young people.

As a result of the sweeps carried out just prior to the time of my reports, scores of Albany's young black men were sentenced to more than 600 years combined in prison for non-violent offenses. In the report, I explain how the actions of the Capital Region officials who conducted those sweeps served to perpetuate the mass incarceration of black and brown people. It was also my intent to enlighten both officials and the community regarding the role of structural racism in the perpetuation of the mass incarceration and to challenge all to participate in collaborative efforts to end this insidious practice.

Immediately following the series, I decided to focus on community policing as a potential pathway to change. After all, this is where the community had voiced its opinion and support for a community policing philosophy to be used in the city's policing efforts. I wanted to promote a discussion on where we were in that current moment and where we had hoped to go.

In that report, I looked at some of the changes that had been made with Police Chief Krokoff at the helm. I concluded that although much progress had been made, I saw a palpable path to a mutually–respectful, police/community partnership in Albany, but there remained much work to be done before community policing could become an everyday reality for black people in the city. Unfortunately, Krokoff did not stay in the chief's position very long. But, I was pleased Brendan Cox, his deputy, was able to step into the position and continue the move toward real community policing and transparency. Along with many others, I developed a strong and positive relationship with Brendan Cox. Although he is no longer chief, we continue to work together in the LEAD program.

In 2018, Mayor Kathy Sheehan selected Eric Hawkins as the city's new police chief. He came into office less than a month after Ellazar Williams was shot and paralyzed by a police detective. He took office a day after the Albany Police Department issued its official report on the shooting. I was asked to attend the public release of the report. Hawkins expressed confidence in the report's findings that the detective was justified in shooting Ellazar. I was shocked that he would take ownership of a report he had nothing to do with. To me this was a mistake. Many in the community could not accept the investigative report and its conclusions. I found the official report lacking in so many ways, so I issued a report of my own critical of APD's report. Soon, a number of community meetings, demonstrations, and rallies were held condemning the report and calling upon the district attorney to drop criminal charges against Ellazar.

Tensions between community members and the police department increased, causing me great concern. I decided to meet with the mayor to discuss the matter. She dismissed my concerns by blaming me for fanning the discontent which she said was caused by me calling Detective Olsen, who shot Ellazar, a liar. Her accusation was untrue, but I did dispute the findings of the police investigative report.

Spurred by growing tensions over the Ellazar shooting, the mayor's reluctance to address my concerns, and a 2019 police brutality incident on First Street in Albany, I decided the Center would carry out another survey to gauge the temperament, attitudes, and feelings of community people about law enforcement and community policing. The resulting survey report is titled, "Pathway to Reformative Change: Public Safety, Law Enforcement, and the Albany Community." That report presented, I believe, shocking findings regarding the level of mistrust city residents - particularly in communities of color - held for the Albany Police Department and the District Attorney's Office. They saw the two entities as lacking in trustworthiness, respect for community residents, treatment of residents in a fair manner, and acceptance of community input regarding police and prosecution policies and practices.

The report was embraced by community members and all but ignored by government officials. I had hoped it would serve as a catalyst for transformative change by sparking meaningful dialogue between officials and the communities they serve. Sadly, the bold experiment in true community policing embarked upon in 2010, seemed of little importance to those responsible for administering the city's criminal justice system.

Disappointed, but undeterred, I published another report in April 2020 calling for a *Recommitment to Community Policing Symposium*. I envisioned a symposium in the fall 2020, co-sponsored by the Center for Law and Justice, the Office of the Mayor, the Albany Police Department, the Albany District Attorney's Office, and the Albany Common Council.

Protests

Meanwhile COVID-19 hit the country, and on May 25, 2020, as the world watched, George Floyd was murdered by Officer Derek Chauvin. This crime prompted one of the largest social justice movements in our country's history. Activists of all colors and ethnicities joined the movement led by Black Lives Matter for transformative change in the nation's criminal justice system.

I heard about several cases like Floyd's, but not exactly like this. This one is the first one that caused me to weep. To see the life being choked out of someone, and for that long period of time, got to me. He symbolized all those things I have been working against, but it is something I did not expect to see like that. I think that is why it had such an impact on this country. We have seen Rodney King brutally battered by police in Los Angeles, California in 1991. We have seen Walter Scott in North Charleston, South Carolina shot in the back by police while running away in 2015. But, this is something we saw and heard in real time - the pain in his voice, the outreach to his mother, and the life snuffed out of him before our eyes. As this all unfolded, I also thought about Jessie Davis, whose case was similar. We knew what happened and how it happened, and it made a connection for me. With all that we had accomplished in Albany and in our nation, we had not come as far as I thought we had. This case had a strong impact on me, as well as others.

Like I said, Floyd's tragic death happened during the pandemic. But that did not stop people from taking to the streets in protest. It caused people to vent their anger in different ways. I waited a few days before I went out. I had gotten a nasty virus on a cruise ship once and did not want to be in that situation again, so I did not go out at first. I eventually went to a demonstration in the South End. My granddaughters went to the demonstration as well. They were 16 and 19 at the time. This was a proud moment for me. I want them to be aware of who they are, where they are, other people's situations, and their responsibility to fight injustice. As someone who has dedicated my life to social justice, I was happy as I could be to see them following in my activism footsteps. And I didn't even prompt them to go! They felt the same heaviness and anger everyone else did. And they acted on it.

There was one night during the uprising in Albany when things were bad. A peaceful march started uptown. There were lots of people there. Later in the evening is when things went sore. I had to be there, so I took the necessary precautions – still aware of a deadly virus encompassing me – and I went. Someone filmed a documentary and interviewed me down there in real time. Being there gave me some perspective on the situation and helped me in responding to officials and the media, as I am often called upon to do.

While being interviewed, I called the situation unfolding before me an *uprising* while everyone else called it a *riot*. There is a difference. People were responding to police. They were upset with the police, not just because of what happened it Minneapolis, but because of what happens in Albany. Yes, there were some people looting, including infiltrators from outside of the community who took advantage of the moment to help themselves. But, looting takes place all the time in different forms. People want to paint the picture that it is just blacks in poor communities. White people loot too. Just in many other ways. But because of stereotypes that associate looting with black people, whites are not identified as looters. I wanted to make that distinction while being interviewed. I was able to bring a historic perspective and my experience to see and interpret what was going on.

The extent of the damage became evident the next day, something only the daylight could reveal. More memorable than the damaged store fronts and sprayed graffiti was the sight of people coming together in the aftermath - sweeping up broken glass from the streets, helping businesses board up windows, and coming together in solidarity. Because of the unrest, Mayor Sheehan put a temporary, emergency curfew in place to try to prevent future looting and damages.

Executive Order 203

The police-involved deaths and racially biased law enforcement could no longer be ignored in the State of New York. On June 12, 2020, spurred by the killing of George Floyd, New York's Governor Andrew Cuomo issued Executive Order 203 – New York State Police Reform and Reinvention Collaborative. This executive order mandated transformative changes in all the state's police departments to address systemic racism and ensure fair and equal treatment of all residents. Specifically, the EO reads in part:

Each local government entity which has a police agency operating with police officers as defined under 1.20 of the criminal procedure law must perform a comprehensive review of current police force deployments, strategies, policies, procedures, and practices, and develop a plan to improve such deployments, strategies, policies, procedures, and practices, for the purposes of addressing the particular needs of the communities served by such police agency and promote community engagement to foster trust, fairness, and legitimacy, and to address any racial bias and disproportionate policing of communities of color.

The mandate gave me great hope that it could function to confirm and support the Center's work for transformative change which it had actively been engaged in for 36 years. The Center took on the responsibility of monitoring the collaborative process and contributing information and advice to its community and law enforcement participants as they went about their deliberations. We were quick to provide critical analysis and recommendations as well. This was the best role for the Center since the mayor did not select us to officially participate in the formal process.

Symposium on Community Policing

Encouraged, the Center entered a collaborative relationship with many local organizations including the New York State Writers Institute, the Times Union, and WMHT television. Together, we held a virtual symposium titled, *The Time for Reckoning*. The pandemic prevented us from gathering in person.

The symposium focused on four themes: the impact of systemic racism on people of color, the issue of trust between a community and its police department, needed reforms to address systemic racism in policing, and the need for police department accountability to the communities they serve. During April and May 2020, the Center had been exchanging correspondence with Albany Mayor Kathy Sheehan, Police Chief Eric Hawkins, and Common Council President Corey Ellis. To our disappointment, District Attorney David Soares did not acknowledge the Center's correspondence, nor our symposium invitations. This was unfortunate, given the DA's office critical role in criminal justice.

I opened the symposium emphasizing why this is the optimal time for a reckoning with our city's past of having strained police/community relations. My unalterable charge is that racism is at the core of what we are experiencing in policing of Albany's black neighborhoods. Our panel of government officials spoke, addressing the four themes outlined above. In turn, a panel of young, black community activists responded remotely to the positions held by the government officials. Paul Collins-Hackett, executive director of The RED Bookshelf literacy program and three members of All of Us Community Action Group - Jamaica Miles, Morgan Jones-Marinia, and Shawn Young - served on the panel.

The Center received financial support from the McKee Foundation for this and other projects. In addition to the symposium, we identified about 15 young people who started projects to tackle racism. I am so proud of what they have done. Some have embarked on community organizing. Some use the arts to focus on systemic racism and racial justice. Some are focusing on the Black Lives Matter movement. They are doing all kinds of positive things with the grant we received. They even have a well-equipped mobile stage. With it, they can transport it from neighborhood to neighborhood for performances, and other special events. They invited me to join them on stage one day during an event and gave me an award for my support.

The big question post symposium is whether the time was a true reckoning of structural racism that blacks had endured since 1619. The swelling activism and public opinion suggested to us that this time was different. But, was it? As I write this, the marches and demonstrations have died down, but we see renewed efforts to deny black and brown people the right to vote; segregation persists; and police are still brutalizing and killing. It has not stopped with the prosecution and sentencing of Derek Chauvin, now sentenced to 22 1/2 years in prison. Our work remains.

But, all hope is not lost. Stirred by George Floyd's murder, The Albany Common Council unanimously passed legislation in 2021 to provide for an independent review board with increased funding and investigative powers. Since former Governor Cuomo's 2020 Executive Order 203 mandated jurisdictions to re-imagine and re-design its police departments, community residents had proposed transformative powers for

Albany's Community Police Review Board that would strengthen its ability to do investigations of potential police abuse and play a significant role in disciplining them. Under existing city law, complaints against police officers fall under the oversight of the Office of Professional Standards, and, if necessary, an independent arbitrator. But with the passage of the Common Council's legislation, a referendum was on the ballot for voters to decide in the general election. A yes vote on Proposal 7 meant voters support increasing the authority of the existing Community Police Review Board to conduct investigations and have oversight over complaints against policy.

Those of us who had been on the frontlines on this issue for decades watched the local elections anxiously and with great expectation. On November 2, 2021, 69.97 percent of Albany's voters cast their ballot in favor of Prop 7! At last! This was truly a win for the community and all who have fought tirelessly over the years. When it finally settled in my mind that Prop 7 had actually passed, I reflected on a time decades ago when the NAACP drafted proposed legislation to create a civilian review board. I thought about the Albany Alliance for A Civilian Review Board and how it pushed hard on this issue. I thought about all the work I did with the New York Civil Liberties Union to bring about an effective review board. I thought about how we fought Mayor Whalen on this but had to settle for a community/police relations board with no teeth. I thought about my time as a charter member of that board and all the frustrations I felt. Because Albany residents voted overwhelmingly to expand the powers of the Community Police Review Board, I know my work on this issue over the past 30 years was not in vain. Jessie Davis, whose case prompted me to start the Center for Law and Justice and whose spirit I will forever be connect to, did not die in vain.

The time for reckoning is not an isolated time in our present. It is an opportunity for action at any time in our future when the legacy of slavery in this country rears its ugly head. That is why it is important for this work to continue. Young people in Albany are getting involved in the social justice movement in a different kind of way, a more exciting way. They have different tools at their disposal like social media. With a quick tweet of 280 characters or less, they can swiftly get a message out to throngs of followers, a more efficient way than the mimeograph newsletters I circulated once upon a time.

We have had a positive influence on the younger generation, and now the old guard is saying, "It's your time." Their agenda is not as structured or single-minded. Where we once focused on single issues such as voting rights, etc., their agenda is more about being an equal partner in society. The City of Albany is in the hands of this new crop of leadership. To those involved in A Village, I see you. To those involved in the African American Cultural Center, I see you. To those involved in Soul Fire Farm, I see you. To those involved in All Of Us, I see you. To all those who protested in 2021 at the South Station and were violently removed, I see you.

I have covered numerous topics in this memoir for you to glean. I hope I have successfully used pieces of my life's story to demonstrate how the criminal justice system impacts the lives of black and brown people, how blacks in Albany rose up over the years to gain some freedom from political control, and how the Center for Law and Justice has been at the forefront in tackling these tough issues for nearly four decades. We have had some losses and some successes, but the important lesson is, we stayed in the fight. For those who are grabbing the baton of social justice, I leave you with 10 top takeaways from this book on how I boldly addressed social, racial, and criminal injustice in the black community. I hope this serves as a model for you and other communities across the state and nation to duplicate.

1. **Make sure you cannot be bought.**
   The Center remains independent; therefore, we cannot be swayed by political or business interests.

2. **Use the media to your advantage.**
   Reporters are always looking for a story. Give them one.

3. **Collaborate with other community organizations.**
   There is strength in numbers.

4. **Empower the residents who are directly affected in the community.**
   They have a right to be a part of the solution.

5. **Do not be afraid to call out the injustices you see.**
   This is the start of change.

6. **Do not be afraid to speak truth to power.**
   Sometimes, that means going toe-to-toe with those in elected offices and other leadership positions.

7. **Find good allies.**
   Embrace allies who can assist, even if they do not look like you. There are people who have your same passion and desire for equality and equity, but they may be of a different race, religion, sexual orientation, or even political affiliation. You will also need to team up with great attorneys. Make sure you have stellar and reputable civil rights and criminal attorneys on your team.

8. **Develop a thick skin.**
   You will need it when the threats, insults, or bad press come your way.

9. **Create your own media to carry your message.**
   If the mainstream media neglects its job of reporting fair and accurate news, create your own media outlet.

10. **Have a passion for what you do and include valuing the lives of all people.**

Understanding your "why" will ensure you are in this fight – with altruism - for the long haul. Your passion in this field will fuel you even when you feel like giving up.

AFTERWORD

On May 25, 2020, this nation was called upon to reckon with the videotaped police murder of George Floyd, the history of black oppression and enslavement, and the continuing systemic racism that plagues all of our social, economic, and political institutions, particularly that which defines our criminal and juvenile justice systems. That vile act of police murder prompted the largest social justice mass movement in our history. And, for a brief moment, we who believe in freedom also believed that the grief black people have endured for centuries might finally be acknowledged, recognized, understood, shared by much of the entire nation's population, and that it would be ended. This, we thought, would be the reckoning so many of us and our ancestors had actively fought for since 1619. It would mean that the fight for the abolition of chattel slavery, the black migration against Jim Crow, the civil rights marches, the prisoner reform movement, the struggles against the police killing of Jessie Davis, Nah-Cream Moore, Brianna Taylor, and many others, and the paralyzing of Ellazar Williams, and the founding and consistent work of the Center for Law and Justice, could, without question, be claimed as victories for freedom and justice.

We activists, who believe in freedom, also wondered whether the nation was now ready to think and act along the lines of embracing reparations for enslavement; securing the right of all to freely vote, including those convicted and imprisoned; ending mass incarceration and the creation of a caste system comprised of formerly incarcerated black and brown people denied entry into mainstream society; and reimagining our policing and criminal justice systems to achieve fairness and equal justice.

While the marches and demands for justice continued, many states seemed open for real change. Then, New York's Governor Andrew Cuomo, issued a bold initiative - Executive Order 203 which read:

Each local government entity which has a police agency operating with police officers as defined under 1.20 of the criminal procedure law must perform a comprehensive review of current police force deployments, strategies, policies, procedures, and practices, and develop a plan to improve such deployments, strategies, policies, procedures, and practices, for the purposes of addressing the particular needs of the communities served by such police agency and promote community engagement to foster trust, fairness, and legitimacy, and to address any racial bias and disproportionate policing of communities of color.

Each chief executive of such local government shall convene the head of the local police agency, and stakeholders in the community to develop such plan, which shall consider evidence-based policing strategies, including but not limited to, use of force policies, procedural justice; any studies addressing systemic racial bias or racial justice in policing; implicit bias awareness training; de-escalation training and practices; law enforcement assisted diversion programs; restorative justice practices; community-based outreach and conflict resolution; problem-oriented policing; hot spots policing; focused deterrence; crime prevention through environmental design; violence prevention and reduction interventions; model policies and guidelines promulgated by the New York State Municipal Police Training Council; and standards promulgated by the New York State Law Enforcement Accreditation Program.

For me, the start of the worldwide demonstrations and the Governor's bold mandate, occurring within days of each other in 2020, provided our greatest opportunity to achieve transformative change, especially in policing and the criminal justice system. We saw both actions as confirming and supporting what we had started to do so long ago to effect change. With that in mind, my staff and I set out to increase and deepen our community activism and involvement. I was there with Center staff at the South End demonstration when police used tear gas against demonstrators on June 6, 2020, and I was there with Center staff when peaceful demonstrators calling for change were violently removed from their encampment in front of the police station with only a 15-minute warning. I am there now working with Corey Ellis, president of the Albany Common Council, to pass Local Law L that embodies our calls for transformative change in the city's policing and public safety structure and operating procedures built upon a stated vision for such change. That vision states:

"The City of Albany envisions a Commission of Public Safety that decouples public safety from policing, centers community voices, and ends systemic racism. The Commission embraces the four pillars of Procedural Justice: treating people with dignity and respect; giving citizens a voice during encounters; being open and transparent in decision-making; and conveying trustworthy motives. The Public Safety Commission will ensure the elevation of the concepts of community policing into the practice of public safety. A guiding principle of the public safety commission is Sanctity of Life: that at the core of an officer's responsibilities is the duty to protect all human life and physical safety." (May 12, 2021)

Using this statement along with a proposed new bifurcated public safety structure that separates policing functions from community public safety functions; we have begun going back into the streets to receive real community input from human beings on our envisioned new structure of policing and public safety. On-the-street approaches to get such input were seriously halted, due in part to the pandemic that silenced many community voices. But, we are determined to see it to the end by actively engaging with the community to push the vision forward and get to a new place that we have not gone before.

Where Must We Go From Here?

On July 4, 2021, two events helped me realize how impactful my activist work, alone and with others, has and continues to be. What we have done can provide support and guidance to others as we go forward to work for change in our community justice systems, particularly in the structure of policing and the delivery of public safety, not only in Albany, but in other communities.

The first event occurred on that very day. The Albany Times Union (July 4, 2021, A1) reported that Albany County has a new program to divert rural residents with mental health issues from the criminal justice system to mental health services. The newspaper acknowledged that the "new" program is built upon the 35-year-old mobile crisis unit formed in "...response to the 1984 killing of Jessie Davis, a mentally-ill man who was gunned down in his apartment by police after neighbors called about a disturbance. His death sparked outrage and was examined in a statewide study of police shootings of Black people." As I mentioned earlier, Jessie's killing prompted the founding of the Center for Law and Justice. Ironically, the county's new program called ACCORD (Albany County Crisis Officials Responding and Diverting) is being presented as a new diversion effort that is doing exactly what the Center and the Albany Common Council are proposing to change the structure of policing in Albany. I was left feeling that our activist work made a difference. But, I continue to recognize how much more needs to happen to bring about the transformative change needed to achieve that which we have strived for over the years.

Where must we go from here to achieve the true freedom we seek? Four hundred and two years is much too long to hold a people in bondage. The demonstrations that swelled on May 25, 2020, have subsided; police still kill black people with impunity, and Albany's collaborative and the governor's mandate proved shallow, failing to provide their promised transformative changes. Over my 36 years of social justice activism, I have tried many approaches and strategies to help bring about that change, offered recommendations from my research, relied upon what I have learned from experience and my intuition, and researched and learned from all the wonderful people I have known, particularly those most directly impacted by racism and the injustices of our criminal and legal systems. I offer several matters that must be addressed to move us forward.

First and foremost, the change we seek can only come from the people exercising the power they have within them and uniting to demand a system that embraces and values its entire people who are treated with dignity, care and respect. The people's actions following the murder of George Floyd showed promise and hope. They need to resume and continue. We were on the right road and headed in the right direction. What will it take to jumpstart the movement? Certainly, the support of engaged and committed individual activists, existing groups organized under the Black Lives Matter Movement, and historical civil and human rights organizations can move this agenda forward.

Second, Governor Andrew Cuomo's Executive Order 203 could have been a powerful change agent. But, many of us question its original intent and the lack of a real incentive offered to successfully make the changes the mandate asked for. The attached threat of loss of funding was far from real and the state provided no way to evaluate the proposals it received from the municipalities.

Although the effort failed, there are ideas and recommendations worth considering and incorporating into a continued attempt to bring about systemic change. Many residents across the state took Executive Order 203 seriously and worked diligently to participate in a major change effort. The people must now demand local and state governments revisit that Executive Order, identify and assess those proposals worthy of consideration for change, and do what they failed to accomplish.

A key issue to be explored fully is systemic racism. Few seem to understand what it is, what it looks like, and how it plays a major role in the lives of everyone, but people of color bear the brunt of its impact and know it well. The State University of New York at Albany recently released a study sanctioned by Governor Andrew Cuomo. That study found a direct link between COVID-19 and structural or systemic racism. The key finding was:

"...COVID-19 did not create disparities in health outcomes but rather exposed and exacerbated them in ways policy makers cannot ignore. ...Systemic racism has produced, and continues to produce deeply entrenched differences in health care and the social, economic, and environmental conditions that account for inequities in longevity and the likelihood of disease. This was true long before the first case of COVID-19 was diagnosed...and will remain true unless the resources and will exist to make systemic changes." (TU, July 6,21, A1). This is true, I maintain, for all the major conditions borne by black and brown people – mass incarceration, and disparities in police killings, violence, affordable housing, education, and unemployment.

A third reality that must be dealt with before transformative change can happen is the legacy of slavery which continues to impact the lives of millions of African Americans today. The problem will not go away; no matter how much many wish it would. Congress is now considering H.R.40 which holds out the possibility that could move America in the right direction for reparations to be made and accountability and justice delivered. The bill proposes a study on the impacts of slavery and a commission to recommend compensations and changes to our current institutions, particularly the criminal justice system.

What is owed to African Americans for their enslavement, loss of labor, and discrimination throughout the years can be mathematically calculated and appropriate ways of compensation be developed and implemented to dramatically improve the horrible conditions affecting these Americans.

There is a fourth action and commitment that must be undertaken to improve the lot of African Americans who are disproportionately arrested, prosecuted and imprisoned. While some positive reforms have taken place in New York State including bail reform, restoration of enfranchisement rights to parolees, and decriminalization of marijuana, much more needs to happen. Of particular importance, we must not be misled by those seeking band-aid solutions to violent crime to declare that crime and violence are the byproducts of criminal justice reform. They are not related. Instead, we must attack those "crime-generative social factors' that are interconnected and often contribute to criminal behavior, including homelessness, lack of affordable housing, poor healthcare, inadequate education, unemployment, poorly funded human service programs, poverty, trauma, racial discrimination, and incarceration. This is the primary point we have tried to make throughout our activist work with advocates, incarcerated people, and the general public.

Another matter of importance individuals and groups must join to defeat is the movement to suppress the right to vote and demand universal suffrage that includes felon enfranchisement. A true democracy demands such a move.

For nearly two decades, the Center has researched and published reports that reveal the disproportionate negative impact of imprisonment on people of color. We also offered a number of recommendations for change. One of these changes calls for attaching racial impact statements to all newly implemented government policies, particularly those related to policing. The purpose of applying such statements to proposed

253

policies is to avoid inadvertently exacerbating the disproportionate representation of people of color in the criminal justice system and to head off discrimination in other community institutions.

I have consistently called for police departments to adopt a community policing philosophy to direct its work. Under community policing, police assist neighborhood groups in crime prevention efforts and problem solving. The two entities work together as equal partners within the community.

I have also taken the position throughout my activist work to encourage communities to stop their reliance upon incarceration. Diversion is always the preferred recourse in all situations. This was my motivation for working the past six or seven years to bring the LEAD (Law Enforcement Assisted Diversion) Program to the City of Albany. It is in its 5th year of operation and is considering program expansion to the county and perhaps diverting persons with more serious crimes than violations and misdemeanors. My ultimate goal would be to divert all cases to community programs and treatment services. I believe we must work to abolish prisons as we know them much as we did chattel slavery. We must immediately stop arresting children below the age of 16. It has already been established that children are not fully developed psychological and mentally. They are prone to making poor decisions. to incarcerate them makes no sense.

The second July 4th event of note is personal and inspiring, one that spoke loudly to the contributions we advocates have made to our community. Although I do not celebrate July 4th because African Americans were not included in the Declaration of Independence, for a number of years, I have visited Lincoln Park to observe the mostly black families who spend much of the day celebrating in the Park with grilling, lively recreating, and positioning themselves for the best view of the annual fireworks display visible from the Empire State Plaza more than a mile away. Due to the pandemic, the event was canceled the previous year, so people seemed excited about its return.

I arrived in the park area two hours before the scheduled 9:15 p.m. fireworks display. Unlike previous years, many of the celebrants positioned themselves on the sidewalk and the grassy edges of the park going down the hilly Morton Avenue to Grand Street. Starting at the top of Morton Avenue, I slowly walked down the sidewalk lined with people sitting, standing, talking, eating and laughing. They were spread out along the lengthy sidewalk. As I slowly made my way down the sidewalk, I was stopped repeatedly; met with hugs, greetings, and thanks for all that I and the Center had done to advance equity, fairness and justice. The people also noted our persistence and consistency for so many years of service. I was recognized and greeted with the kindest remarks and expressions of appreciation for the work I do and have done. Many bowed to me, hugged me, and showered me with expressions of love. I was constantly thanked for working "to help our people." It was absolutely amazing and a little embarrassing to be showered with such great attention and affection.

After a while, I headed back up the street through the park. I stopped to observe a large family at the top of the park hill. The family included people of all ages with the youngest being a two-year-old girl. As I got near to them, they recognized me, and the male head of the family called on his family members to recognize me and pay homage to me. He introduced me to the younger members as the greatest civil rights leader who has been working for years to help black people. "She is a genuine freedom fighter," he said. I smiled at the mention of "freedom." Then, I heard the voice of Nina Simone who sings the song, "Wish I Knew How it Would Feel to be Free."

I wish I knew how
It would feel to be free
I wish I could break

WE WHO BELIEVE IN FREEDOM

All the chains holding me

I wish I could say
All the things that I should say
Say 'em loud, say 'em clear
For the whole round world to hear

I wish I could share
All the love that's in my heart
Remove all the bars
That keep us apart

I wish you could know
What it means to be me
Then you'd see and agree
That every man should be free

I wish I could give
All I'm longin' to give
I wish I could live
Like I'm longin' to live

I wish I could do
All the things that I can do
And though I'm way over due
I'd be starting anew

Well I wish I could be
Like a bird in the sky
How sweet it would be
If I found I could fly

Oh I'd soar to the sun
And look down at the sea
Then I'd sing 'cause I know, yea
Then I'd sing 'cause I know, yea
Then I'd sing 'cause I know

I'd know how it feels
Oh I know how it feels to be free
Yea yea! Oh, I know how it feels

Yes I know, oh, I know
How it feels
How it feels
To be free, Lord, Lord, Lord

Many people ask me, "Why do you continue to be an activist, and how do you handle the great disappointments that come with such work?" My response is, "We who believe in freedom cannot rest until it comes."

ACKNOWLEDGMENTS

Very early in my career as a social justice activist and community organizer, I learned that change only comes when people work together to make it happen. I have been fortunate to work and associate with hundreds of incredibly wonderful, committed people involved in the struggle for black freedom. Many of them contributed to this book in ways they may not know or recognize. Here, I mention only a few of the many who gave me encouragement, support and assistance. I am pleased that this current exercise provides me another opportunity to thank them.

I am so grateful to - first and foremost - my husband, best friend, and social justice partner, Charles Touhey. He provided the great support of listening and critiquing that is invaluable. Janet Rothacker, another key partner, shared her magnificent organizational skills. She is a strong social justice advocate and one of the best researchers and writers anywhere. Dr. Lawrence Sturman readily shared his valuable insight and research materials on Albany's history. Others in my corner include: Katie Agar, Imam Yassin Muhiddin Aref, Sarah Birn, Nicholas Connolly, Carol Coppolla, Brendan Cox, Mardi Crawford, Mark Dunlea, Robert Elmendorf, Marco Flagg, Mary Ellen Frieberg, John Green, Paul Grondahl, Joseph "Jazz" Hayden, Jean Hynes, Naomi Jaffe, Darryl Johnson, Reverend McKinley Johnson, Reverend Samuel Johnson, Lorenzo Jones, Thomas Keefe, William Kennedy, Alice King, Steve Krokoff, Joan Lee, Tor Loney, Lauren Manning, Roger and Maria Markovics, Jack Mayer, Mark Mishler, Lewis Oliver, Anne Paden, Duke Paden, Cheryl Randall, Gabriel Sayegh, Merton Simpson, Barbara Smith, Michelle Stroe, Martha Swan, Anita Thayer, Earl Thorpe, Leon Van Dyke, David Walker, and Larry White.

I continue to remember and acknowledge those who gave me support and guidance but are no longer with us - Brother

Yusuf Burgess, Richard Collins, Dr. and Mrs. James Cunningham, Rev. Henry Johnson, Charles LaCourt, Rev. Robert Lamar, Michael Nardolillo, Margaret Sim, James Sotis, Dr. Hans Toch, Lila Touhey, and so many others.

BIOGRAPHY

Alice P. Green is the executive director of the Center for Law and Justice, a civil rights organization she founded in 1985 in Albany, New York. For nearly 40 years, the Center has been the foremost change agent in working to transform policies, practices and people in the areas of social justice, criminal justice and prison reform. The Center provides community education on civil and criminal justice, legal guidance and advocacy, crisis intervention, and community planning and organizing around criminal justice, civil rights, and civil liberties issues concerning poor and communities of color. As a result of her effective work with incarcerated people, she has been banned from all state prisons in New York since 2000, but the Center continues to work on behalf of people who are incarcerated and returning to the community.

A staunch advocate for implementing community policing, eradicating police brutality, and dismantling systemic racism, Green's career highlights include serving as legislative director for the New York Civil Liberties Union, deputy commissioner of the New York State Division of Probation and Correctional Alternatives, a member of the Citizens Policy and Complaint Review Council of the New York State Commission of Corrections, and executive director of Trinity Institution – a youth and family services center. She is also the founder of the African American Cultural Center in Albany's South End.

Green writes and lectures on racism and criminal justice, often providing commentary and analysis for many newspapers, television, and radio programs. With Dr. Frankie Bailey, she co-authored the book, "Law Never Here: A Social History of African American Responses to Issues of Crime and Justice" (1999 Greenwood Press), "Wicked Albany," (2009) and "Wicked Danville" (2011 History Press) – the latter two on Prohibition. In addition, she wrote the afterword for "Blacks in the Adirondacks" (2017).

In 1997, Green founded - in collaboration with the Center for Black Literature housed at Medgar Evers College in Brooklyn and Plattsburg State University - the *Paden Institute and Retreat for Writers of Color*, located in the Adirondack town of Essex, New York. There, writers get technical assistance and a free, serene writing environment. She is the current president.

Green's other literary accomplishments include creating and editing several community newspapers throughout her career: The Voice of the South End, The South End Scene, and The Advocate, also distributed to persons imprisoned across New York State.

In July 2021, Green was inducted into the Essex Literary Wall of Fame at the Belden Noble Library in Essex, New York, a recognition reserved for notable authors hailing from that area. She also was recognized as a Literary Legend by the Friends and Foundation of Albany Public Library in 2018. Green has earned a doctorate in criminal justice and three master's degrees — education, social work, and criminology.

Stay connected with Alice P. Green and the Center for Law and Justice:
Website: www.cflj.org
Email: info.cflj@gmail.com - Phone: 518.427.8361
Facebook: Center for Law and Justice
Instagram: cfljalbany

APPENDICES

Appendix 1: Newsletter below was distributed by imprisoned men at Green Haven Correctional Facility. Alice P. Green is banned from all state correctional facilities because the state accused her of disseminating contraband (this newsletter). By request, the Center for Law and Justice merely added pictures to the cover page and retyped the illegible copy.

WAKE UP!!!

As you probably have been noticing, since Governor Pataki became Governor in January 1995, it has become harder and harder, month after month, and year after year to be released on parole in New York State. In the year 1992-93, two years before Pataki took office as Governor, 60% of violent felony offenders were paroled after serving their minimum sentences (*DOCS Today, 4/99 p.9*). Today, violent felony offenders are forced to sign out on conditional release (CR), and those of us with a life sentence are being denied parole repeatedly.

Executive Law 259.I, the law which governs the parole board, says, among other things, that if we behave and program, we should be released at our court imposed minimums. Why are we not being released at our minimums – especially when we comply with 259.I? In addition, violent crime in New York State has been at it's lowest (29%) since *1970 (DOCS Today, 2/99, p 12)*. There is a big contradiction here! We comply with 259.I and violent crimes are at their lowest in thirty years. And to contradict things even more, Governor Pataki is building more prisons. Before Governor Cuomo left office in 1995, he had already built 29 prisons! So why does Governor Pataki want to build more prisons?

> Why should we be the raw materials in the DOCS prison industrial corporation which only serves politicians to be elected into office, and to provide jobs for rural Northern New Yorkers?

The justification made by Governor Pataki for not releasing us and for building more prisons is that crime is down because he is keeping us in prison longer. But the real reason crime is down is because of three factors: 1) the CIA has stopped bringing cocaine into the USA, which it did during the 1980's to finance their Contra War in Nicaragua, thus there is no more crack epidemic; 2) the economy is doing well (when the economy is good, crime is low and vice versa); and 3) the demographic age group of 15-24 who are the most crime-prone, have aged (*FAMM-Gram, Vol. 9, Issue 1*). So once again we ask - WHY ARE WE NOT BEING RELEASED?

The reason we are not being released is because the Department of Correctional Services (DOCS) has become a prison industrial corporation, and prisoners have become its assets or valued commodities. DOCS does not want to release us because we are their moneymakers.

We hear the oft-repeated phrase, **prison industrial complex (PIC)** when anyone is talking or writing about the mushrooming of prisons across America, and the negative consequences of runaway prison expansion on taxpayers, and the social programs of the poor. But what is this PIC? The PIC can variously be defined in psychological terms as a complex or a spectre created by abnormal fear of crime and criminals (especially Blacks and Latinos) which is generated by politicians to obtain votes, and aided by their mass media lackeys who fan the flames of this phantom to the point of general hysteria, bordering on paranoia, in the minds of the American

Appendix 2: A collage below of the various iterations of the newspaper Alice P. Green started at Trinity Institution: The Voice of the South End, South End Scene, The Scene, and The New Scene.

Appendix 3: The Advocate newsletter featured information to education the community and people imprisoned about the criminal justice system.

THE CENTER for LAW & JUSTICE, Inc.

| Community Education |
| Mobilization & Empowerment |
| Change in Criminal Justice |

ADVOCATE

Winter, 1992   Volume 1   Number 2

Long-term prisoner, Eddie Ellis, posed with fellow board members of the Center for Law and Justice. From left to right are Rev. Henry Johnson, Dr. Frankie Bailey, Mr. Ellis, Dr. Alice Green, and Attorney Ralph Byrd.

EDDIE ELLIS -

SERVING THE COMMUNITY

By Kathleen L. Ryan

ALBANY, NY -- Eddie Ellis, who has served more than 23 years in prison, is now back in a Harlem community doing what he does best -- "serving people."

A member of the Board of Directors for The Center for Law and Justice, Ellis is now serving as a community worker for The Harlem Neighborhood Defense Services as part of a prison work-release program. The program allows Ellis to work a regular job. According to a recent report in the "Daily Challenge," the incarceration rate for U.S. Black males has risen to 3,370 per 100,000, compared to 455 per 100,000 people for all other racial groups. The Black incarceration rate for men in this country is five times greater than that of their counterparts in racist South Africa.

"We hope to change these statistics with the help of Mr. Ellis," notes Alice Green, Executive Director of The Center for Law and Justice in Albany, NY. "It's interesting to note that the first state prison was built just one year after slavery was ablished in New York. And yet, we continue to build new ones to use as our 'plantations'."

The fate of Ellis began taking a turn for the worse in the midst of the Civil Rights Movement in the 1960s. Ellis, a well-spoken, dapper, young president of his own public relations

Don Jackson To Speak in Albany

The Center for Law and Justice will present a program on "Racism, Law Enforcement and Violence on Friday, February 19, 1993 at 7:00 P.M. at The College of St. Rose in St. Joseph Hall Auditorium on Madison Avenue. The Graduate School of Criminal Justice of the Rock feller College will co-sponsor the program. Don Jackson, a nationally recognized Black police officer whose beating by white police officers was captured on videotape, will speak. He will be joined by his wife Tyra Ferrell Jackson, an actress and expert on racism. For additional information, please contact The Center at 427-8361.

firm, was placed on the FBI's Security Index List in 1967 because of his writings and associations as a Harlem activist.

Under the FBI's counter intelligence program (COINTELPRO), Ellis was slated for "emergency detention" in the event of urban uprisings in New York City. He was also placed under physical and electronic surveillance. It was during this time that Ellis also served as national news editor for Liberator Magazine and as an officer for the New York Black Panther Party. He also was associated with members of the Revolutionary Action Movement (RAM).

Then in 1969, Ellis was arrested and convicted of killing a stranger. According to published reports, there was no physical evidence presented to link him to the crime. No plausible motive was ever offered for the killing and his

EDDIE ELLIS continued on page 5

Inside

Malcolm X: Review

The Effects of Long Term Imprisonment

Minority Participation in Jury Duty

Appendix 4: Advertisement for the 9th Annual Capital District Community Conference on Criminal Justice.

NINTH ANNUAL CAPITAL DISTRICT COMMUNITY CONFERENCE ON CRIMINAL JUSTICE
April 26 & 27, 2002
At
Albany Law School
80 New Scotland Avenue

Presented by
The Center for Law and Justice, Inc.
Pine West Plaza, Building 2
Washington Avenue Extension
Albany, New York 12205
(518) 427-8361

CITATIONS

Chapter 1

Reid, I. (December 1928) *The Negro Population of Albany, New York: A Survey.* The Urban League

Green, A. (May 1991) Racism Kills: The Tragic Death of Raymond Stallings. The Scene, Volume 15, Number 5

Mason, J. (2012, March 23) Albany cop cleared in fatal shooting. *The Daily Gazette.*
https://dailygazette.com/article/2012/03/23/0323_shooting

Chapter 2

Waller, C. (1990) *Slavery Time When I Was Chillun Down on Marster's Plantation: Interviews with Georgia Slaves.* Beehive Press

Schmidt, W. (1984, February 13) *NYT Southern Practice of Eating Dirt Shows Signs of Waning.* SOUTHERN PRACTICE OF EATING DIRT SHOWS SIGNS OF WANING - The New York Times (nytimes.com)

It's Easy to Register!!! (PDF)
https://www.crmvet.org/info/gavr_training.pdf

Onion, R. (2013, June 28) *Take the Impossible "Literacy" Test Louisiana Gave Black Voters in the 1960s.* Slate.
https://slate.com/human-interest/2013/06/voting-rights-and-the-supreme-court-the-impossible-literacy-test-louisiana-used-to-give-black-voters.html

(2021, June 28) *Felon Voting Rights*. National Conference of State Legislatures. https://www.ncsl.org/research/elections-and-campaigns/felon-voting-rights.aspx

Chapter 3

Grondahl, P. (2018, November 13) Grondahl: Documenting the fight for racial justice in Albany. *Times Union.* https://www.timesunion.com/local/article/Grondahl-Documenting-the-fight-for-racial-13388172.php

Grondahl, P. (2016, March 19) Waves of immigration shape region over 400 years. *Times Union*. https://www.timesunion.com/tuplus-local/article/Waves-of-immigration-shape-region-over-400-years-6924205.php

Churchill, C. (2010, December 5) Food Deserts in the land of plenty. *Times Union.* https://www.timesunion.com/business/article/Food-deserts-in-a-land-of-plenty-860634.php

History.com editor (2009, November 13) Mobster Dutch Schultz is born. *History.com.* https://www.history.com/this-day-in-history/dutch-schultz-is-born

(2003, October) Obituary Edmund P. Ted Flint. *Times Union.* https://www.legacy.com/obituaries/timesunion-albany/obituary.aspx?n=edmund-p-ted-flint&pid=1471265&fhid=5016

(2020, July 6.) Understanding the stress response. Harvard Health Publishing. *Harvard Medical School*. https://www.health.harvard.edu/staying-healthy/understanding-the-stress-response

Chapter 4

History.com editors (2010, July 21) Riot at Attica Prison. *History.com.* https://www.history.com/this-day-in-history/riot-at-attica-prison

George, Alice (2018, March 1) The 1968 Kerner Commission Got It Right, But Nobody Listened. *Smithsonian Magazine.* https://www.smithsonianmag.com/smithsonian-institution/1968-kerner-commission-got-it-right-nobody-listened-180968318/

History.com editors (2010, July 21) Kerner Commission Report Released. *History.com.* https://www.history.com/this-day-in-history/kerner-commission-report-released

Kennedy, B. (1965, November 11) Siena Priest Ordered to Curtail Rights Work. *Times Union.*

Kennedy, B. (1965, July 25) 45 S. End Families Air Housing Complaints. *Times Union.*

Weber, C. (1965, December) Mayor to Give 6 Answers. *Knickerbocker News.*

Chapter 5

Weisman, Steven R. (1976-06-24). *"Albany Mall Is Enjoyed by Friend and Foe Alike".* The New York Times.

Miller, P. (Director) (2014) *The Brothers: The Forgotten Struggle for Civil Rights in Albany* [Film] University at Albany.

Sanzone, D. (2020, July 10) Albany Councilman was the First Openly Gay Black Person Elected to Public Office in the U.S. *wmht.* https://www.wmht.org/blogs/local-history-blog/albany-councilman-was-the-first-openly-gay-black-person-elected-to-public-office-in-the-us/#:~:text=One%20historical%20claim%20to%20fame,city%20of%20Albany's%20South%20End.

Biography.com editors. (2021, January 28) 17 Inspiring Martin Luther King Jr. Quotes. *Biography.com.*
https://www.biography.com/news/martin-luther-king-famous-quotes

Chapter 6

Martin, D. (2005, February 24) Nathan Wright Jr., Black Power Advocate, Dies at 81. *New York Times.*
https://www.nytimes.com/2005/02/24/obituaries/nathan-wright-jr-black-power-advocate-dies-at-81.html

George, A. (2018, March 1) The 1968 Kerner Commission Got it Right, But Nobody Listened. *Smithsonian Magazine.*
https://www.smithsonianmag.com/smithsonian-institution/1968-kerner-commission-got-it-right-nobody-listened-180968318/

Poor People's Campaign. The Martin Luther King, Jr. Research and Education Institute, Stanford University.
https://kinginstitute.stanford.edu/encyclopedia/poor-peoples-campaign

Covert, B. (2019, July 2) *The Myth of the Welfare Queen.* The New Republic.
https://newrepublic.com/article/154404/myth-welfare-queen

Sit, R. (2018, January 12) Trump Thinks Only Black People Are on Welfare, But Really, White Americans Receive Most Benefits. *Newsweek.*
https://www.newsweek.com/donald-trump-welfare-black-white-780252

Noonan, B. (2016, April 29) *New York State Increases Minimum Wage and Enacts Paid Family Leave.* JD SUPRA.
https://www.jdsupra.com/legalnews/new-york-state-increases-minimum-wage-98715/

Tsuchiya, K. (2007, January 23) *National Welfare Rights Organization* (1966-1975). Black Past.
https://www.blackpast.org/african-american-history/national-welfare-rights-organization-1966-1975/

Nathan Wright Jr. Biography. Jrank.org.
https://biography.jrank.org/pages/2999/Wright-Nathan-Jr.html

Terkel, S. *A Black Power Scholar and Advocate*. Chicago History Museum.
https://www.chicagohistory.org/a-black-power-scholar-and-advocate/#:~:text=Wright%20served%20as%20the%20chairma
n,1%2C000%20delegates%20representing%20286%20organizati
ons.

Chapter 7

Churchill, C. (2017, October 23) Churchill: Remembering the woman who dared challenge the machine. *Times Union*.
https://www.timesunion.com/local/article/Churchill-Remembering-the-woman-who-dared-12300649.php?converted=1#photo-14407060

Blumenthal, R. (1972, December 26) State Study Finds Albany 'Fleeced' by Machine's Rule. *The New York Times*.
https://www.nytimes.com/1972/12/26/archives/state-study-finds-albany-fleeced-by-machines-rule-democratic-party.html

Grondahl, P. (2016, June 16) The best political races in Albany's history. *Times Union*.
https://www.timesunion.com/tuplus-features/article/The-best-political-races-in-Albany-s-history-8210458.php

Chapter 8

Carroll, M. (1985, February 6) Police Chief in Albany Resigns in Policy Clash. *The New York Times*.
https://www.nytimes.com/1985/02/06/nyregion/police-chief-in-albany-resigns-in-policy-clash.html

(1984, September 14). Mayor's Plan Gets Lukewarm Reviews. *Schenectady Gazette.*

Mahoney, J. (1985, May 22) Residents Oppose Police-Review Plan. *Times Union.*

(1985, February 20) Albany Police Department: Room at the Top. *Knickerbocker News.*

Chapter 9

Mann, B. (2013, February 14) *The Drug Laws That Changed How We Punish.* NPR. https://www.npr.org/2013/02/14/171822608/the-drug-laws-that-changed-how-we-punish#:~:text=Rockefeller%20launched%20his%20campaign%20to,of%20marijuana%2C%20cocaine%20or%20heroin.

Giovannitti, S. (2020, December 17) *A Conversation with Larry White; The Radical Anti-Prison Activist and Teacher for Life.* SSENSE. https://www.ssense.com/en-us/editorial/culture/a-conversation-with-larry-white-the-radical-anti-prison-activist-and-teacher-for-life

Arthur O. Eve Bio. Uncrowned Community Builder. Uncrowned Queens Institute for Research and Education on Women, Inc. https://www.uncrownedcommunitybuilders.com/person/arthur-o-eve

From Criminal Justice to Human Justice. Center for Nu Leadership on Human Justice and Healing. https://www.nuleadership.org/ https://www.nuleadership.org/assets/downloads/Hyperlink_EddieEllisBio_EEmemorialProgramFINAL.pdf

Chapter 10

Jochnowitz, J. (1987, July 21). Police, fire AIDS lists assailed. *Times Union.*

(2019, October 10) *History of AIDS and HIV Overview.*
Avert. Avert.org.
https://www.avert.org/professionals/history-hiv-aids/overview

About HIV. Centers for Disease Control and Prevention.
https://www.cdc.gov/hiv/basics/whatishiv.html

Wexler, R. (1991, January 8) Jail death spurs blacks' protest
against police. *Times Union.*

Staff writer. Three Albany Detectives Face Harassment Counts.
The Buffalo News.
https://buffalonews.com/news/three-albany-detectives-face-
harassment-counts/article_62bab76f-5f13-5531-9558-
5fa61fc3443a.html

Seiler, C. (2020, June 11) Why does it feel like 1991? *Times
Union.*
https://www.timesunion.com/opinion/article/Why-does-it-feel-
like-1991-15321177.php

Moran, J. (1991, January 9). Arbor Hill crowd rallies against
police 'brutality'. *Daily Gazette.*

Seruton, B. (1987, July 21). NAACP member scores AIDS list. *The
Knickerbocker News*

(1987, August 8) Rights groups press Albany to clarify its AIDS-
list policy. *Times Union.*

Chapter 11

McDowell, G. (1996, January) Like Dr. King, Alice Green spoke
truth. *The Sunday Gazette.*

Hill, M. (2000, July 12) Longtime activist now fights for herself.
Associated Press.

(2000, June 8) Department of Corrections denies prisoner
advocacy group access to state inmates. *Metroland.*

Chapter 12

Lyons, B. (2011, December 31) Other toll of a fatal bullet. *Times Union*.
https://www.timesunion.com/local/article/Other-toll-of-a-fatal-bullet-2435206.php

Shabazz, S. (2004, August 17). Muslims' arrest in Albany raises concerns. *The Final Call*.

Axel-Lute, M. (2004, January, 15). Time to Push the Envelope. *Metroland*.

Sahn, A. Case Closed, Questions Open. *Metroland*.

Goodwin, M. (2004, January 5) Call for external probe of shooting. *Times Union*.

Duggan, E. (2004, January 20) Sharing a legacy of hope, peace. *Times Union*.

Patrick, J. (2004, November 28) Inmates wearing stripes again. *Daily Gazette*.

Nearing, B. (2004, September 14) Truancy plan under fire. *Times Union*.

Karlin, R. (2004, September 30) Plenty of work on streets for truancy patrol. *Times Union*.

Green, A. (2004, October 20) Truancy isn't a law enforcement issue. *Times Union* commentary.

(2001, June 19) Statement from the Police Union - *Times Union*.

Carleo-Evangelist, J. (2010, February 17). Albany chief's job attracts varied lot. *Times Union*.

Chapter 13

Dunham, R. (2010, April 5) An illegal immigrant from Mexico dies at the hands of a cop, and questions arise about porous borders, police conduct. *Chron.com.* https://blog.chron.com/txpotomac/2010/04/an-illegal-immigrant-from-mexico-dies-at-the-hands-of-a-cop-and-questions-arise-about-porous-borders-police-conduct/

Gavin, J. (2012, January 7). Activist backs chief, but urges 'right thing'. *Times Union.*

Green, A. (2012, January 9). Albany needs trust and truth. *Times Union.*

History.com editors (2021, January 19) *Little Rock Nine*. History. https://www.history.com/topics/black-history/central-high-school-integration

Chapter 14

Alexander, M. (2012). The New Jim Crow: Mass Incarceration in the Age of Color Blindness. The New Press.

History.com editors (2010, March 4). LAPD officers beat Rodney King on camera. History. https://www.history.com/this-day-in-history/police-brutality-caught-on-video

Carballo, R. (2020, May 30). In wake of George Floyd killing, hundreds rally for justice in Albany. *Times Union.*

Policing Reform and Reinvention. NYCOM.org https://www.nycom.org/2-uncategorised/1485-police-reform-and-reinvention

Van Slyke, N. (Producer) (2020) *The Time for Reckoning* [Video]. *New York NOW from wmht.* https://youtu.be/H_pxkyQ9pzw

Green, A. (August 2019). Pathway to Reformative Change: Public Safety, Law Enforcement, and the Albany Community. Center for Law and Justice. www.cflj.org. http://www.cflj.org/cflj/CFLJ-Pathways-to-Reformative-Change-2019.pdf

Green, A. (2013). Pathway to Change: African Americans and Community Policing in Albany. Center for Law and Justice. www.cflj.org. http://www.cflj.org/cflj/PathwaytoChange.pdf

Green, A. (October 2012). What Have We Done? Mass Incarceration and the Targeting of Albany's Black Males by Federal, State, and Local Authorities. www.cflj.org http://www.cflj.org/cflj/what-have-we-done.pdf

Green, A. (July 2012). The Disproportionate Impact of the Juvenile Justice System on Children of Color in the Capital Region. www.cflj.org http://www.cflj.org/report/juvenile-justice.pdf

Green, A. (February 2012). The Disproportionate Impact of the Criminal Justice System on People of Color in the Capital Region. www.cflj.org http://www.cflj.org/wp-content/uploads/2012/05/The-Disproportionate-Impact-of-the-Criminal-Justice-System-on-People-of-Color-in-the-Capital-Region.pdf

Rizzo, S. (2021, November 2) Capital Region ballot proposals in the 2021 General Election. News10. https://www.news10.com/news/your-local-election-hq/capital-region-ballot-proposals-in-the-2021-general-election/

CPSIA information can be obtained
at www.ICGtesting.com
Printed in the USA
BVHW061003100222
628588BV00002B/103